ENGLISH LANGUAGE SERIES

The English Language in West Africa

The English Language in West Africa

EDITED BY
JOHN SPENCER

The School of English, University of Leeds

LONGMAN

LONGMAN GROUP LIMITED *LONDON*
Associated companies, branches and representatives throughout the world

© Longman Group Ltd 1971

First published 1971

ISBN 0 582 52215 3

Made and printed in Great Britain by
William Clowes and Sons, Limited, London, Beccles and Colchester

Foreword

A few years ago, *The Times* published a full-page map of Africa and captioned it 'The Bright Continent'. This was not merely a verbal play on the new attitude that the world was taking to this immense conglomeration of exotic cultures, fauna and geophysical wonders. It was a vivid summary of the experiment and excitement, the thrust and new development characterising the recently independent African countries as they faced the invigorating gusts of the winds of change.

The 'anglophonic' territories south-west of the Sahara by no means add up to Africa. Nor are the emerging patterns of English use by any means coterminous with the bright continent's new development. But the position of the English language in West Africa as a medium of utilitarian communication and of aesthetic expression alike, as the instrument of national unity, of African faith in a corporate, unified future, and of contact with the world at large, is decidedly central to all the developments, both political and economic, in which Africa's hopes reside.

The description of the varieties of English involved in the many cultures and for the many purposes involved is a task of such magnitude that no single scholar can be expected to be equipped for it. And there are other desiderata which make the field still more obviously one for collaborative scholarship on a broad basis: an account of the place that these varieties of English occupy in African societies, an estimation of current trends, and perhaps an informed speculation concerning the linguistic future. Our object – already optimistic enough – has therefore been to persuade an expert to undertake the task of selecting relevant topics covering some of the major issues and of recruiting specialists who could contribute chapters studying such topics. It has been our good fortune that John Spencer allowed himself to accept this difficult role of surveyor, selector and co-ordinator, and we should have found it hard to specify superior qualifications to those that he possesses for the work. After some years of university experience in India and Pakistan, he moved to Nigeria and the beautiful Ibadan campus (where he was head from 1959 to 1962 of what is now the Department of Linguistics and Nigerian Languages). He soon had close ties with the leading linguists and educationists in West Africa as a whole and actively joined in their work. He became the Chief Examiner in Oral English for the West African Examinations Council and he played an important part in the West African Languages Survey (1960–3). These concerns have persisted unabated since his return to Britain and his appointment in the School of English at Leeds University. Since 1963 he has edited the *Journal of West African Languages* and been editor (with Joseph H. Greenberg) of the *West African Language Monograph Series*. He was joint organiser of the successful 1964 Conference on Commonwealth Literature, held at Leeds. He has paid frequent visits to Africa, lecturing, examining, inspecting and advising.

This work has naturally enabled him to remain in close friendship and academic association with the scholars, African and expatriate, most concerned with the areas of specialised observation and research that are represented in this volume. It says much for his stature that he has been able to persuade these distinguished and busy contributors to join him in the present venture. All of them write with the authority that proceeds from unique, personally conducted research in their respective fields.

The present book is the first in our series to deal with English as it is used and being developed outside native English-speaking environments. More must certainly follow. As English has increasingly come into world-wide use, there has arisen an acute need for more information on the language and the ways in which it is used. The English Language Series seeks to meet this need and to play a part in further stimulating the study and teaching of English by providing up-to-date and scholarly treatments of topics most relevant to present-day English – including its history and traditions, its sound patterns, its grammar, its lexicology, its rich and functionally orientated variety in speech and writing, and its standards in Britain, the USA, and the other principal areas where the language is used.

University College London   RANDOLPH QUIRK
August, 1970

Preface

When planning this volume several years ago, it seemed clear that the subject could best be dealt with by means of a series of separate studies. This was partly because the subject is a many-sided one, with perhaps no single scholar at present equipped to handle adequately all its aspects. The method has obvious disadvantages; different points of view and, more particularly, different styles of presentation may cause unevenness and lack of uniformity. I am grateful to the contributors for giving me considerable freedom to edit their chapters, and I would like to think that wherever I have exercised this freedom it has been in the interests of uniformity, not at the expense of their material or point of view. If the volume as a whole lacks an overall unity of treatment the fault must therefore partly be mine.

Undoubtedly, there are aspects of the subject which have been left unexplored, and some which have been more fully treated than others. In particular, I am very conscious that there is scarcely anything here about the English language in Liberia. A treatment of this aspect of the subject would obviously have been of considerable interest, especially as Liberia's links have been with America and American English rather than with Britain. Unfortunately I failed to find a specialist who could contribute a chapter on this topic; and I myself could not discover anything substantial in the way of published material on which to draw.

No apology is needed for the emphasis throughout this volume on the social and cultural setting of English in West Africa. At this stage sociolinguistic elucidation must precede detailed descriptive work. If West Africa is a significant growing point of the English language to-day, the factors which cause and direct this growth must be made clear. It is therefore as important to understand the function of English in West Africa, the roles it plays, and the contacts it has with other languages in the lives of those who use it, as it is to enumerate and classify the particular lexical or syntactical or phonetic characteristics which it displays in the various speech communities of the area.

This volume can best be seen as an exploration. There is a relative lack of historical evidence about English in West Africa; sociological studies which might throw light on language habits and language attitudes are very few; and so far there are only scattered studies of the actual forms which English takes in the varied linguistic life of the West African societies which use it as a second language. There is therefore no question of a summing-up. The observations and documentations presented here are unavoidably rudimentary and tentative. But they suggest, I submit, that in West Africa we have, as it were, a piece of linguistic history of a complex kind in the making, under pressures and in circumstances which, while not altogether without parallel, are certainly not to be found in the annals of traditional linguistic histories. If our explorations prove to be of interest to the non-specialist, while at the same time stimulating the specialist to embark upon further research, we shall be very well satisfied.

I am grateful to all the contributors to this volume. Some have had to be patient while other contributions were being completed. All of them have had to be patient while I completed the rather lengthy process of editing. I would also like to express my particular gratitude to the General Editor of this series, Randolph Quirk. He has been long-suffering, for the volume has taken longer to complete than we imagined. He has also been very generous of time and advice at various stages of its production. Without his help and counsel it would have been a much less satisfactory book. For her care and collaboration in preparing the final manuscript for the printers, I am also grateful to Peggy Drinkwater, of the Longman Group.

University of Leeds   JS
August, 1970

Contents

Acknowledgments

We are grateful to the following for permission to reproduce copyright material: William Heinemann Ltd. and Astor-Honor Inc for extracts from *No Longer at Ease* by Chinua Achebe.

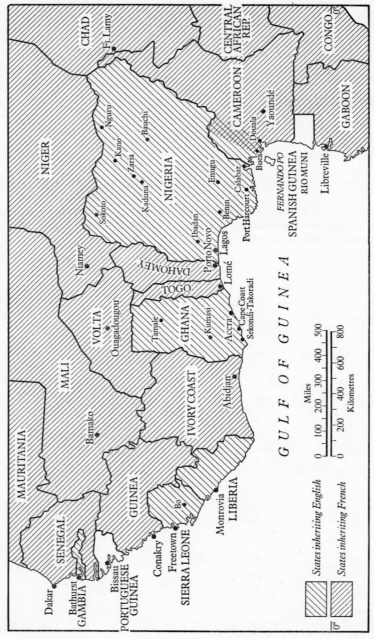

West Africa

John Spencer

West Africa and the English Language

The continent of Africa, year by year, supplies new and wondrous forms, the examination of which will upset many favourite theories ...
Robert Needham Cust, 'On the Progress of African Philology', 1895

As in so many other areas of life, the twentieth century brings to bear upon the evolving ecology of languages influences which are unique in both their strength and their nature. In consequence, languages are subject to demands and pressures unforeseen by traditional linguistic historians. The inner formal characteristics of languages may, it is true, continue to be subject to change of a kind similar to that observed in past ages, even though at a faster or slower pace. But the social and functional configuration of languages and dialects, relative to one another and to the activities of the societies they serve, is likely to become in many parts of the world more complex than ever before. The linguistic life of more and more individuals and communities will as a result become more complicated than was the case in the relatively static, less developed and isolated societies of the past.

A paradigm case of this new complexity is constituted collectively by those societies in West Africa which use English for educational, administrative and many other official and unofficial purposes, against a background of extreme multilingualism in vernacular languages: the Gambia, Sierra Leone, Liberia, Ghana, Nigeria and, subject to the additional complexity of the coexistence of English with French as its two official languages, the Cameroon Federation.

These societies are changing fast. As a result of economic, political, social and technological pressures, their sociolinguistic patterns are being constantly modified. The place of English within their total language configuration is not therefore static, nor are the attitudes of their peoples towards English constant. Its position, function, prestige and value relative to the truly indigenous languages are neither uniform throughout any one of these societies nor variable in any degree predictable by reference to region or social class. Any attempt to treat in detail, and from the many relevant aspects, the multiform life which English leads in West Africa today must thus inevitably have the appearance of an interim report, and requires at the same time contributions from several hands: one individual could hardly be expected to present the English language in West Africa, in the past and in the present, in all its manifestations and guises, in functional as well as in formal terms, clearly and as a whole.

Perhaps because of the fact that many hundreds of languages are native to West Africa, English has become relatively at home there. If hundreds of thousands of Africans in these societies know no English at all, and if, in the mouths or at the pens of thousands more, English can seem awkward or ill-at-ease, many others seem very comfortable indeed with the language, even though it is not the mother tongue of more than a tiny proportion of them. Newspapers are produced in English, journals in English grow in number year by year, parliamentary debates are for the most part held in English. West Africans are contributing, often through the medium of an impeccable English, to scientific thought and historical investigation; and the new poetry, drama and fiction in English which is now emerging from West Africa is catching the imagination and commanding the admiration of the English-reading world. English in West Africa cannot thus be seen as a temporarily borrowed language. On the contrary, it is by now part of the linguistic property of those who use it, and if it is not a mother tongue it is not thereby a foreign language. For in as much as it is widely used, it is often used with a creativity and ebullience which must spring from a confident sense of ownership.

That this creative ebullience exists at the grassroots of English in West Africa as well as in the realm of literary art may be instanced – to move from generality to particularity – by a line from a popular Ghanaian song of some years ago. The song refers to someone who is, so the refrain goes, 'Been-to, jaguar, fridgeful'; all attributives of worldly success much used in Accra and elsewhere at that time. To construe these slang expressions: *been-to*, used as both noun and adjective, implies education or training in Britain, and thus membership of a westernised élite; *jaguar* means that this paragon possesses the prestige of a high quality car, the Jaguar being then in West Africa (by a now defunct process of imperial preference) what a Mercedes seems to be today, the ultimate in four-wheeled status symbols. Of his heroine Jagua

Nana, in the novel of that name (1960), Cyprian Ekwensi writes that 'they called her Jagua because of her good looks and stunning fashions. They said she was Ja-gwa after the famous British prestige car.' Finally, *fridgeful* suggests, with an interesting sharpening through its attachment to a material object (itself another status symbol) of the indistinct possessive sense of the suffix *-ful* in such words as 'beautiful', 'graceful', that he (or possibly she) has the attributes of the class which can afford refrigerators. With regard to the widely used term *been-to* for an England-returned[1] graduate or trained man, it was believed in Ghana some years ago that a feminine form, *beentress*, also existed in popular usage. It is probable that this particular instance of what one might call 'rule-bending creativity', however, was in reality an apocryphal joke among the linguistically sophisticated, especially the British. Just how much condescension and how much admiration was mingled in the telling of this little linguistic joke it would be difficult to judge.

Yet, despite creative originality in its use, from the demotic to the literary ends of the scale, English in West Africa can hardly be equated with other regional Englishes, and treated on all fours with, for instance, Australian English or Jamaican English. If West Africa has inherited English, the process of inheritance has been very different from that which has caused Australia or Jamaica to become English-speaking nations. There has been neither the direct father-to-son inheritance of the settler-dominated communities, in which English was carried overseas from the mother country and implanted by native speakers, nor the assimilative inheritance, whereby those speaking a variety of tongues lost them over the course of generations and took to English, either through the bitter detribalisation of slave plantations in the New World, or through the kindlier processes of voluntary immigrant acculturation. The terms of the West African inheritance of English are different from either of these.

In West Africa English exists alongside a multitude of other languages, languages which constitute the mother tongues of practically all the peoples of those states which retain English as an important auxiliary, or sometimes as an explicitly national, language. English thus complicates what is already, in terms of vernacular languages, one of the most multilingual areas of the world. For, while it may be said in some senses to simplify communication in and between these societies, it complicates their total linguistic patterns by adding, not just one more language to the many already in use, but a new dimension of complexity. As these societies develop, as their populations become socially and geographically more mobile, as institutions and organisations spread and multiply, and as group interacts with group in the process of modernisation, so the place of English gets more interwoven with the lives of more and more people. It is normally through English that an individual breaks the bonds of West African traditional life and enters into some kind of relationship with the westernised sectors of his society. Through English he obtains the education which is the road to the kind of success which awaits him beyond the village or the tribe. Through English of one kind or another he communicates with fellow citizens from language groups other than his own, or with foreigners. English is the language of institutions implanted by colonialism: the law, large-scale business, formal education beyond the first two or three years of primary school, science and technology, central administration and politics. Yet his mother tongue, denied the opportunity of serving him in many of these fields of activity, must remain the language of child-hood memories, and of the endearments and emotions of home. How far the children of educated West African parents are nowadays being brought up bilingually in the home – in English and the vernacular – it is impossible to say; but for the majority of adult English-using West Africans today, English is primarily the language of the westernised areas of their lives, an institutional rather than a domestic tongue.

At this point it is relevant to pose the question: What kind of English are we discussing? To this there is no simple answer. If we look at the school syllabus, past or present, we get one kind of answer. Schools have been teaching the English of the textbooks, of Wordsworth, Shelley and Tennyson, of *The Mill on the Floss* or of *Black Beauty*; as well as, until recently, the English of Nesfield's *Grammar* (whence *beentress*, perhaps, whether fact or fiction). In church, and also at missionary schools, it was the English of the hymn-book and the Bible, except where the ver-nacular was used for worship and religious teaching. A colleague who endured a painful overnight journey by ambulance in Northern Nigeria told me that the kindly Nigerian nurse attending him began to comfort him as the journey wore on with the expression 'the night is far spent', thus assuring him that they would soon reach Kano Hospital. It was to these kinds of English that the children were exposed, if they ever had a chance of schooling. They learned, not always perfectly, a standardised written English: and they heard in the classroom, and, if they were churchgoers, in sermons in English from the pulpit on Sundays, a formal spoken English – though not always from a native speaker of English. West African children thus did not usually have much opportunity to acquire a grasp of the colloquial ranges of English as used by native speakers. They did not, after all, have very much need of this area of linguistic competence in English, unless they went abroad; social mixing between Englishmen and Africans was not very widespread in West Africa during the colonial period.

If, on the other hand, one listened to children in the playground in certain urban areas of coastal West Africa, one might hear another language, closely related in some ways to English, but certainly unintelligible to native English speakers from outside West Africa: Pidgin English. Where it existed as a lingua franca in local community life it was forbidden in classroom and, hopefully, in playground and dormitory too. It was frowned upon by the schoolmaster and swept under the carpet by almost all colonial educationists. Many Africans who made use of it were also made ashamed of it. From the point of view of formal education Pidgin, as well as Krio, the creole language of Freetown, lived an 'underground' existence. Those who represented the colonial educational establishment, African and European, believed there to be only one English worthy of the name: that which they conceived they themselves used, or which corresponded in their minds with the 'correct' English of the textbooks and grammars, or the English of great literature, or of polite society – depending upon whichever criterion their background or education suggested.

The English-based demotics, Krio or Pidgin, have yet to come fully into their own. They belong to those areas of West Africa which have had relatively long contact with Europe; and they represent the very earliest period of English language implantation. A descriptive linguist might wish to group them all together as a West African dialect cluster or continuum. Certainly Pidgin exists in considerable variety, separable by register as well as by region. A recent sociolinguistic sketch of the western Cameroon area (Mbassi-Manga, 1968) suggests that besides an 'anglophone Pidgin' and a 'francophone Pidgin' distinguishable according to the degree to which English or French influences the lexicon, there is also a distinctive 'liturgical Pidgin', established by the Catholic Church in its catechisms and sermons, and a 'drover's Pidgin', used by the Bororos who bring cattle on the hoof from the northern savannahs to the coast: all dialects or registers of Cameroon Pidgin, and each being lexically, and perhaps also phonologically, marked as distinct, while retaining a sufficient common linguistic core to remain reasonably inter-intelligible.

Clearly then, a considerable range of English faces us in West Africa, from the home-grown pidgins and creoles at one end of the spectrum to the universally accepted formal written registers of standard English in which almost all scientific, scholarly, literary and legal writing is done. Between the two ends of the spectrum there are many gradations, especially in speech. The various kinds of English are not always struggling against one another for mastery, however; in the life of the individual they usually have complementary roles, and he is able to switch as occasion demands from, shall we say, Pidgin – or Pidgin-flavoured English – to more standard forms shared by most English speakers everywhere, or into a technical register of English.

> 'Good! See you later.' Joseph always put on an impressive manner when speaking on the telephone. He never spoke Igbo or pidgin English at such moments. When he hung up he told his colleagues: 'That na my brother. Just return from overseas. BA (Honours) Classics.' He always preferred the fiction of Classics to the truth of English. It sounded more impressive.
> 'What department he de work?'
> 'Secretary to the Scholarship Board.'
> ''E go make plenty money there. Every student who wan' go England go de see am for house.'
> ''E no be like dat,' said Joseph. 'Him na gentleman. No fit take bribe.'
> 'Na so,' said the other in disbelief.

As this revealing passage from Chinua Achebe's novel *No Longer at Ease* (1960) suggests, English is only part of the total linguistic activity of a typical educated urban West African. Pidgin, and of course his maternal language, whether Igbo or any of the several hundred others, also have significant roles to play which English cannot replace; in addition, he may be able to call into use, at some level of proficiency, other West African languages which he has learned and needs on occasion to use. Circumstance, convention and convenience will determine which language or variety of a language he chooses out of his total armoury of linguistic competences.

Languages are thus continually in contact within the lives of an increasing number of West Africans, as more and more of the population becomes bilingual or trilingual. English will therefore, in certain of its uses, tend to naturalise itself: lexical, phonological and syntactic influences from vernaculars may operate upon it; semantic shifts will occur as the pull of the mother tongue and the mother culture overrides the patterns of meaning taught at school; and new slang or colloquial expressions will arise as the need is felt to create a less formal instrument for shared communal experience, banter or group solidarity in English-using institutions such as the school, the university and the army. Likewise, the vernaculars will receive their impact from English, as the place of English in everyday life grows in proportion to the penetration of the traditional by the modern. As always, when languages live side by side within the lives of individuals and societies, a constant reciprocal seepage takes place. Over many years permanent effects upon the language behaviour of communities will be seen, and also a degree of stabilisation may occur. Because this process has been going on for a long time in parts of West Africa, and has left its indelible mark on certain varieties of spoken and written English, one is perhaps justified in using the term West African English to refer to such local particularities as may be observed in the use of the language. It is a term best used with caution, however, as is implicit throughout this volume. The West Africans who know and use English do not constitute a homogeneous speech community, in regard either to their mother tongue or to English. In an area so large and varied, it is extremely difficult to say without much more investigation how widespread a particular local feature of English is. Nor can one be sure how far such particularities of language behaviour command the linguistic loyalty of those who use them. Before we can understand the processes of stabilisation and change in the English of West Africa, we need a great deal more sociolinguistic evidence. It is perhaps relevant therefore at this point to turn away from the present and future and look briefly backwards, at the implantation of English in West Africa by mercantile contact, colonial rule and missionary activity.

*   *   *   *   *   *

The earliest contacts between Europe and West Africa were developed by the Portuguese in the fifteenth century. The captains of Prince Henry the Navigator reached Cape Verde in 1444, Sierra Leone in 1460 and the Gold Coast in 1471. In 1460 they began to colonise the Cape Verde Islands, using them as a base for settlements south along the coast. Within eleven years of their first landfall on the Gold Coast, they had begun the construction of their headquarters for that stretch of the coast, the fort of São Jorge de Mina, now known as Elmina. Before the century was out they had set up a station at Gwato, the port of Benin, and colonised the island of São Thomé as a centre for their Niger-Cameroons trade. And this was only a small part of their astonishing voyaging. By the first decade of the sixteenth century they had establish-ed, however flimsily, settlements, forts and trading stations down the western and up the eastern sub-equatorial coasts of Africa, had reached Goa and Calicut on the Malabar coast of India, and by 1511 were at Malacca on the Malayan peninsular.

When the English language was first heard along the West African coast it is not possible to discover with certainty. According to Hakluyt, William Hawkins the Elder made three voyages to Brazil between 1530 and 1532, each time calling at the Guinea Coast en route for the New World. In 1555–6 William Towerson made the first of three trading voyages to the Guinea Coast and, as reported in Hakluyt (1598, Vol VI), encountered in the neighbourhood of Elmina a young African who had escaped from the castle, where he had learned a little Portuguese:

> This fellowe came aboord our shippe without feare, and assoone as he came, he demaunded, why we had not brought againe their men, which the last yeere we tooke away, and could tell us that there were five taken away by Englishmen: we made him answere, that they were in England well used, and were there kept till they could speake the language, and then they should be brought againe to be a helpe to Englishmen in this Countrey: and then he spake no more of that matter.

If what Towerson told the African was true – and there is little reason for it not to be, for the Portuguese had been training African interpre-ters for themselves in this manner since the beginning of their contact with Africa – these must have been some of the earliest West Africans to learn English; indeed, the first (though involuntary) *been-tos*. Clearly Towerson had not himself been responsible for sending them to Eng-land, for he had not previously been on the coast. But in reporting his second voyage to Guinea, in 1556–7, he constantly refers to 'our owne Negros', who were manifestly sailing with him, one of them being mentioned as 'George, our Negro'; and it is they who, when the Mina region of the Gold Coast is reached, appear to act as interpreters for the English traders.

The Portuguese had a monopoly of Guinea trade, however, and it was not until 1631 that the first English fort was built, at Cormantine on the Gold Coast. With the establishment of English settlements in the West Indies in the first decade of the century, slaves were needed for the sugar plantations, and interest in England in the West African trade, which had been fitful before, received fresh impetus. The English became active around the mouth of the Gambia river and on Sherbro Island south of what is now Freetown in Sierra Leone, as well as on the Gold Coast. Unfortunately, contemporary records of European voyages rarely offer clues about the languages in which trading and other contacts were carried on. In a work by Peter de Marees of 1602, originally written in Dutch and later printed in English (Purchas, Vol vi, 1619) as 'A Description and Historicall Declaration of the Golden Kingdome of Guinea', we learn that in the 'Kingdome of Mellie [the old kingdom of Mali, around the Senegal river] their language differeth in the one place from the other: but moste of them speak a little French, by reason that they are used to deale much with the French men, and so get some part of their speech, as they on the gold Coast also doe, who likewise speake a little Portugall, by reason also that the Portugalls in times past used to Traffique there much.'

Christophersen (1953) has suggested that a pidginised form of Portuguese (often referred to as Negro-Portuguese) was used for contact between Englishmen and Africans on the Guinea Coast from the earliest times until well into the eighteenth century. This seems a doubtful hypothesis, however. Without question some knowledge of Negro-Portuguese would have been useful in those parts of the coast where the influence of Portugal had been extensive. But this would not imply that English was rarely used as a contact language until late on in the eighteenth century, when, according to Christophersen, a pidginised form of English supplanted Negro-Portuguese as the trading lingua franca of the coast. The development of a contact language based on English must almost certainly be put back a century or more. Probably, pidginised forms of several European languages developed quite early in West Africa, and coexisted along the coast; thus accounting, among other things, for the survival into present-day English-based Pidgin of a number of common words of Portuguese origin. A. P. Kup (1961), writing on the early history of Sierra Leone, tells us that from the seventeenth century onwards 'there grew up a professional band of interpreters who would keep a sharp lookout for approaching ships, and, meeting them in their canoes, offer their services for the ensuing palavers; often they carried credentials in the form of certificates issued by previous captains'. If Towerson's assertion is true that as early as 1554 Africans were taken back to England to learn English, in order to assist future trading expeditions as interpreters, it is unlikely that there was not, by the seventeenth century, a scattered band of Africans capable of inter= preting between English and a number of the vernaculars. With Euro- pean forts and trading stations in considerable numbers established along the West African coast by the middle of the seventeenth century,[2] interpreters must have been at a premium on both sides; and it is very doubtful whether English sea captains, traders and the governors of the English forts would long have been content to use a form of Portuguese as the entrepreneurial and diplomatic language in their dealings with Africans. African traders who rose to wealth and power along the coast had often begun their careers as servants in the European forts, famil- iarising themselves by this means with the language, the customs, and the weaknesses, of those with whom they were later to trade.

Nevertheless, it is still extremely difficult, with the paucity of evidence available, to picture in any detail the nature of African–European con- tact at this time, or the manner in which this contact, from a linguistic point of view, was sustained. It is clear that it is from this mercantile period that the pidgin and creole languages of West Africa derive; but precisely in what way the various pidgins arose is not at all clear – and is, indeed, a matter of some dispute among linguists. In simple terms, it may be said that the controversy over the origins of the pidgins and creoles to which European mercantile activity and slavery gave rise is between two opposing theories: the diffusionist view, which considers all such pidgins to be descendants of a single 'ur-pidgin', a late medieval Mediterranean sailors' lingua franca; and the 'baby talk' theory, which considers that all these pidgins arose independently, and that the similarities among them result from the common habit of European traders and sailors of talking to the peoples of Africa and Asia, whom they tended to despise, as if they were, linguistically, small children. That the contacts involved were far from civilised, at least on the European side, and that their main purpose, especially from the seventeenth century on, was the brutalising trade in human beings, is not in doubt. Perhaps the best hint of the kind of relationships we can expect the Europeans to have developed on the West African coast during these centuries is offered by a majestic paragraph from a little-known preface to a book of travels, written by Dr Samuel Johnson (1759) almost exactly three hundred years after the Portuguese first made landfall on the peninsula they named Sierra Leone:

In 1463, in the third year of the reign of John II, died Prince Henry, the first encourager of remote navigation, by whose incitement, patronage, and example, distant nations have been made acquainted with each other, unknown countries have been brought into general view, and the power of Europe has been extended to the remotest parts of the world. What mankind has lost and gained by the genius and designs of this prince, it would be long to compare, and very difficult to estimate. Much knowledge has been acquired, and much cruelty been committed, the belief of religion has been very little propagated, and its laws have been outrageously and enormously violated. The Europeans have scarcely visited any coast, but to gratify avarice, and extend corruption; to arrogate dominion without right, and practise cruelty without incentive. Happy had it been then for the oppressed, if the designs of Henry had slept in his bosom, and surely more happy for the oppressors. But there is reason to hope that out of so much evil good may sometimes be produced, and that the light of the gospel will at last illuminate the sands of Africa and the desarts of America, though its progress cannot but be slow, when it is so much obstructed by the lives of Christians.

From these early centuries date some of the most characteristic Pidgin words, known and used by almost everyone, English or African, who has lived in the coastal areas of West Africa: *dash*, n and v, '(to give) a gift, bribe, tip or commission'; *pickin*, n, 'a young child'; *palaver*, n, 'talk, argument, trouble', and compounds such as *mammy-palaver*, 'woman (or wife) trouble', *belly-palaver*, 'stomach trouble'; *chop*, n and v, 'food' and 'eat', and its recent extensions in phrases such as *small chop*, 'cocktail eats', *chop box*, 'food box for use on trek, originally for head loading', etc. The difficulty of tracing the origins of some of these words (others are clearly of Portuguese origin), and of dating their entry into coastal Pidgin or into English generally, may be illustrated by the word *dash*.

The *Oxford English Dictionary* gives its first occurrence as 1788, with an earlier citation of *dashee* in 1705. The etymology is in dispute; some consider it to have been a corruption of the Portuguese phrase *das-me*, 'give me', while the *OED* derives it from an alleged 'native' word (language unspecified) *dashee*. Christophersen (1953), rejects both the African etymology implied by the *OED* and the direct transfer from Portuguese. He points to a word similar in form to *dash* which existed in a number of late medieval Romance dialects, meaning 'toll' or 'tribute'. Whatever its origin, it certainly occurs in print earlier than the *OED* claims; thus, it appears in the *Purchas* version (1619) of Peter de

Marees's 'Description and Historicall Declaration': 'And when they [ie the Africans] have bestowed their monie, then we must give them some-what to boot, which they call Dache.' The word as spelled in *Purchas* occurs in German, as early as 1603, in a work about the Guinea Coast by Johann Theodor and Johann Israel von Bry; but they may have had it from the Dutch original of the Marees account, which appeared in 1602. If one wished to confuse the issue further one might draw attention to a list of eight words given by Towerson, whose accounts in Hakluyt of his voyages in 1555–7 have already been referred to. These eight words he thought to belong to a language local to the Mina district of the Gold Coast; but as they include *bassina*, 'basins', and *molta*, 'much', 'of great store', Hakluyt is almost certainly justified in his marginal comment that 'this language seemeth partly to be corrupt'. Included is a form *dassee, dassee*, which Towerson glosses as a form of thanks. It is just this side of the wildest conjecture to wonder whether Towerson mistook a parting request for commission for a thanking formula. But such fancies cannot be given lexicographical credence! Current investigations, however, are beginning to suggest that *dash* originated in a West African language, and it appears that the *O E D*'s conjecture of just under a century ago is likely to be justified in the end; as well as, one must hope, made rather more precise. (The exact contemporary meanings of *dash* in the context of West African life also raise problems; sometimes, indeed, of an ethical as well as a semantic kind. The unravelling of the reasons for its untranslatability might give a sociolinguist interested in semantic relativity a pleasantly complicated and rewarding task.)

As the traffic in slaves expanded to appalling dimensions in the eighteenth century, West Africans engaged in trade with Europeans found it increasingly expedient to acquire a knowledge of their languages. The Europeans were still, as they had been for centuries, merely fleeting visitors to the coast, and sons of Efik traders at Old Calabar, where trade with the British throve, were often sent off to England to learn English and book-keeping. Archibald Dalzell, for many years a governor at Whydah and a resident at Abomey, reported to the African Association in 1804 that 'at Bonney and Callabar there are many negroes who speak English; and there is rarely a period that there are not at Liverpool, Callabar negroes sent there expressly to learn English' (Hallett, 1964). Schools were established at Old Calabar by some of these returned Africans to teach the rudiments of English and the keeping of accounts – including, presumably, slave-trading accounts.

The kind of English learned there, as well as through intercourse with British sailors and traders, may be glimpsed in the remarkable diary of Antera Duke, written in the latter part of the eighteenth century in a large folio volume given to him by one of the officers of a slave-ship anchored off Duke Town, Calabar. It was published for the first time quite recently (Forde, 1956), and the following entry for 8 February 1786 may give some idea of Antera Duke's English:[3]

> at 5 am in aqua Bakassey Crik and with fine morning and I git for aqua Bakassey Cril in 1 clock time so I find Arshbong Duke and I go Longsider his Canow so I tak Bottle Beer to Drink with him and wee have call first for new Town and stay for Landing come way so wee go town in 3 clock time so we walk up to plaver house sam time to putt grandy Egbo in plaver house and play all night Combesboch go way with 639 slave & Toother.

The regularised modern version of this passage runs as follows:

> At 5 am in Aqua Bakassey Creek; it was a fine morning and I arrived at Aqua Bakassey corral at 1 o'clock. I found Archibong Duke and went alongside his canoe. I took a bottle of beer to drink with him and we called first at New Town and stayed at the landing and then went to town at 3 o'clock. We walked up to the palaver house to put the Grand Ekpe in the house and played all night. Combesboch went away with 639 slaves and Toother [proper name].

*   *   *   *   *   *

The foundation of the Freetown community in 1791, and its subsequent use throughout a good deal of the nineteenth century as the base for the educational and evangelical work of the Church Missionary Society in the whole area, marks an important shift in the history of English in West Africa. In the missionary schools of Freetown and in the churches, what one might call 'establishment English' was used. No longer the brutal commercial exchanges of the slavers; the 'civilising mission' of Europe had begun. The English of the school primer, of the sermon, of the Bible and the hymnal – each, of course, a distinct variety of English – was now to be propagated. English was to become the language of salvation, civilisation and worldly success, a splendid nineteenth-century combination. Reporting to the C.M.S. headquarters in London on the progress of education in the Abeokuta area of Nigeria in 1862, a missionary wrote of English as a 'language which seems of itself to raise the person who is acquainted with it in the scale of civilisation' (quoted in Ajayi, 1965). The telling phrase 'of itself' was apparently added to the letter as a significant afterthought.

At the same time the English which was the home language of the original groups settled in Freetown – the 'black poor' from London (the true and original 'settlers'); the 'Nova Scotians' who, having escaped from the slavery of the southern states of America, had fought on the British side in the War of Independence and been temporarily settled in Nova Scotia, of all places, before being shipped to Sierra Leone; and the Maroons (escaped slaves) from Jamaica – emerged as very different indeed from standard metropolitan English. We may assume that London English, creolised English of the slave plantations of Carolina and elsewhere in the southern states, Jamaican English-based creole, the existing pidginised English of West Africa, the speech of British sailors, and other influences equally various, all contributed their quota to the language which eventually crystallised as Krio, the creole tongue of many Freetown people today. As the small groups of original settlers were swelled by the addition of Africans taken off slave-ships by British navy vessels patrolling West African waters after the abolition of the slave trade, the assimilation of these newcomers, most of whom had only just been sold into slavery and knew no English, contributed to Krio a very considerable amount of African, and especially Yoruba, linguistic influence.

These liberated Africans were taught in different schools from those attended by the offspring of the original settlers. Many of the former were of course young adults, and may only have been enslaved a short while previously. The extraordinary distances some of them had been forced to travel from the deep interior of Africa, and the variety of tribes they represented, is strikingly evidenced in Koelle's famous *Polyglotta Africana* (1854), wherein he presents word-lists from over one hundred African languages, all of them collected from the lips of liberated African slaves in Freetown in the years 1851 and 1852. They were taught English, but how well it is not easy to say. Robert Clarke (1843) commented that the liberated Africans 'have the faculty or organ of language well developed, as they acquire in a few weeks a sufficient smattering of English to be able to communicate their ideas'. He also gives us one or two glimpses of local English, which include familiar words such as *ju-ju*, *chop* (as a verb) and of course *dash*, from which there was no escape; and the colourful expression used to him by a liberated African, for reasons the author does not disclose: 'You scowl me much, why you can curse too bad?'

The missionary teachers were thus faced in Freetown with a community which spoke a creolised form of English. Their efforts to teach a standard form of English in school, to give high prestige to the latter and allot very low prestige to the former, laid the foundations of a classic case of *diglossia*[4] which persists to this day. However, the missionaries and educationists were by no means the only culprits. Perhaps more insidious was the Englishman's (and Englishwoman's) patronising superiority to what they conceived to be a 'low' and 'corrupt' form of speech; transferring to West Africa the attitudes they held towards rural dialects at home.

In the travel books of the period we find plenty of evidence of this archetypal linguistic snobbery, disguised as curiosity mingled with exasperation, towards the language of their servants. The following passage, from a letter by a 'Lady' who stayed in Sierra Leone in the eighteen-forties (Norton, 1849), is perhaps typical:

> Then all my perplexities in endeavouring to make myself understood by native servants! Not one single sentence that they utter can I as yet comprehend, and they seem quite as confused at my mode of speech. I hear other people talk to them in such strange phrases, perfectly unintelligible to me, and am told that until I too can talk 'country fashion' there is no chance of my household being conducted with regularity or comfort. My directions are constantly mistaken. On asking one of the servants to bring me a breakfast cup, he first brought a cream-jug, and then, on repeating slowly and distinctly that I wanted a large blue cup, he returned with a dessert-plate; and not till the command 'Go fetch big tea-cup, he live in pantry', had been issued by lips initiated in the mysteries of African *patois*, did the boy understand and obey accordingly. There is no neuter in negro-grammar, and everything is endowed with animation; for instance, they say of dinner, 'he *live* on table'.

A more penetrating observer of a few years previously (Rankin, 1836) had discovered that differences in the use of English also distinguished different groups among the Freetown settlement, indicating that the historical division (and antagonism) between the Settlers proper and the Maroons had already been buttressed by conscious distinctions of linguistic usage:

> Shortly after arriving, when Settlers and Maroons were to me as equally black and indistinguishable as Soosoos and Ibbos, I innocently inflicted deep injury on the sensitive mind of the laundress by

inquiring why she had omitted to bring home some particular article of dress. In conversation the whites show deference to the blacks by adopting the 'talkee-talkee' *patois*; and, to do as others did, I had sagaciously stored my memory with a few fashionable local phrases. In endeavouring to render myself intelligible, I became obscure, and, what is still worse, offensive. The exact idiom which wounded the pride of the Settler has already been forgotten; it was either 'What *matter* for you no done bring him?' instead of the correct diction, 'What *fashion* for you no done bring him' or some nicety equally important, and of similarly difficult discrimination. It had the effect, however, of changing the mild maiden into a fury; 'What! white man come for insult me! leff me, leff me!, bad man, dis man, for true, 'peak a me so! me no Maroon, me tink! me Settler-girl and you sabby.' She departed in dudgeon. Not a little surprised at wrath apparently spontaneous and unprovoked, I sought my host, who at once perceived that I had ignorantly addressed the Settler in a Maroon idiom, and who intimated the chance of my being denounced by the whole Settler population if the same chose to make the worst of the affair. I repeated the exact words, and the mistake was instantly detected and explained. The difference between the complimentary and the insulting, the Settler *patois* and the Maroon, was so slight and so non-essential that a professor of languages need not have blushed at the mistake. Explanation melted the moody maiden and reconciliation was not denied, strenuous and persevering hatred of white men not being an attribute of the sable ladies: she only observed, 'Why for, den, you no can 'peak a me like Settler-girl? Why for you done curse me wid Maroon word? pish, phoo, for true; me sabby de English good; no talk bad-palaver like Maroon girl'; and the linen was henceforward duly honoured by her destructive care.

In the first half of the nineteenth century Freetown was also a base for British political influence along the coast. By an Act of 1821, the British government took over all British trading settlements in West Africa. Thereafter, British control began to expand and consolidate itself, and the colonial period, in the political sense, may be said to have begun. With the missionaries and the administrators, and sometimes in advance of them, went traders, teachers, preachers and functionaries drawn from the Freetown Creole community. They traded up the Gambia and at Bathurst, along the Liberian coast and in Monrovia itself, that other English-speaking African community, founded by freed negro slaves from America in the early part of the century. There were Creoles from Freetown on the Gold Coast and at Lagos. The mission to the Niger, led by Bishop Crowther, himself a freed Yoruba slave educated by the Church Missionary Society in Freetown, attracted evangelists and traders. A fairly large offshoot of the Freetown community settled in Fernando Po, and a smaller one opposite on the mainland at Victoria; and their descendants speak Krio to this day. Not all these members of the Freetown diaspora were without knowledge of the African languages in the areas in which they settled; many were, like Bishop Crowther, first generation liberated slaves who had never lost their mother tongue and returned to work among their own people. But having learned English at school, and having assimilated also a knowledge of Krio, their influence upon the spread of English in West Africa must have been considerable, especially as they are likely to have prized their knowledge of English as a mark of their affiliation to the colonial and missionary establishment. They must in some areas have greatly outnumbered native Englishmen, and become the natural intermediaries in trade, missionary effort and administration.

Nevertheless, it would be false to assume that the missionary educational effort did much more than scratch the linguistic surface. The vast mass of African peoples who came under British colonial rule along the coast and inland during the nineteenth century had little need and less opportunity to learn or use English. Even in Freetown, African languages were widely used, and standard English as spoken by the missionaries, not all of whom were English, was not readily understood even by Africans who had some knowledge of the language. Hannah Kilham, the Quaker missionary who felt the need for teaching Africans to read and write their own vernaculars, and who was one of the first Europeans to collect African language material as a basis for designing school books, wrote on her last visit to Freetown in 1832:

> I still hear the old sound of 'This colony is an English colony, and for our own people we do not need the native languages'. The manner in which English is understood and spoken here is grievous. I believe the people singing hymns often remember but very few of the words given out in two lines, and either use other words, or sing a part of the tune without words.[5]

However, missionaries were not always aware of their proselytes' lack of competence in English. The American Southern Baptist missionary T. J.

Bowen, who spent many years in West Africa, made the following percipient comment in 1857:

> Most of the missionaries in Africa preach in English. In Sierra Leone, Liberia, and at some other places, the native must understand English or live and die without hearing the gospel, though it is administered regularly in his town. Very few of those who pretend to understand English, can comprehend what is said in the fine classical style of the missionary. Sometimes the preacher is a German, whose accent would puzzle an Englishman, much more an African. Vast amounts of preaching are thrown away by missionaries. At Cape Coast Castle and other places, a native man interprets from the lips of the English-speaking preacher. What the interpreter calls 'high English', or 'deep English', is often an unknown tongue to him, and of course he cannot tell the people what the preacher has said, though he is sure to tell them something.

Yet, as Bowen reports, there was also current a good deal of linguistic awareness as to the different regional varieties of English:

> When we arrived in Freetown several boatmen boarded the ship to convey passengers to the shore, one of whom approached us and said,
> 'Plenty American man live ashore.'
> 'How do you know we are American?' we enquired.
> 'By de tongue,' he replied.

The problem of vernacular teaching became a real one for the missionaries as their activities preceded or followed the British flag. The missionary societies remained responsible for almost all education in the British West African territories until well on into the present century. Evangelically there were obvious advantages in teaching children to read and write their own tongue. As early as 1816 the Church Missionary Society had drawn the attention of its West African mission at Freetown to 'the advantage, and indeed the necessity of teaching the children to read their own language in order to their being useful to their parents and other countrymen, by reading the Scriptures and religious Tracts'. But little was known of the vernaculars at that time, and Africans did not fail to see the advantages of learning English.

In certain areas of the coast, at least, English seemed to be spreading apace. It was reported that by the latter end of the nineteenth century so much English was spoken in the southern region of the Gold Coast that the Wesleyan Mission, which was active there, did not need to use the vernaculars much, even their African clergy doing most of their preaching in English. On the other hand, the Basel Mission claimed, in a letter of protest to the German Colonial Office in 1913 about an order by the Governor of Kamerun forbidding education in anything other than German, that if the British had been so unsuccessful after so many years in spreading English in the Gold Coast, the Germans could hardly be expected to do any better in the Cameroons with their language.[6] While using English for some levels of education in both the Gold Coast and the Cameroons, the Basel Mission was a prime protagonist of vernacular education, as compared with the Wesleyans; but it must be remembered that most of the European preachers and teachers of the Basel Mission were not native speakers of English. A Ghanaian writing on this subject not many years ago (Asamoa, 1955), noted that 'until quite recently the Basel Mission (now Presbyterian Church) schools used to be looked upon as unprogressive by their Methodist brethren (whose education was almost entirely in English) because of the comparatively high value they placed on the vernacular.' Between these two extremes, it may be added, the Anglicans often characteristically tried to find a reasonable *via media*.

Much of the pessimism or optimism expressed at this time about the future spread of English in West Africa was presumably the result of attempts to justify a particular language policy; or else the product of English language loyalty combined with British cultural imperialism, masquerading as a 'civilising mission'. Hope Waddell, the pioneer Church of Scotland missionary in Eastern Nigeria, wrote in 1848 that children in missionary schools 'are taught in English, not merely from necessity on our part, nor solely because some knew our tongue a little and all wished to learn it, but also from a conviction of the great importance ... of promoting among them a knowledge of our own language.' What he called 'broken English' was, he claimed, already spoken along the coast from the Gambia to Gaboon. English was not therefore starting from scratch in the missionary schools; it already existed, even if in a 'depraved' form. It was the task of missionary effort to purify and extend it:

> By the aid of missionaries and schools (English) may be made the common medium of communication, yea, the literary and learned language of all Negro tribes as the Roman language was to the modern European nations of Europe while yet the modern European languages were in an infantine and unwritten state. (Quoted in Ajayi, 1965.)

3

Hope Waddell's sanguine prediction has, in some measure, been realised. A darker prophecy of some decades later, however, made in sorrow rather than in hope, has fortunately not been fulfilled:

> ... the hand of death is necessarily upon many African languages: they have neither the strength derived from civilisation, nor that infusion of elements of a more powerful, or a dead language, which will enable the Languages of India to resist for all time the invasion of the English Language.[7]

As more and more of the West African hinterland came under British rule, the conviction became stronger that the vernaculars must be given some place in education. By the latter part of the nineteenth century a good deal of information had been gathered, in the main by missionary linguists, about some of the major languages of West Africa. Primers, tracts and gospel translations had been produced in many of them, and at least one objection to vernacular teaching, that there were few if any books available, was in these cases invalidated. With the colonial governments beginning to establish some kind of control, however attenuated, over missionary education, clearer statements of policy began to be adumbrated.[8] The 1927 Report of the Advisory Committee on Native Education (HMSO, 1927), set up three years earlier by the British Secretary of State for the Colonies, recommended the use of vernacular languages as well as English in primary schools in Africa. But the Report admitted that one of the major incentives for Africans to send their children to school was the opportunity it offered for acquiring a knowledge of English. To delay unduly the switch from the vernacular to English as a primary school medium of instruction would, the Report goes on, be interpreted by Africans as 'an attempt of Government to hold back the African from legitimate advance in civilisation'.

Thus it was that vernacular languages tended to be used for the first few years of primary school, wherever teachers with the requisite language skills and linguistically homogeneous classes made it possible. Unlike the French, therefore, who would permit nothing but the French language to be used in their colonial schools, the British paid some lip-service to the vernaculars in education. Whether this was because of a genuine solicitude for vernacular languages and cultures on the part of the British; or because of their experience in India, where the disregard for the vernaculars in education in the nineteenth century was seen by the beginning of the twentieth to have done considerable educational and social damage; or simply because, unlike the French, the British never accepted the notion of Africans becoming totally anglicised, and always planned for 'separate development' rather than cultural (and hence, objectionably to many, social) assimilation – it is not easy to decide.[9] It was probably a mixture of many motives, and perhaps partly pure chance. In any case, education in British West Africa never overlooked the need to teach through English after the first year or two. In the westernised sectors of West African life, English was of course at a high premium. For an African who had access to education the English language was a means of advancement; it was the gateway to a government or commercial office job, to the professions, and to social and geographical mobility. The prestige of English in West Africa was less the result of its being the language of the colonial establishment *per se*, still less the fact that it was the language of Shakespeare and John Stuart Mill, but more because of the educational, and hence material and status advantages, which a knowledge of it conferred. The West African peoples are nothing if not realists.

Educational opportunities were, however, very limited. Only a small proportion of African children had until quite recently the opportunity for formal schooling, and thus the chance of learning English in the classroom. Of those few who were fortunate enough to obtain some education, only a tiny minority were able to proceed beyond the primary to the secondary stage, where their embryonic proficiency in English would of course be consolidated and extended. In order to view in some kind of perspective the growth of facilities for learning English through formal education, it may be worth briefly citing a few statistics from forty or so years ago. In 1928, there were in the Gambia, out of a total population of almost 207,000, only 1,300 children at school. Total government expenditure on education for that year, including grants-in-aid to the missions, was just over £9,000. In the Colony of Sierra Leone (the area around Freetown), with a population of 85,000, there were 6,000 children in school; but in the Protectorate, which includes all the remaining territory of present-day Sierra Leone, and with a population estimated at 1,500,000 or so, there were only 5,500 children receiving education. The Gold Coast, with a population of perhaps three million at that time, had just under 70,000 at school, but of these only a few thousand were at secondary stage. In Nigeria as a whole, not much more than 100,000 were estimated to be receiving education, out of a total population of over twenty million; even so, Northern Nigeria, containing over half this population, had only some 10,000 at school.

Liberia, which had been an independent republic since 1847, had not at this point extended education very far; for a long time the descendants of the original Creole settlers had maintained themselves within a kind of coastal enclave, and had done little for the remainder of the country over which they were nominal rulers. In 1928 it was estimated that about 5,000 Liberian children were receiving education in the Republic out of an estimated population of a million or so.[10]

It may be seen that in as much as the attainment of a writing and speaking knowledge of English was dependent upon opportunities for formal education, the extension of the language was not at that point proceeding very fast, and could hardly have touched more than a minority of the population throughout the previous century. With the approach of political independence in the British territories in the years following the Second World War, the expansion of education in the West African territories proceeded at a rapid rate. Primary school development accelerated; secondary schools sprang up and expanded with great speed; and university colleges were founded in Nigeria and the Gold Coast (shortly to become Ghana). Even this late spasm of colonial effort was rapidly outstripped by expansion after independence arrived in the late fifties and early sixties, and in some areas of West Africa it is now hoped to achieve free, compulsory primary education for all within the course of the next few years. University expansion since independence has been even more dramatic; Nigeria, which had one university (Ibadan) in 1960, now has five, with the present number of undergraduates probably eight or nine times what it was then. This clearly must alter the picture as far as English is concerned; for there has been no marked shift in policy towards the vernaculars in education since independence, except, if anything, to reduce still further the amount of time devoted to it. How great a strain English teaching, and teaching through English, will be upon such expanded and still expanding educational systems, only the future will tell. Certainly, the problems involved in introducing English to a very wide section of the population have until recently been masked by the very paucity of the educational opportunities offered during almost the whole of the colonial period.

*   *   *   *   *   *

A somewhat simplified view of the implantation and extension of English in West Africa might see it historically as marked by phases in a struggle between local, naturalised forms of English and an external, élitist variety of the language. The pre-colonial period, with its brutal traffic in slaves, gave birth to the pidgins and creoles of the West African coast. The abolition of the slave trade, the founding of Freetown and the Republic of Liberia, and the extension of colonial political control and missionary activity through much of the area, ushered in the next phase. Now the pidgins and creoles were driven underground. The spread of British-style law and order, the so-called 'civilising mission' of the colonial power and the associated evangelical and educational work of the missionary societies, called for the suppression of the 'debased' forms of English, as they were conceived to be, and their replacement by 'correct' bourgeois English. Thus was engendered, at least on the coast, the diglossia which is exemplified in the low status allotted to demotic Englishes, and the high status of literary and book-learned English. A third phase is now beginning, with the achievement of political independence. This gives a chance for the West African societies to free themselves from the cultural bonds which, under colonial rule, tied them to the controlling metropolitan power. There is now no reason, apart from prejudices which several generations of exposure to cultural imperialism may have induced, why the varieties of English now in use in West Africa, as well as Pidgin and Krio, should not coexist in reasonable comfort, each performing the tasks which, at any given time, it can most conveniently and efficiently accomplish. As the Prospero-Caliban psychology of colonialism begins to fade, one can hope for a more fruitful and creative relationship among the languages and dialects of the area.

However, while such a synoptic view may be suggestive, like all simplifications it conceals almost as much as it reveals. For one thing, for much of the area we are considering there has never existed a diglossic situation, with varieties of Krio and Pidgin competing against the English of the classroom and the written word. The former are peculiarly coastal phenomena. The hinterland, which was exposed late to colonial rule and English education, reveals little diglossia in relation to English, except where, as is the case in Sierra Leone and the western part of the Cameroon Federation, an English-based pidgin or creole serves as a lingua franca for the whole territory. This contrast between the coastal and inland situations of English – as well as other more political nuances – is hinted at in a new translation of Aristophanes' *Lysistrata*, first staged in 1965 at the Ahmadu Bello University in Zaria in the north of Nigeria (Harrison and Simmons, 1966). Athens is represented as a Northern Nigerian emirate, and its citizens speak a standard, literary

English. The citizens of Sparta, on the other hand, are presented as Southerners, and speak the strong and bawdy Doric of Nigerian coastal Pidgin, to the great delight of those in the audience able to understand it.

In the second place, even where Pidgin or Krio does exist, there is by no means always a simple dichotomy between it and the more normative English taught as standard. Many gradations between the two are possible, especially of course in speech. Spoken English is obviously permeable to Pidgin or Krio, in varying densities; and vice versa. As we know from other areas of the English-speaking world, local colloquial or dialectal elements can, when occasion permits, be amalgamated in varying degrees with the more universally shared elements of English. In a sense there are no truly discrete codes distinguishing standard from nonstandard varieties of English, or separating off one register from another. All varieties of English are porous, in spite of what the purists believe, and it is perhaps not very useful therefore to apply the term 'code-switching' to the way in which so many speakers and writers of English seem able to swerve, sometimes almost imperceptibly, from one register or style to another, as need arises. This seems to occur in West Africa with English among many of those who use it, and the facility and readiness with which it is done seems likely to increase rather than diminish, as English users more and more see and accept their heritage of English as a whole.[11] Writers such as Wole Soyinka in the drama and Chinua Achebe in the novel are able to manipulate the speech of their characters, as circumstance, comedy or dramatic tension require, by moving differentially between a relatively normative kind of English and a Pidgin-impregnated English. Versions of English with a local West African flavour are also now being used by advertising copywriters. A well-known poster not long ago advertised the efficiency of a particular brand of petrol with the slogan BP PASS ALL. This phrase, which is of course revealed as demotic only by the uninflected form of the verb, effectively utilises the dual Pidgin sense of *pass*, meaning both to 'pass (someone, something) physically' and to 'surpass', as well as the dual sense of *all*, meaning both 'all people' and 'all things', including, of course, all other brands of petrol. It will also be seen from this instance that Pidgin can retain older English meanings now obsolete or obsolescent elsewhere.

It is necessary not to be confused by the pseudo-Pidgin often used by Europeans to their African servants. In this extremely restricted jargon *pass* has a further meaning, that of to 'serve' or 'proffer', deriving from Pidgin, which took it from a now obsolete English meaning of this verb.

Pass chop, boy! or *Pass whisky!*: thus would an Old Coaster (an Englishman long resident in West Africa) call for food or drink. Water, it must be added, was also occasionally proffered as a result of a similar command, to the embarrassment of guests unfamiliar with the linguistic usages of the Coast! Even baths were *passed*, especially in the days when this required the steward (or more likely the *smallboy*, the steward's assistant) to heat the water in old kerosene tins over the kitchen stove. The small quota of imperative expressions and special idioms which so many Europeans in West Africa made use of for such purposes bears about the same relationship to true Pidgin as the 'kitchen Hindustani' of many a memsahib bore to the Urdu of northern India. Perhaps the old servants will keep these phrases alive for a time – except the offensive term *boy*, used often enough, here as in other parts of the world, to servants old enough to be the father of the 'master'; and possibly members of the American Peace Corps and young English students on voluntary service will find themselves initiated into this peremptory imperialist jargon, if they can ever afford a servant.

As there are many possible gradations between the extremes of English in West Africa, so everywhere are there variant pronunciations of English to be heard. The phonology of a second language will almost always receive some imprint from the phonology of the mother tongue. The number of languages native to the area we are considering must run into several hundreds, and each West African who learns English is subject to a variable amount of exposure to that language, and presumably also possesses a degree of motivation and a capacity for imitating native English speech which varies from individual to individual. Theoretically, therefore, there are as many variant pronunciations or accents of English in West Africa as may be computed by taking the number of vernacular languages and multiplying them by some arbitrarily chosen figure to represent the aggregate of the 'exposure variable', the 'motivation variable' and the 'imitative capacity variable', all these being of course interrelated. Each idiolect of English in West Africa is thus, potentially, phonologically *sui generis*. Yet observation seems to suggest that there is more homogeneity in the pronunciation of English throughout West Africa than might be assumed from the above computation. Homogeneity in pronunciation can, it is true, be more apparent than real to the subjective observer; accent homogeneity may lie more in the ear of the hearer than in the mouths of the speakers. If, however, the pronunciation of English in West Africa does have some overall and very general characteristics which give it a degree of unity throughout the whole area, this might not, after all, be so surprising; though it would be extremely premature at this point in time to speak of such a thing as a West African accent of English.

The first reasons one would adduce for any such relative homogeneity would lie in a number of phonological characteristics which many West African languages appear to have in common. Rhythmically, a high proportion of them seem to conform to a basic pattern which has been termed 'syllable isochronicity', whereby in any evenly flowing utterance the syllables will succeed one another at approximately equal intervals of time. English conforms to an opposite kind of rhythmic pattern based on 'stress isochronicity', in which it is the stressed syllables which succeed one another at approximately equal time-intervals – speed of utterance being constant – with the intervening unstressed syllables fitted in as best they may. All West African languages except Fulani appear to be tonal – including Krio and some varieties of Pidgin – in that they use the relative differentiation of pitch on successive syllables to distinguish lexical items and also, in some cases, to make morphological or syntactical distinctions; although the degree and manner in which this operates varies from language to language. Most West African languages have a simpler range of syllable structures, viewed as segmental phoneme sequences, than English; it is very rare to find languages in this area which contain the kind of complex initial or final consonant clusters of which English makes use. Many of the languages have also a rather smaller set of contrasting vowels than English, especially than British Received Pronunciation, which is a particularly complex accent in this respect. Many of them, however, have oral and nasalised vowels in phonemic contrast, which English does not.

If the above generalised prosodic and systemic statements are valid for a fair number of the West African vernaculars, it would not be surprising if phonological 'interference' by these languages upon the English of learners tended to push in the same general direction.[12] It will be likely to produce a syllable-isochronous rhythm; it will also give a prosodic pattern in which the stressed syllables will be primarily marked by being on a higher pitch than the adjacent unstressed syllables, since the English stress-accent seems to be identified by most West Africans with their own high tone. Initial, medial and final consonant clusters of the more complex kinds are likely to be simplified or sometimes lost altogether, as a result of a tendency which certainly operates in some languages to approximate to a syllabicity of CV-CV-CV-. English vowels followed by nasal consonants, especially in weak, unstressed position, as in *flying*, for example, may well be realised as a nasalised vowel and the nasal consonant lost. Finally, the reduction of the vowel contrasts of English, in conformity with a more restricted oral vowel system in many of the vernaculars, may produce similar convergences, with such pairs as *ship* and *sheep*, *rub* and *rob*, *bird* and *board*, etc, becoming homophonous.

Nor should one overlook the relevance of 'interference' from Pidgin, even at long distance; since the Pidgin- and Krio-using areas of West Africa supplied many of the early African teachers (and evangelists) who went into the inland regions with the missionaries. In the areas where today Pidgin is still widely used, and where many children will come to school with a knowledge of Pidgin, then this will certainly place its imprint on the learning of school English, in particular because of the close relationship between many simple words in both which will be manifest to the child.

Yet, although inter-lingual 'interference' and 'transfer' operate in the pure sense only within the linguistic life of the individual, and tendencies in communities which result from such influences are merely aggregates of individual but similar cases, there is a very important sociolinguistic aspect; and this is extremely significant where a second language is widely used within a community as well as for external communication, and where the language is felt, ambivalently it may be, as a possession over which certain rights can be exercised. In these circumstances, which are *par excellence* those of English in West Africa, 'interference', 'drift', 'transfer' and 'convergence' are sociolinguistic as much as, if not more than, purely linguistic phenomena, for communal factors are very powerful in affecting and modifying speech habits. There is always a tendency to imitate others in their use of a language, whether it is our own or a second language; and a West African does not need to choose to imitate an English public schoolboy's accent if it reminds him and his fellows of some former unloved District Officer rather than an admired schoolmaster. Imitation is stimulated by many motives; but one is surely the desire to gain admittance to a group of which the key to membership seems to be a particular form of behaviour – and West Africa is beginning to have many English-using groups of its own. Deviations in speech behaviour are thus often constrained by the limits of group tolerance; and if a body of students, or an army mess, for instance, develop a communal resistance, expressed as ridicule or disapproval, towards both extremely British speech behaviour and strongly Pidgin-marked speech, then members of these groups are likely to try to keep their pronunciation inside these limits. How far such group attitudes are developing within the westernised sectors of West African life only research by social psychologists could discover. Finally, the need to remain intelligible to one's fellows, and especially to those with whom one converses most frequently, also acts powerfully against undue diversity in language behaviour, and is presumably the basic cause of all linguistic homogeneity. Radio, television and travel can also act similarly across very considerable distances.

Some of these factors may be seen as countervailing forces, tending to limit or reduce the centrifugal pull exerted by the mother tongue upon the second language; others as forces tending to increase homogeneity locally, but sometimes at the expense of the larger homogeneity of the English-speaking world. What will be the final outcome of the struggle between the centripetal and the centrifugal influences on spoken English in West Africa, it is not yet possible to predict. Whatever happens, West Africa must surely in the long run find its own norms for English, and some of them will probably not be so very distant from those in other regions of the English-speaking world.[13] More investigations of such matters would be of the greatest value in guiding teachers of English; and would also contribute to our understanding of the forces which act upon an inherited second language, and determine its patterns of ultimate naturalisation.

There is certainly a sufficiency of terms and expressions peculiar to the use of English in this region to justify the term West Africanism, even if it is not in many cases easy to say how widespread they are or how permanent they are likely to be. As one might expect, there are well-established terms necessitated by the use of English in a natural and cultural environment previously foreign to it. A new flora and fauna had to be coped with: hence such items as *silk cotton tree*, a pleasant arboreal oxymoron for a very elegant tree, not, however, exclusive to West Africa; or *cutting-grass*, a small West African rodent. In addition there are the compounds which have been created to refer to objects or institutions which are either truly indigenous, or the result of the syncretism arising out of the meeting and mingling of European and African cultures: such terms as, for example, *chewing stick* (a piece of wood from a particular kind of plant or tree used for cleaning the teeth), *head-tie* (length of cloth tied decoratively round the head of a woman), *market mammy* (woman trader), *mammy wagon* (a hybrid vehicle with a locally built body serving as both lorry and bus, and capable of carrying goods and – very uncomfortably – passengers from town to town), *talking drum*, *head-load* (a term now surely becoming obsolescent with the advent of mechanical modes of transport), or *fetish priest* (the first element being of Portuguese origin). A number of such terms are likely to be calques; others descriptive compounds originated by Europeans. A very useful one which might be recommended to English-speaking communities elsewhere is the expression (to be) *on seat*, as in a sentence such as 'The Deputy Secretary is back on seat today'; meaning he is in the office, or generally available, as opposed to being absent. This phrase neatly completes a three-term 'locative' set very useful in any society where officials are not always on hand when required: *on tour*, *on leave* and *on seat*.

Then there is the range of English terms whose meanings have been slightly pushed out of place as a result of semantic influences from the vernacular culture pattern. Kinship terminology is an obvious case where this is likely to happen. *Sister* is widely used in certain areas as a term of respect for an older woman, though such usage is not unknown in English outside West Africa. *Cousin*, as it was once explained to me, has a specificity of kinship reference highly variable in proportion to the distance from home at which an encounter takes place: in the home village two men are cousins if they are related in ways not dissimilar to those which define English cousinhood; away from their village, in Accra or Lagos, say, any two men from the same village may refer to each other as cousins; and in England or America, this term could be applied to any man or woman of the same tribe or ethnic group. Phatic expressions and greeting and leave-taking formulae never precisely match across cultural borders. In English we have no fixed formula for expressing sympathy with someone who suffers a sudden minor misfortune, like slipping on a banana skin or spilling a cup of coffee on someone else's carpet (or one's own, for that matter), except 'Hard luck!', which has a rather cynical and masculine ring to it. Many West Africans will be heard to cry *Sorry*! when observing such petty catastrophes – and to one Englishman at least, with peculiarly comforting effect – and this is the result of their search in English for a formula which their own languages certainly possess.

Finally it is necessary to refer to a penumbral area in which semantic, grammatical or collocational 'errors', either through false analogy within English or transference from the mother tongue, gradually become entrenched and widely used. It is never easy to tell when this kind of structural shift or extension has taken firm root, and for how long it remains, or ought to be treated as, remediable. The errors which learners may perpetrate are of course legion, and specimens of some of the most typical will be found elsewhere in this volume, and their causes expounded in greater detail. At this point attention need only be drawn in passing to the sector of the total spectrum of potential errors which is most likely to be the source of widespread and perhaps permanent deviations in West African usage, at least in speech and the more colloquial registers of written English. This is the range of shifts in grammatical pattern, semantic field, collocational relation or idiomatic formulae which, while originally made perhaps in error through false analogy or under vernacular influence, remain insidiously subtle and delicate, representing the kind of 'rule-bending creativity' to which I have earlier referred in another, similar connection. Two examples will suffice. It is to be expected that English phrasal verbs will provide West African learners, like learners all over the world, with very irritating and, it must often seem, unfair difficulties. It is not therefore surprising if in West Africa the use of *dress up* for the verb *dress*, as in a sentence such as 'Every morning I wake and dress up before breakfast' is sometimes to be heard, and quite often finds its way into school compositions. After all, the British and Americans confuse a similar issue by refusing to permit the phrasal verb *wash up* to mean the same activity on both sides of the Atlantic. Also, perhaps, the distinction between plain 'dressing' and elaborate 'dressing up' is not quite the same in the English and the West African cultures. Nominalisations such as *the absents* and *the presents* for children absent or present at, for instance, school roll-call must be a convenience; the adjectival-to-nominal shift is well established in English, and is common in the vernaculars too. One wonders whether in these and similar cases, other English-speaking communities might well do tomorrow what West Africans do today.

*   *   *   *   *   *

In view of the dominating position which English holds in the world today, it is unlikely that the place and function of English in West African life will diminish, even if there are readjustments of role as well as of attitude vis-à-vis the vernacular languages. English continues to be extremely useful in West Africa, internally as well as externally; and God, to adapt a phrase, seems to be more than ever today on the side of the big linguistic battalions. One comfort at least must be that this colonially imposed language, by a fortunate chance of history, happens to be one of the most useful of all languages in the modern world. However much the West African peoples and their governments may wish to offer a more prestigious and significant role to their major vernacular languages, they are not likely to risk their developmental aims by seriously impeding thereby the spread and efficiency of English.

The English-using states of West Africa are intermingled, as may be seen on a map, with French-using states. This is a further cause of difficulty, because bilingualism in French and English is up to the present comparatively rare among West Africans, though urgent steps are being taken to remedy this in all territories. The reason is not far to seek. In the colonial world all roads, linguistic and otherwise, led to the metropolis of the controlling power, never to that of the rival colonial ruler next door. In one West African country, however, the Cameroon Federation, these two colonial traditions and languages confront one another within the borders of a single state. When independence was achieved in 1961 English and French were made joint official languages of this federal state. This was in recognition of the fact that the Federation came into being through the union of the southern part of the former British Cameroons and the whole of the former French Cameroons, both of which had formed the larger part of the German colony of Kamerun before 1918. The official policy of bilingualism in two European languages on top of a very complex infrastructure of scores of vernacular languages as well as a number of regional lingue franche – one of which is Pidgin – is a special kind of complexity which inevitably causes many additional problems of an educational and administrative kind. For not only do two European languages confront one another – thus presumably intensifying any loyalty felt towards each by those who have used it at school; but also two inherited educational systems, each very different from the other, and two attitudes to the language of primary education. The process of *harmonisation*, to use the convenient bilingual word adopted by the Federal Government of Cameroon for the protracted business of mutual adjustment between the two traditions, will need much patience and skill. It is only when one sees the confrontation of two different inherited European languages, educational systems and social values, incarnated within one state in post-colonial Africa – and with only forty odd years between their replacement of yet another, earlier colonial system, the German, and the coming of independence – that one realises just how deeply they have penetrated.

The future of English in West Africa, its manner of use, the roles it performs within these societies, and the contribution its users make to the growth of the language and literature of the English-speaking world, will all depend upon what Deutsch (1953) has called the 'mobilised sector' of these populations. The graduates, the teachers and professional men, the administrators and higher commercial cadres, the technologists and the technicians – it is they who will increasingly dominate the governmental, commercial and educational structures. It is they who will constitute the growing urban, mobile élites of the new societies of West Africa. And it is they who use English and know it best. The future of English in West Africa is largely in their hands, and it is theirs to mould and fashion as it seems most convenient for them and their peoples, both for communicating with the rest of the world and for conversing among themselves. West Africa is certainly one of the growing points of English in the world today. More scholarly documentation and research would be of great benefit, not only to teachers, but also to students of language everywhere; for it may be that as we follow the many interwoven strands of social and linguistic change in these new, yet very old, societies, we shall learn things about the nature of language and linguistic behaviour that we did not know before.

Notes

1 The very term *England-returned* suggests itself to me as a possible West Africanism, but perhaps not exclusive to the area. Trying to ascertain from memory whether it is so or not, with personal experience of English from four continents to choose amongst, as well as literature from a fifth, is a task I find neither easy nor conclusive. Anyone who travels much assimilates a good deal of what, to him, is peripheral English, in the form of local terms and idioms. He is often hard put to recall where precisely he came across them, and without documented lexicographical evidence to support or contradict his memory, he is often at a loss. This kind of difficulty in establishing the regional provenance of a word or idiom, especially now that they can travel from one area to another with great speed by means of radio and television, as well as through journalism and literature, should be kept in mind throughout this volume, which is written in advance of extensive and detailed investigations of English in West Africa.

2 In 1662 the English trade with the Gold Coast was intensified by the founding of the Company of Royal Adventurers of England Trading to Africa. The founding members included James, Duke of York, later to become king in succession to his brother Charles II. Its charter gave it a monopoly of trade along the coast of Africa from Gibraltar to the Cape of Good Hope. It was to supply 3,000 slaves annually to the West Indies, take over the fort of Cormantine and build new forts or lodges at Cape Coast, Anashan, Egya, Kommenda and Winneba along the Gold Coast. In 1663 the company built Cape Coast Castle and lodges at the other places mentioned. These forts and bases often changed hands in the succeeding decades as the English, the Dutch, the French, the Danes, and the Portuguese fought over the West African trade or extended their European squabbles to

Africa. The Royal Adventurers were replaced in 1672 by the Royal African Company, which it is estimated exported 140,000 slaves to the New World between 1680 and 1700.

3 This diary, written in Antera Duke's own hand, was taken to Scotland some time during the nineteenth century by a missionary, deposited in the library of the United Presbyterian Church in Edinburgh and then transferred to the offices of the Free Church of Scotland after the union of the former with the latter. Eventually its interest was appreciated and before the Second World War a Scottish missionary, formerly of Calabar, made copious extracts from it, and drew the attention of the International African Institute to its existence. However, during the war the offices of the Church were bombed and the diary destroyed. All that remains of it are the extracts taken from it by the missionary, and it is these portions which are published under Daryll Forde's editorship, together with a modern translation and linguistic and ethnographic notes by D. Simmons, from whose modernised text the regularised form of the quoted passage is taken, with acknowledgments. The story of how almost accidentally this diary came to light after lying in a library for many decades, must cause one to wonder how much information of linguistic relevance to West Africa may be lying in European mercantile, church and governmental archives. Historians have searched a good many of these archives for their own purposes; but few linguists, whether interested in the implantation of European languages on the coast or early records of vernacular languages, have so far investigated them.

4 Diglossia is a term coined to denote situations in which two distinct languages, or related but relatively discrete dialects, are used by the same community for different purposes; one of these languages or dialects having a high prestige, the other a low prestige. Pidgins and creoles, which commonly coexist in such situations with a standard, classical or literary form of the base language, or another language of prestige, almost always have a low status relative to the other. See Ferguson, 1959, and Hymes, 1964, *pp* 429–439.

5 Quoted in Groves, 1948, Vol 1. One must ask, however, whether the situation described by Hannah Kilham was very much different from that of illiterate dialect speakers in England at the time, who must also have gained somewhat garbled notions from the remote language of many hymns.

6 Letter from the Basel Mission to the Berlin Colonial Office, quoted in Mbassi-Manga, 1968.

7 Cust, 1895. Robert Needham Cust was not a missionary, but a distinguished member of the Indian Civil Service. He was a fine Sanskrit and Persian scholar, with a wide knowledge of Indian and European languages. On his retirement he travelled extensively, including visits to West Africa. Between 1870 and his death in 1909 he wrote more than sixty volumes on Oriental philology, comparative linguistics and religion, among them a two-volume *Sketch of the Modern Languages of Africa* (London, 1883). His observation in one of his essays on the English of people in Freetown and Monrovia, presumably on the basis of personal experience, may be noted: 'The West Africans of Sierra Leone and Liberia speak excellent English, as their only language, and enjoy an English culture . . .'

8 A defined relationship between British colonial governments and missionary schools, concerning financial aid and inspection, was instituted by the West African Education Ordinance of 1882.

9 For a comparison of colonial policies towards languages in Africa see Spencer, 1970. See also Tiffen, 1968, for a fuller exploration of British policy in education in Africa, with special reference to language.

10 The figures quoted are taken from the Annual Reports for 1929 by the Directors of Education for the respective territories.

11 Thus, for example, the early hostile reactions of many West Africans to the idiosyncratic prose of Amos Tutuola, neither true Pidgin nor traditional literary
English, seem now to be giving way to a calmer assessment. Much of the original
antagonism was, it is true, really directed against the English critics, who, on the
appearance of *The Palm Wine Drinkard* in 1952, hailed it enthusiastically with
what may have seemed a Prospero-like patronage. For a most perceptive recent
examination of this and other related matters by a distinguished Nigerian writer,
see Clark, 1968.

12 It must be appreciated that, apart from such general characteristics in common
among groups of languages, the languages of West Africa display great variety in
their detailed phonological composition. See Ladefoged, 1968.

13 For a salutary reminder of the dangers of premature christenings of new regional
Englishes, see Prator, 1968.

Ayọ Bamgboṣe

The English Language in Nigeria

Of all the heritage left behind in Nigeria by the British at the end of the colonial administration, probably none is more important than the English language. This is now the language of government, business and commerce, education, the mass media, literature, and much internal as well as external communication.

For purposes of government and administration, English is the official language, though this is not stated in the Constitution. Government records, administrative instructions and minutes, legislation, court records and proceedings (except in the customary courts) are all in English. In business and commerce too, the situation is the same: business records, contracts, and most advertisements are written in English.

The entrenchment of English is perhaps most noticeable in the field of education. English is introduced as a subject in the first year of the primary school, and from the third year of the primary school up to and including the university level, it is the medium of instruction. This in effect means that the Nigerian child's access to the cultural and scientific knowledge of the world is largely through English. Since the products of the schools will be absorbed into types of employment where English is the official medium of communication, and where, consequently, proficiency in English is a necessary qualification, the pre-eminent position of English in the educational system is likely to remain for a long time.

In the mass media, English is again in a predominant position. All the national newspapers are published in English. On the radio, most of the non-musical programmes such as the news, announcements, reports and feature talks are in English. Television is almost entirely in English, especially since most of the films shown are imported from either Britain or the USA. Like television, the cinema is also dominated by English language films, and where non-English films (such as Indian films) are shown, the sub-titles, if any, are always in English. Although there is a

4

lot of drama in some of the local languages, and sometimes in Pidgin, plays in English (especially those by Shakespeare and by Nigerian playwrights) are very popular.

Very few of the local languages have any appreciable written literature. The best-known literary works so far produced in the country are all in English. These include novels, short stories, plays and poems. They range from folk literature, often in sub-standard English (for example, the well-known Onitsha market fiction, written, published and distributed in and around Onitsha in Eastern Nigeria), to the more sophisticated works of leading writers such as Chinua Achebe and Wole Soyinka.

By far the most important role of English in Nigeria today is its use as a medium of social communication. It is estimated that there are about 400 different local languages in Nigeria. Three of these languages (Hausa 15,000,000 speakers; Yoruba 10,000,000 speakers; Igbo 6,000,000 speakers)[1] are often referred to as the major languages of the country; but very few persons speak more than one of these three languages. In practice, therefore, English is the only effective medium of communication between Nigerians from different linguistic backgrounds. This is why national activities have to be conducted in English. And this is not only true of official activities. In social gatherings, such as private parties, English is usually the medium of communication. This is often the case even when the guests have a common language other than English. The feeling seems to be that a party can only be formal if the official language of the country is used. The many send-off parties, naming ceremonies, wedding receptions, house-warming parties which are a regular feature of life in the towns and at which English is invariably the medium of communication are a testimony to the role of English in the social life of educated Nigerians.

As a medium of communication, English has an important role not only internally but also externally, that is, for contact between Nigeria and the outside world. Because English is a 'world' language, Nigerians who know English are able to communicate with colleagues in other countries. At the United Nations, at Commonwealth and other international meetings, Nigerians have no language other than English for taking part in the deliberations, except for the small minority who know French.

Yet it is all too easy to get a false impression from the foregoing paragraphs, unless one can make some sort of estimate of the number of Nigerians actively involved in the use of English. This kind of estimate is very difficult to make, because there are varying standards of English and different levels of attainment by the users of the language. Excluding Pidgin English, which is a semi-official language in certain areas and in certain institutions (such as the Nigeria Police), the question of what variety of English should be accepted as standard in Nigeria still remains to be tackled. Hardly anyone would hesitate to rule out the market women's *patois* which many market-goers in the large towns are familiar with. These market women will call out, in their own peculiar way of speaking English, such phrases as *Customer, buy here; My friend, buy from me; Look tomatoes; What of oranges?; Madam, I have good pawpaw o!* Beyond these phrases and a few greetings, most of them know no other English. In any estimate of speakers of English, it is obvious then that these women cannot be included.

A ready measure of proficiency in English is educational attainment. In Nigeria, this ranges from primary-school to university education. The question then is: where does one draw the line? The primary-school leaver in most areas has had at least five years of English. Should he be considered a speaker of English? Many headmasters of secondary schools complain that when the primary-school leaver comes to them, his English is extremely inadequate. The following is a letter written to me by a boy who had successfully completed a primary-school course:

Dear Sir,
    With much pleasre and respect I inscribe you this few lines and with the hope that it will meet you in good condition of health.
    The reason why I write you is to tell you about my work which I wrote the first to you sir and I have resign from Textile work and go for Electronic Servise that is radio and T.V. mechanic for three year and its remain for my money for apprentiseship and books and tools so next Monday is the last promise we made for my work before I start that I will complete both money and books – tools, but I have recived the list from Manager, and all my mates there have paid their money, and if I beg them to manage with them to study with their books manager will tell me to buy my own so I beg you by the name of God to help me for the money and books and tools and I hope that you will help me and I don't want to miss this work at all.
                                        I am yours truely,
                                        David

The writer of this letter had a good (Grade A) certificate. This suggests that the English of many of his fellows must be worse than his. I have in fact seen samples of written work by many primary-school children; and what passes for English in them is hardly recognisable as such.

There is one other difficulty about making educational attainment a yardstick for determining proficiency in English. On the one hand, there are many persons of poor educational background who have subsequently had an opportunity of improving themselves educationally, either through their work or by private study. The civil service and other institutions in Nigeria are full of the old Standard vi (Primary School) Certificate holders who can hold their own against much better qualified newcomers. On the other hand, there are quite a few people of good educational standard whose English hardly reflects their educational attainment. On a recent tour of Nigeria as one of the members of the Ford Foundation English Language Survey Team commissioned to look into the problems of English language teaching in the country, I took the opportunity to observe the use of English by many educated Nigerians (mainly teachers, civil servants and university lecturers). One of the school teachers whose teaching I watched used the following expressions within a period of less than ten minutes: *think it, think your own, they are having a king, last time I collected a news.* This teacher held the Grade i Teacher's Certificate. Another person, a very senior civil servant and university graduate, used the following expressions at an interview: *For the senior ones, they have no time, but for the junior ones, they do (For the senior ones* = As far as the senior ones are concerned); *the girls in this lower class, they like French; Can they fit to go back to the same position?* Perhaps the point should be made here that I am not suggesting that these two people are in any way typical. But the fact that some people who have had a reasonable standard of education talk like this underlines the difficulty of relying completely on educational attainment as the determining factor of proficiency in English.

The answer to the question 'How many speakers of English?' thus depends on how wide one casts the net. If one includes the level of proficiency generally attained by primary-school leavers, perhaps ten per cent of Nigeria's population of fifty-five million may be said to know English. If the criterion of proficiency is raised to exclude anything lower than the standard expected of a secondary-school leaver, it is doubtful whether the number of competent users of English would be higher than five per cent of the whole population. It must be said, of course, that there are hardly any quantitative data on which to base these estimates. In 1965, the number of children in primary schools was three million. It is estimated that this number represents only thirty per cent of the children of school-going age. The output of children from all the primary schools in the country in 1965 was lower than 250,000 (Fuller, 1966). It is from these that candidates for secondary school education, and in fact any other kind of training, are drawn.

Although, in comparison with the total population of the country, the number of users of English is thus very small, their influence is of course tremendous in view of the official position of the language. The English-speaking group, in fact, forms an élite which is constantly being added to as education reaches more and more people. Those who do not know English are at a disadvantage, for at one time or the other they are inevitably involved with matters which require some knowledge of English: for example, with things like licences, electricity bills, telegrams, taxes, various government forms and official letters.

Nigerian English

In a situation where English is in contact with many local languages, and where English is a second language, it is to be expected that the kinds of English found will be different from the varieties of English spoken in countries where English is the mother tongue. The point about English in Nigeria is not just that it is different from British or American English. It is rather that there are several varieties of English 'ranging from something very near standard English to the patois of the market place' (Grieve, 1964). In this kind of situation it is difficult to know where to draw the line – what to accept as standard Nigerian English and what to reject as sub-standard. The well-known Nigerian novelist Amos Tutuola writes in a most peculiar kind of English. Here is a passage from his novel, *The Palm Wine Drinkard* (1952):

> After a little we came from the farm to the house, but at the same time that he saw us, he left all the people with whom he was fighting and met us, so when we entered the house, he showed us to everybody in the house saying that these were his father and mother. But as he had eaten all the food which had been prepared against the night, then we began to cook other food, but when it was the time to put the food down from the fire, he put it down for himself and at the same time, he began to eat that again as it was very hot, before we could stop him, he had eaten all the food and we tried all our best to take it from him, but we could not do it at all.

Should this kind of English be accepted as standard in Nigeria? Most people will say it should not. Yet, this kind of English is not restricted to one writer only. There is a growing tradition of folk-writing in English – short stories, plays and other imaginative writing – associated with little presses and publishers in Onitsha, Eastern Nigeria. These pamphlets, with such curious titles as *Miss Cordelia in the Romance of Destiny*, *Nancy in Blooming Beauty*, *The Joys and Sorrows of Man and Woman*, *Congo Damsel in Love Drama*, *Veronica My Daughter*, *How to Fall in Love with Girls*, *The Sorrows of Love*, run into more than 200 items, and they are all written in a type of English which many people would consider sub-standard. At one level of literacy, however, these books are regarded as classics. Here, for example, is a description of the love between two young people as seen by the girl (Nwosu, n.d.):

> Can ever two people live so happily, letters flowed from one to each other, the contents of which I should not disclose. Our love spread in the town like Radio Newsreel.

and a critique on love by the same girl:

> So the type of love I needed was not the kind you could pick or drop on the wayside any time according to your discretion. Some boys are unchristian of course, who call themselves diamond chasers – boys who would not keep to one friend alone are not at all diamond chasers but traders in love credit and cash.

At the other end of the scale, the type of English one finds in government reports, learned journals and the more sophisticated novels is hardly different in any way from standard written English from any English-speaking country. Here, for example, is a passage from Chinua Achebe's *No Longer at Ease* (1960):

> Going from the Lagos mainland to Ikoyi on a Saturday night was like going from a bazaar to a funeral. And the vast Lagos cemetery which separated the two places helped to deepen this feeling. For all its luxurious bungalows and flats and its extensive greenery, Ikoyi was like a graveyard. It had no corporate life – at any rate for those Africans who lived there. They had not always lived there, of course. It was once a European reserve. But things had changed, and some Africans in 'European posts' had been given houses in Ikoyi. Obi Okonkwo, for example lived there, and as he drove from Lagos to his flat he was struck again by these two cities in one. It always reminded him of twin kernels separated by a thin wall in a palm-nut shell. Some-

times one kernel was shiny-black and alive, the other powdery-white and dead.

Between the two extremes, there are various admixtures – sometimes close to the Onitsha market fiction variety and sometimes nearer to the more standard type of English. The newspapers provide excellent samples of the various kinds.

The problem posed by the coexistence of these varieties is probably most keenly felt by examiners of English who are forced to decide between right and wrong English. On the whole, the attitude of the West African Examinations Council examiners has been that while standard English should form the basis of examinations and tests, variants which experience has shown are acceptable to educated members of the appropriate community may be accepted for examination purposes (Grieve, 1964). In practice, this solution is not easy to apply. As noted above, it is difficult to decide what standard of education should be used to define the educated members of the community. How much local variation should be accepted? What is genuinely a local variant and what is merely an error? A Chief Examiner for English in the 1965 West African School Certificate and GCE examination pointed out that the expression 'It was my first time of going to hospital', used by many candidates with the meaning: 'It was my first visit to a hospital', would definitely be marked wrong by London or Cambridge examiners; but in Nigeria, most examiners would probably accept it as a local variant.

Nevertheless the problem of a standard is, on the whole, easier as far as written English is concerned. In the case of spoken English, there are two acutely important problems. One is the problem of intelligibility; the other the question of acceptability. How much local variation can be allowed without reducing the ability of the Nigerian speaker of English to communicate effectively with speakers of English from other countries? What pronunciation model should teachers aim at? It is generally agreed that the aim is not to produce speakers of British Received Pronunciation (even if this were feasible!). But until a local variety of English pronunciation can be evolved such as will satisfy the minimum requirements of national and international intelligibility, a point of reference has to be found in some existing variety of spoken English. In this connection, it is important to stress that acceptability is almost as important as intelligibility. Many Nigerians will consider as affected or even snobbish any Nigerian who speaks like a native speaker of English. It is also true to say that most Nigerians prefer a British accent to an American one. These are sociological factors which cannot be ignored in English language teaching and examining in Nigeria.

The major differences between English in Nigeria and English in other countries are to be found mainly in the spoken form of the language. The greatest influence on the pronunciation of English by Nigerians is the sound systems of the vernacular languages. Most of the phonetic characteristics in the English of Nigerians can, of course, be traced to the transfer of features from their first language. Many people claim that they can tell what part of the country a Nigerian belongs to from the way he speaks English. This kind of skill, in so far as it exists, is due to the recognition of typical interference features in the pronunciation of English by the speaker involved. One example of such a typical feature is that Igbo speakers of English, even well-educated ones, tend to transfer the vowel harmony system of their language into English. They say [folo] instead of [fɔlou] for the word 'follow' because the sequence of /ɔ/ and /o/ in two successive syllables is not permissible in Igbo. Hausa speakers of English tend to insert a vowel between a syllable-final consonant and the initial consonant of an immediately following syllable; for instance, [rezigineiʃən] instead of [rezigneiʃən] for the word 'resignation'. Yoruba speakers of English generally nasalise English vowels which are preceded by nasals. For example, they say [mɔ̃nĩn] for English 'morning' [mɔ:niŋ].

In spite of the existence of features restricted to the speech of persons from particular language backgrounds, there are nevertheless features which are typical of the pronunciation of most Nigerian speakers of English. For example,

1 there are certain characteristic stress patterns for certain words, eg: maˈdam, mainˈtenance, ˌtriˈbalism, ˈcircumference;
2 English is spoken with a syllable-timed instead of a stress-timed rhythm;
3 compared with most varieties of English, the Nigerian variety has a more restricted system of intonation and a smaller number of vowel distinctions;
4 there is generally an absence of word-final syllabic consonants since a vowel is usually inserted before such consonants, eg: [bɔtᵘl] for 'bottle', [litᵘl] for 'little', [lesⁱn] for 'lesson';
5 unstressed syllables which have vowels such as /i/ or /ə/ in British English generally have other vowels in Nigerian English, eg: [kɔnˈsist] for [kənˈsist], 'consist', [ˈbraitest] for [ˈbraitist], 'brightest',

[ˈdraivə] for [ˈdraivə], 'driver', and [aˈraival] for [əˈraivəl], 'arrival'.

Typical features of this kind tend to show that there are standardising factors which could lead to the emergence of an Educated Nigerian variety of English pronunciation. An interesting example is the case of the phonemic distinction between /iː/ and /i/, as in *beat* and *bit*. Most Yoruba speakers of English do not make this distinction because it does not exist in their first language. But in Hausa and Igbo there are vowels similar in quality to the vowel /i/ in English as well as /iː/. In spite of this, many Hausa and Igbo speakers of English do not make this distinction. The same is true of most speakers of English from other language backgrounds. What seems to be happening here is the development of a standard local variety.

The other major area where the emergence of a Nigerian variety of English may be observed is in lexical usage. Apart from features which may be traced back to the influence of the local languages (and which will be mentioned later), many lexical items have developed special meanings in Nigerian usage. The following are some of the more common examples:

fellow =	any person (including a female)	(David is going to marry that fellow)
branch =	call (on one's way to another place)	(I am going to branch at my uncle's house)
drop =	alight (*eg* from a car)	(I will drop at the roundabout)
lesson =	private tuition	(My daughter goes to lesson after school hours)
themselves =	each other	(My parents love themselves)
against =	for	(You should prepare this against next session)
chase =	try to win a girl's affection	(I am going to chase that girl)
globe =	electric bulb	(We had no light because she broke the globe)
cup =	drinking glass	(He drank a cup of water)

Perhaps more important than single lexical items are the idioms

which have developed in Nigerian English. The following are a few
typical examples:

to be on seat = to be in the office	(The director is not on seat)
to take in = to become pregnant	(My wife took in last month)
to be with = to be in one's possession	(It is with him = He has it)
a been-to = a person who has travelled overseas (usually to Britain)	(Stop talking like a been-to)
all what = all that	(I believe all what you say)
to move with = to associate with	(That boy moves with the wrong company)

Another difference between Nigerian English and other varieties of
English is the difference in appropriateness of certain expressions for
particular situations. For example, in Nigerian English, the expressions
sorry and *welldone* are often used as greetings – the former as an expression of sympathy (*eg* to a person who sneezes) and the latter as a greeting
to anyone at work. The use of these expressions in similar situations
in British or American English would be inappropriate.

Thus, in answer to the question, Is there such a thing as Nigerian
English? one can point to the features which are becoming typical of the
varieties of English spoken in Nigeria. But much research is still required in order to determine what really constitutes 'Nigerian English',
and which variety of it should be accepted as the standard.

English and the Nigerian languages

Because the vast majority of Nigerians do not know English, the medium
of communication for most people is a Nigerian language. English is
therefore a minority language. Since almost every Nigerian speaker of
English has a vernacular language as his mother tongue, an interesting
aspect of the study of the role of English in Nigeria is the relative use of
English in relation to a vernacular by those who know both. There are
two kinds of general situation in which such language use may be observed. One is the case where the participants do not share a common
vernacular. In this sort of situation, if the whole group is expected to be

involved in the act of communication, the only medium possible (whether written or spoken) is English. The second kind of situation is that in which the participants share a common vernacular. Here, the choice of language depends on a number of factors. If the communication is written, the chances are that the medium will be English. This is generally because many persons lack adequate skills in writing their own vernaculars. Also, in a number of cases, either no orthography has yet been devised for the vernacular, or such as has been devised is unsatisfactory. It is therefore not unusual, indeed quite common, for a husband to write to his wife in English, even though they share a common vernacular. In the case of oral communication, the choice of medium tends to depend on the degree of formality or informality required by the situation. If the participants wish to be formal, they generally speak in English; if they wish to be informal, they speak in the vernacular. There is, however, a further constraint imposed by the subject of discourse. If the discussion is on a technical subject, the tendency will be for English to be preferred; the only way of showing familiarity or informality in this situation is to dilute the English with the vernacular. This mixture of languages is, in fact, very common among the better-educated classes. Sometimes, however, switching between English and the vernacular may be due to purely linguistic reasons. I myself have found, for instance, that in talking to a Yoruba person whom I am not sure whether to address as 'you-singular' or 'you-plural' (the choice of which depends on status, age, familiarity, etc), I often either talk in English or, if I wish to be less formal, talk in Yoruba but switch over to English whenever I have to use the second person pronoun singular!

In the school curriculum, English occupies a more important position than any of the vernaculars. Apart from the use of some of them as a medium of instruction in the first two years of the primary-school, the majority of vernaculars only exist as a subject in the primary-school curriculum. In the secondary school, four of the vernacular languages (Efik, Hausa, Igbo and Yoruba) may be offered as optional subjects in the West African School Certificate and GCE examination. In the 1964 examination, passes in these languages were as follows: Efik, 87; Hausa, 395; Igbo, 1,568 and Yoruba, 3,323. The total number of passes was 5,373. This is less than fifty per cent of the total number of passes in English, which was 11,524 in the same year.[2] At university, English is a very important subject. All the five Nigerian universities have departments of English. In 1966, the number of final year students majoring in English in the universities (excluding the University of Lagos, which had no final year class until 1967) was 129. The only Nigerian languages taught at university level are Hausa, Igbo and Yoruba, and so far one cannot take a degree in the first two; a course leading to a BA degree in Yoruba was introduced at the University of Ibadan in the 1966–7 session.

In spite of the inferior position of the vernaculars in the school curriculum, they are of course important socially. As soon as pupils leave the restriction of the classroom, they usually revert to the vernaculars or, in some areas, to Pidgin. One of the constant problems of the school teacher (especially the primary-school teacher) is the limited opportunity his pupils have of using English. In most cases, the pupils speak only the vernacular in the home. Even in some boarding schools where pupils are fined a penny whenever they speak in the vernacular, the use of the vernacular outside the classroom is still quite common.

On the radio and television, there are news broadcasts and feature programmes in the major Nigerian languages. In Yoruba, there is a thriving tradition of folk drama, and plays in Yoruba are constantly produced for the stage and television. There are also weekly newspapers in Hausa and Yoruba.

In view of the existence of Nigerian languages alongside English, the suggestion has often been made in the legislatures and also in the newspapers that the country should decide on a national language. It is generally agreed that the choice is between one of the local languages and English. Given the official position of English as the language of government, commerce, industry, learning and national and international communication, it is not surprising that many people would favour the choice of English as a national language. But there are others who feel that one of the local languages should be selected. They say, for instance, that it is ridiculous that Nigerians should have to talk to each other in a 'foreign' language. It is true that there is one advantage in choosing a Nigerian language as the national language: any major Nigerian language chosen would probably have many more speakers than the number of persons who now speak English in the country. But there are serious problems involved in such a choice. Since the speakers of a Nigerian language generally constitute an ethnic group, one would be putting the ethnic group whose language is selected at an advantage over the others, and it is unlikely that the other groups would willingly accept such a situation. Another major problem would be how to produce technical works in the national language (textbooks on most subjects are available only in English); and, of course, there would still be a continuing need for a world language (like English) for the purposes of international communication.[3] It is probably because of these complex problems that the government has so far avoided taking any decision on the national language question. And the prospect for the foreseeable future is that a decision on the question will continue to be avoided.

In a language contact situation such as exists in Nigeria, it is to be expected that there will be an interaction between the vernaculars and English. The influence of English on the vernaculars (which is the topic of one of the sections of this book) is most obvious in lexical borrowings and in the mixture of English and vernacular expressions in speech. The influence of the vernaculars on English is more relevant here, especially in view of the earlier discussion of local variants in Nigerian English. Basically, what happens is that patterns of the local languages – phonological, grammatical and lexical – tend to be transferred into English. Some of the more common lexical forms include borrowings, *eg: kiakia bus* (a Volkswagen bus; *kíákíá* is a Yoruba word for quickly, and the bus is so named because it goes very fast); and idiom translation, *eg* the common greeting exchanged by two people on meeting: *How? Not bad*; which is a near-translation of the Igbo *Kèdú? ọ́ dị̀ m̀mà* (How are you? It is good); or the expression *I hear the smell* where *hear* is a literal translation of Yoruba *gbọ́*, 'hear', or Hausa *jí*, 'hear, feel'. Sometimes, the translation is indirect. There may be a situation in the vernacular for which there is an appropriate expression. If there is no such expression in English, an existing expression may have its meaning extended to cover the situation. Such a case is the use of *sorry* or *welldone* mentioned above.

In urban areas where many vernaculars are represented, the pressure to use English is greater. But in a town where there is a dominant vernacular, the tendency for persons moving into such areas is to pick up expressions in this vernacular as well. However, immigrants to an urban centre hardly ever give up their own languages. Sometimes the speakers of the same vernacular settle together in the same part of the town, but more commonly they live in different parts of the town while continuing to meet socially. In any case, the vernacular language is usually preserved in the home. Children from such homes generally become proficient in the dominant vernacular of the area in addition to their own language and English. Since opportunities for using English are much greater in the big towns, many adults who have never been taught English, tend to pick up some form of spoken English. Those who already know English are able to improve their performance. The net result is that the standard of competence in written and spoken English is much higher in urban areas.

   From this brief account of the position and role of English in Nigeria certain broad conclusions may be drawn. English is firmly established as a second language in Nigeria. It is the official language, and is likely to remain so for a long time. In view of the existence of many mother tongues in Nigeria, the English spoken and written in Nigeria is bound to be influenced by these languages; new features are bound to develop, and are in fact already developing. In time, many of these features are likely to become stable and ultimately standardised, and a distinct Nigerian variety of English, probably associated with a certain level of education, will then emerge.

Notes

1 These figures are based on the 1963 Census figures as given in a paper read by C. Okonjo at the First African Population Conference at Ibadan in January 1966, 'A Preliminary medium estimate of the 1962 mid-year population of Nigeria'.
2 These figures are taken from the Annual Report for 1965 of the West African Examinations Council.
3 Many of the factors to be considered in the choice of a national language, and the consequences of such a choice, are listed in Spencer, 1963, *pp* 129–35.

L. A. Boadi

Education and the Role of English in Ghana

There is not much that is unique about the history, development and present position of English in Ghana. One can readily cite languages like Latin, Greek, Arabic and Turkish all of which have, with varying degrees of success and for different periods of time, been imposed on alien peoples (Brosnahan, 1963b). In more modern times one obvious result of European expansion has been the spread of languages like Spanish, Portuguese, English and French to the Americas, Asia and Africa.

In the case of Ghana English was imposed as the language of administration by colonialists, their immediate practical aim being to bring together the separate political units which they had won either by conquest or treaty. This was inevitable. For quite apart from the well-known fact that colonial rulers were often both unwilling and too busy to learn the language of the ruled, in Ghana the various ethnic groups spoke, as they do now, a very wide range of languages.

The official use of English in administration on the large scale that we have it now was made possible by the introduction of schools by missionaries, particularly along the coast and in one or two places inland where English was formally taught as a second language. Sections of the community who had the benefit of a western education became bilingual.

After independence from colonial rule in 1957 the language of the colonial rulers is still a cohesive force internally, and is used in a wide range of activities, but it must have been clear even from the beginning of the cultural contact that English was not going to be used in the Gold Coast in all spheres of life. The indigenous languages, of which one can count more than forty, are still used and are, in many cases, being deliberately cultivated; no less than six of them – Akan, Gã, Ewe, Nzima, Dagbani and Hausa – are regularly heard on the radio. The Ghana

Bureau of Languages has devised orthographies for some of the more obscure of these languages and has turned out pamphlets giving brief sketches of their linguistic structure. There is no indication that any of the local languages is likely to disappear or that the importance of the vernaculars as a whole in the life of the people will diminish. Rather than recede into the background, it is clear from all observable evidence that the indigenous languages are going to receive greater prominence in the practical as well as the cultural life of Ghanaians than was accorded them during the colonial period. Talented Ghanaians now write poetry and plays in their own native languages – an activity which, though possible, was uncommon before independence.

These and other facts suggest that since independence Ghanaians have become more sharply aware of the possibilities of the indigenous languages, and of their existence as separate linguistic entities. Clearly, the results of any attempt to impose one local language on everybody would be disastrous. There was talk a few years ago of making Akan, the most widely spoken of the languages, the lingua franca of Ghana, but this was more a political wish than a well thought-out attempt to make the country officially monolingual; and although the subject was brought up for discussion in the National Parliament once, it was not pursued with the vigour and enthusiasm which a topic of national importance would otherwise have deserved. Even the most fervent of the Africanist politicians were aware that to attempt to give one of the local languages such national importance would be doing great harm to the very concept of the African personality whose interest such a move was supposed to serve.

Since, as far as one can see, the adoption of a local language as the lingua franca is not envisaged, the English language is the most obvious choice for general internal use. This was clear even before independence. The politicians who sprang up after the war condemned colonialism both on the political platform and on paper with all the animus and vehemence they could command. But, ironically, their eloquence and debating powers could find expression in no other medium than one of the legacies of colonialism, the English language – not because they were not competent in the use of their own first languages but because they had to reach the largest possible number of people within the shortest possible time and at the least expense.

Many of the newly independent states of Africa are going to have to accept the international status of English for years to come, not only for internal administrative purposes but also for contact with the outside worlds of learning, politics, commerce, science and technology. More people are going to school today in Ghana than ever before, and they learn there to use English for reasons which are bound up with independence from alien rule. The position seems to have been accepted by the élite in the newer nations that national boundaries need not coincide with linguistic ones. At a conference on African literature in 1963 one delegate brought this point home clearly when he said, 'The problem is to make the people of England realise, and in France for that matter, that their languages are no longer their sole property, because they have almost defeated themselves by their own success in propagating their language . . .'.[1]

It is not easy to make a simple overall statement about the varieties of English to be found in Ghana because the users of it range from the most educated to the totally illiterate. It is enough for our present purposes to distinguish arbitrarily between educated and uneducated varieties, and regard them for convenience as the extremities of a graded continuum, the least educated being the least internationally acceptable and the most educated the most widely understood in the English-speaking world.

Of the varieties which cluster around the former one can easily cite a very important representative, commonly referred to as *Kru* English or Pidgin, and associated with the uneducated sections of the population – labourers, traders, mechanics, stewards and so on. Pidgin as used in Ghana exhibits a number of structural affinities with the creolised varieties of English of Jamaica,[2] and of places along the West Coast of Africa where English is the official language. We have to note, however, that whereas in places like Freetown in Sierra Leone creolised English is used in the home as a first language and very often between educated people, in Ghana *Kru* is rarely, if ever, used between speakers of the same local language or between educated people. It is used, for example, between the educated master and his steward if they happen not to speak the same language; between labourers and artisans in a factory or workshop, and between buyer and seller in the market, and, less commonly perhaps, in the larger department stores. As would be expected, it has considerable currency within the army and the police force.

The vocabulary is very mixed, although it is preponderantly English. Word order is basically that of standard English, but the grammar exhibits marked deviations from that of educated standard English with respect to certain syntactic features. For example, since there is a limited use of inflectional affixes in this variety of English, rules of selection like

5

concord and government are of little importance. Unlike Freetown and other places in the Commonwealth where similar varieties of language are used, Pidgin very seldom occurs in written form in Ghana. A few years ago one local newspaper had a regular column written in Pidgin, but the aim was more to entertain the public than to keep it informed.

In larger towns where Pidgin is very widely used teachers and parents have expressed anxiety about its possible adverse effects on school children's learning of standard English. While one would be inclined to sympathise with these fears, it would be overhasty, perhaps, to adopt a rigidly uncompromising attitude towards this variety of speech, in view of our present state of ignorance about its possible influence on the more prestigious varieties of English used by the educated sections of Ghana. What is required is research aimed at determining the socio-linguistic facts of Pidgin English usage, facts which would help in answering such questions as the following: What is the attitude of the educated sections of the population towards Pidgin? What Pidgin forms are passing into educated usage? Under what circumstances is Pidgin acquired? (There seems to be a widespread belief amongst educated Ghanaians that one does not need to have been exposed to Pidgin for any reasonable length of time in order to be able to use it, provided one can already speak standard English. All one needs to do is ignore certain restrictional rules involving inflexion. It is doubtful whether this is the case.) What is the attitude of users of Pidgin towards standard English? In what situations is Pidgin used? Answers to these questions would be useful about a language variety whose importance as a communication medium in Ghana cannot be overstressed. Nobody would attempt to make a wedding or after-dinner speech in Pidgin, it is true, but it plays a considerable role in reducing some of the linguistic barriers which exist in Ghana.

At the other pole of our continuum are clustered the educated varieties of English, some of which are acceptable internationally. These varieties, written and spoken, are used for administrative purposes, at social functions and weddings, for preaching sermons, for journalism and so on. They are also being used by the new generation of creative writers. It is difficult to make any generalisation based on fact about these educated varieties, other than that they are all, in different degrees, approximations to educated British standard English and that their users have received formal education, the most internationally acceptable varieties being associated with the most educated sections.

In recent years the question as to what constitutes educated Ghanaian

English has been much discussed. A variety of opinions has been expressed on the subject, and only a few are mentioned here. Of those who have shown an interest in the subject there is a considerable minority who would like to see English used by educated Ghanaians in what they describe as the 'African way'. Some of the questions that have been put to those who hold this view are: Is there one unique African way of speaking and writing English? and, assuming for purposes of argument that there is, Why is it necessary to speak English the African way? Answers to these questions have not been clearly formulated by those who make the claim, but it is generally argued that it would be desirable for educated Ghanaian users of English to impress their African personality on the language by stripping it of all traces of affectation and artificiality. It is further contended that educated Ghanaians lose some of their African identity in their efforts, in using a language which is alien to them, to ape native speakers.

It is possible that this view is not very different from other more liberal ones which argue that the English language in Ghana – and, for that matter, West Africa generally – will inevitably develop along lines different from those in other English-speaking areas. However, one would first like a few points clarified. For example, it has never been made clear by the propounders of this view whether this educated African way of using English already exists or is to be deliberately cultivated. One would also like to know to what extent this standard, imaginary or real, should be allowed to deviate from other educated varieties in the rest of the English-speaking world.

The second view that we shall mention here is the antithesis of the first. It argues that English is a borrowed foreign language, and if Ghanaians are going to continue to enjoy the privilege of using it without offence to the lenders they had better use it properly. The proper way to use the language is not the educated American or Canadian or Australian way: it is the educated British way. Those who hold this view are not prepared to accept American forms of English. Clearly, this view is too uncompromising and fails to take into account a number of factors; for example, the fact that there are more American teachers in the schools today than ever before.

Another view is that the linguistic backgrounds of educated Ghanaians are too varied to enable any investigator to come out with a useful characterisation of a Ghanaian brand of English. Those who hold this view point out that since the first language of each educated user of English affects his use of English, there are theoretically as many types of English as there are indigenous languages in Ghana. They would argue, for example, that not only do Ewe and Gã speakers of English differ in their use of English, but also that speakers of Twi and Fante, which are dialects of the same language, differ markedly in the way they speak and write English. It is difficult to refute an assertion like this, for it is literally true. Nobody today would wish openly to oppose the view that first-language habits interfere with the learning of a second. It should be remembered, however, that the importance of first-language interference can be exaggerated; and one is inclined to think that any serious attempt to define educated Ghanaian English can most easily be thwarted by a preoccupation with relatively trivial distinctions between speakers from different linguistic backgrounds. What we must look for are the broad similarities which set together users of English belonging to the various professions and levels of education – lawyers, doctors, university lecturers, post-primary and post-secondary school leavers, etc. It is very likely that there are widespread peculiarities in their use of vocabulary, idiom, grammar, intonation and rhythm which these groups of educated Ghanaians share in common.

These casual observations are mere impressions, and their value is therefore limited. However, those who claim to have thought about the problem with any care and in any detail are of the view that there *are* educated varieties of English used by Ghanaians which conform to international standards. What is needed now is a thorough study of the problem. Until this has been done a great deal of our discussion of the subject is bound to lack substance. A pertinent question in this connection is which sections of the community one would wish to classify as educated. The difficulty of drawing a line between educated and uneducated users of the language has often been noted. A few years ago most people who had spent eight to ten years in an elementary school could get a reasonably good job because they could claim they were educated. Now the position is different; present-day primary-school leavers and certain categories of GCE 'O' level holders are said for many purposes to be 'illiterate'. In a desperate effort to look for the educated norm, some people have turned to university graduates and sections of the community who have professional qualifications. The difficulty with this criterion is that it leaves out a relatively large section whose use of English is undoubtedly what one would like to describe as educated. On the other hand, there is no guarantee that a graduate, or someone with a professional background, will not be restricted in range and variety in his use of English. As a matter of fact, this is common. It is not unreasonable to require that the educated members of the community who set the fashion in usage be able to use different varieties of English in appropriate situations.

Any discussion of the English language in a former British colony is bound to concern itself with the position of the language in the schools. It is the schools and other higher educational institutions that aim at fostering varieties of English that are internationally usable. Further, not only do the schools set the standards and determine the varieties that are to be used in other sectors of public life: they teach the language most formally and most purposefully. Almost every adult non-native user of English has either received formal education at school or has been taught by someone else who has himself been to school.

It would be superfluous to stress the by now widely recognised importance of language in education, and labour the point that to put one's ideas across forcefully and effectively one has to command a sure grasp of the language one is expressing oneself in. We have all had the common experience, at one time or another, of having to struggle hard to express clearly conceived ideas in our own language: the ideas run faster than we can organise the resources of language to express them. The problem is much more complex and acute if the medium is a second language. This is why countries like Ghana, where English is taught as a foreign language as well as used as a medium of instruction in schools, should be urged that whatever educational policy is pursued it should clearly recognise the unique position of this language in the curriculum. It would be a mistake to regard English at the primary and post-primary levels as a school subject in the same sense as geography or history.

Governments in developing Africa are all too ready to introduce huge schemes for training scientists, doctors and economists and, in Ghana in particular, a number of stratagems have been resorted to in recent years to encourage schools and universities to foster the teaching of the sciences. This bias towards the sciences, if somewhat exaggerated, is fundamentally sound. But schools and educational bodies must not lose sight of the fact, that governments can derive the fullest rewards from the huge sums invested in such educational schemes only if those in charge of directing educational policies are prepared to reorganise their thinking about the present medium of instruction. We do not need to reflect long before realising that a pupil's successful understanding of scientific notions is to a large extent determined by his degree of competence in the language in which he is taught.

One might have thought this to be too obvious for comment; but in

Ghana it does not seem to have been clearly appreciated by the Ministry of Education and other educational authorities. There is a general demand from all quarters for improvement in the standard of written and spoken English in the schools and universities. University teachers, finding their freshmen insufficiently equipped to understand and write English at the level required for advanced work, blame the low standard on the secondary schools. They argue that secondary-school teachers are not as conscientious as they used to be, or, possibly, that children take less interest in reading widely than they did previously. Teachers in secondary schools, on the other hand, admit that something radically wrong is happening to the teaching and learning of English, and that this is adversely affecting standards at all levels. But they see the cause of all this in the handling of the subject in the primary schools. They expect pupils who come from the lower schools to have attained a certain level of competence in oral and written English before they ever begin secondary-school courses. Present standards in the use of English, they argue, can be improved by reorganising the teaching in the primary schools. Being in the unhappy position of receiving children directly from the home the primary schools are unable to shift the blame further back. It has occasionally been pointed out that the teacher training colleges are either not producing specialist teachers in sufficiently large quantities to fill vacancies in the primary schools; or at best must be doing their work only half-heartedly, in view of the poor quality of teachers they are at present producing.

It would certainly be unjust to blame the lowering of standards on any one educational stage. It was inevitable that the Accelerated Educational Development Plan, embarked upon in the early fifties by the Gold Coast Government of the time, should cause a general lowering in standards. As a result of this scheme the country suddenly became flooded with new primary schools and school children to an extent that had not been anticipated. Not only were there no adequately furnished classrooms and other facilities for the majority of these children; it was also suddenly realised, a little late perhaps, that there were not enough teachers with sufficient training and experience to staff the new schools. The only choice open to the authorities, if the plan was to be implemented, was to employ primary-school leavers as teachers; and most of them were barely good enough to be admitted into secondary schools and training colleges. These pupil teachers, as they were called, were to teach English to beginners. As a result a lot of harm has already been done, and the right thing now would be for all levels of education to contribute their part in remedying the situation. It would be wrong, in any case, to assign such an important task to one level. We shall return later to the question of the roles to be played in teaching English by the various stages of education. Meanwhile, we may usefully look a little more closely at what actually happens at each stage.

The official policy is that English should be introduced as a medium of instruction in the primary schools as early as possible. This gives teachers too great a latitude, and leaves too much to their discretion because, depending on the location of the school and the teacher's competence and interest in the language, English may be used in the teaching of other subjects any time after the third year. As a rule, children are gradually introduced to a few simple sentences right from the beginning, while the vernacular of the area is used as the medium of instruction during these early years. The vernacular is expected to play a less important role as the pupil goes up the school and more English is introduced. In larger towns where the children in a class do not share a common local language the tendency is to introduce English as early as possible. The position is naturally the reverse in the smaller towns and villages: there the vernaculars may be used for six or seven years.

Mention may be made here of a group of schools generally known as International Primary Schools. These form a class on their own as far as the teaching of English is concerned at this level of education. Naturally, because the teachers in these schools are either expatriates or have been trained abroad, the children get introduced to English very early and are taught in it. This early introduction to and use of the language is also encouraged by the fact that the pupils are drawn from varied linguistic backgrounds. Some of these schools have day nurseries attached to them where teaching is done in English, so that before the children begin actual primary-school work they already understand and speak English fluently, even if they happen not to have been introduced to it at home. This gives them considerable advantages over children who attend government-sponsored primary schools. Their performance in spoken and written English is naturally better and they thus have greater chances of being admitted to secondary schools on the basis of the Common Entrance Examination. Because of the expensive fees, admission into these privately run primary schools is severely restricted; children in these schools are obviously going to remain in a minority.

As far as the majority of primary-school leavers is concerned, if there is any agreement about the level of attainment which they reach in English, it is that this is low and inadequate for most ordinary purposes.

As pointed out earlier, secondary-school teachers and employers have had unflattering comments to make about the English of primary-school leavers. Admittedly, some of these criticisms are based more on impression than on hard facts, but this does not necessarily invalidate them. If it is true, as the teachers claim, that primary-school leavers fifteen to twenty years ago could write more adequate and acceptable English than their counterparts today, then the concern shown about the present state of affairs and what may be happening in the schools is justifiable.

In many ways the climate is much more favourable now for English language learning than it was twenty years ago: teaching methods have improved, there are more library facilities, and radio programmes are accessible even to some of the remotest villages. There is no reason to believe that children in primary schools are poorer or less willing learners. The truth is that although the number of trained teachers today far exceeds that of twenty years ago, the number of classrooms in which teachers of the same calibre and level of training are needed is disproportionately higher.

While admitting that the weight of responsibility for teaching the language which is the medium of instruction should be evenly distributed throughout the various educational stages, one must not ignore the fact that a good start in the language is ideally what should be aimed at; and, to the extent that this is a valid assumption, that the primary schools have a considerable responsibility to fulfil here. A good start at primary school should not be taken to mean large amounts of English. What the educational authorities should aim at is to give children in the early years a very firm grasp of a restricted range of the spoken and written language, so selected as to be of use to them and, consequently, providing them with the necessary incentive to go on learning. One can hardly hope to come anywhere near achieving this by perpetuating the present situation in which pupil teachers continue to teach the language itself as well as other subjects through it. A lot of reorganisation is called for. Until our teacher training colleges have the facilities for turning out trained personnel in sufficiently large numbers, it would not be unrealistic at all, as a short-term measure, to concentrate the few available trained teachers in the upper levels of the primary schools, while keeping the untrained ones in the lower classes. If this distribution were instituted as an interim measure, the latter would have nothing to do with the ultimate medium of instruction: all their teaching would be done in the vernaculars so as to prevent adverse effects upon the pupils' learning of English when they came to the upper grades, where the language would be taught by competent, trained teachers.

This is probably all that can be proposed for the primary schools at the moment. The root of the problem, however, is in the teacher training colleges, and that is where we should look for a solution to the allegedly low standards of English in the primary schools. It is most important that the role of the teacher training colleges in the task of raising English language standards be clearly defined. It is high time now that planners of teacher training courses draw a distinction between equipping teachers with English language skills (spoken and written, which should form part of the subject matter of their teaching) and teaching them the methodology of language instruction. The trained teacher needs both, but in different proportions: the first is much more important than the second. Unfortunately the teacher training colleges are giving teachers too much methodology of language teaching and not doing enough to develop their actual skills in the use of English. At present far too much incompetence is hidden behind the guise of language-teaching methodology. A teacher can hardly hope to teach English if his mastery of it is inadequate. On the other hand we should expect methodology to evolve naturally out of the subject matter if the teacher knows his subject at least to the level expected of him. So much for the primary schools.

The standard of attainment in learning English ought to be more encouraging in the secondary schools if we take into account the number of potentially favourable factors which operate there. In the first place, the selection of primary-school leavers for these schools is based on a highly competitive Common Entrance Examination which a pupil can pass well only if his control of English at this level is reasonably good. In addition to being able to understand English well enough to answer written questions in the arithmetic, general knowledge and English papers, he is expected to perform creditably in oral English at an interview where the final selection is made. Having been admitted into a secondary school, the pupil begins, for the first time, perhaps, to hear English spoken by native speakers and educated Ghanaians every day, and finds himself surrounded by other pupils who cannot, or will not, speak to him in his first language. And not only is he expected to look for information independently in textbooks and other sources, and do all his writing assignments in English, but he also finds himself in a position where he has to listen to lessons in English and answer questions orally in English. Ideally, he now reads a greater variety of prose and, if he is in one of the better schools, he can borrow suitable and interesting material to read from the library.

Potentially, then, there are more opportunities in the secondary school for raising the standard of English. Indeed, the difference in the level of attainment of some of the pupils after a year's work in secondary school is remarkable, and if this standard could progressively rise amongst a reasonable percentage of pupils throughout the country for the five years they spend at secondary school, most of the criticisms would not be valid. Unfortunately, however, there have been other factors at work. Of these, we mention only three: (i) the lack of qualified staff to teach English, which is itself the result of the rise in the number of secondary schools; (ii) the lack of clearly formulated teaching aims; and (iii) the content of the courses. In the early fifties the number of recognised secondary schools into which primary-school pupils could seek admission through Common Entrance was about twelve. These were the schools which provided the University of the Gold Coast with its intake for undergraduate work. It is not surprising that the standard of attainment in English by pupils in these schools was high: they had most, if not all, of the expatriate teachers in the country, as well as the non-expatriate Ghanaian teachers who had been educated abroad and who spoke and wrote almost native-like English. In addition to the twelve 'recognised' secondary schools, there were large numbers of so-called 'unrecognised' ones, which admitted pupils who had either failed the Common Entrance Examination or, for one reason or another, had not taken the examination at all.

The number of Common Entrance Examination candidates had trebled by the beginning of the second half of the fifties, as a result of the Accelerated Development Plan in education. The Government's answer to this sudden post-primary explosion was to raise the status of some 'unrecognised' schools to 'recognised', and then to build fresh 'recognised' ones. A number of competent teachers left the older schools for the newer ones, where prospects for promotion were greater. On the whole, however, the number of qualified teachers did not rise correspondingly. Staffing has always been a problem. The schools have relied on the University of Ghana but also, to a very large extent, on foreign countries for the supply of teachers. The country cannot hope to rely for ever on foreign sources for the supply of specialist teachers of English (who are needed all over the world). The Government and the Ministry of Education are aware of this. They are also aware that more and more teachers are leaving the teaching profession to join the Civil Service and the Corporations for better conditions of service. It should be clear to the Government by now that they cannot persuade qualified graduate teachers to remain in the profession by merely appealing to their supposed missionary zeal and inherent sense of duty. The only way to fill vacancies in the schools with really good teachers is to make the teaching profession more attractive than it is now.

In addition to staffing difficulties there is the problem of the adequacy of courses. One feature of the teaching of English at secondary level which has recently invited criticism, and which has been blamed, at least partially, for the lowering of standards, is the lack of clearly defined aims and objectives. Questions like the following do not seem to have received enough attention from teachers of English in the schools: What are we teaching English for? What demands are going to be made on our pupils' command of English while at school and when they leave it? That is, what level of attainment are we aiming at? Having got our aims clearly defined, how do we achieve them? For example, what do we include in the syllabus and what textbooks do we need in order to teach the syllabus? Leaving aside for the moment questions relating to the model of English to be taught in the schools, for which no clear answers can be provided within the next few years, these are some of the more immediate questions to which the schools might usefully address themselves. What is required in the secondary schools is a much more practical view of the English language. Many advantages would be gained if future syllabuses and teaching concentrated on giving pupils in secondary schools a command of the varieties of English which they will need while still at school, as well as when they have entered the outside world. It is here that maximum co-operation between the schools and the public examination bodies is called for. We cannot run away from the fact that examination syllabuses and past examination questions are continually having a backwash effect on teaching and learning in the schools, and it is desirable for this reason that public examination bodies build into their examination syllabuses requirements which will direct the teaching of English in the schools towards more utilitarian ends. Happily, one can already see signs of this. The new West African Examinations Council syllabuses for English have recently been modified with these aims in view.

Details of the English courses need replanning, too. We have already alluded to the need for giving pupils the types of language skill that they will need later in life. The schools can hardly achieve useful results in this direction if they continue to adhere in every detail to the present syllabus in English, with all its imbalance. One manifestation of this imbalance is that spoken English is hardly, if ever, taught in the majority of schools, because the syllabuses do not make it a compulsory section of the English language paper. On the other hand, a disproportionate amount of time is spent on teaching the section of the syllabus concerned with English literature, and which requires candidates to read a maximum of three or four works from among authors like Shakespeare, Milton, Wordsworth, Keats and Jane Austen. Teaching pupils to appreciate works of literature is not to be discouraged, but to require foreign learners of a language to read three or four set books in two years is the most effective way of encouraging them in slow reading habits. It would not be unwise to suggest that the present 'O' level syllabus for English literature either be abolished or modified drastically. What seems to be needed is a scheme which would require all pupils to read a wide range of prose written in present-day English. The study of literature, in the sense of a minute line-by-line scrutiny of texts, archaic for the most part, could be usefully postponed to sixth form and university work.

For some obscure reason it is generally taken for granted by many people, including some university teachers, that success in the GCE 'O' level English Language paper guarantees a candidate's linguistic adequacy for undergraduate work. This belief has led them to pass harsh comments on secondary schools for not preparing students satisfactorily for work in the university and other institutions of higher education. What these university teachers are in effect demanding is the unreasonable requirement that a freshman should, before being admitted to the university, be fully equipped to deal with every problem of communication in English, at all levels of undergraduate work, by virtue of his having gone through a set of English courses prescribed for secondary schools. As pointed out earlier, the schools should have their own teaching aims and objectives, and these need not stretch to cover all the demands made by university work. If it is a fact that freshmen in Ghana's universities do not have enough English to cope with degree work, it is only reasonable that the universities themselves do something to improve their English. It should surprise nobody to hear that a freshman's English is not adequate for handling work in literary criticism, linguistics or genetics.

Departments of English in African universities must continue to teach English language and literature as pure academic subjects. This should be one of their functions – and a very important one – as university departments. However, present needs require that, in conjunction with other related departments, they provide practical remedial courses in English to students who will need it for university courses. This should not be considered retrograde. We do not have to be reminded that a foreign learner of English who is graded 'good' in the language at, say, the GCE 'O' level, may sound very incompetent linguistically when it comes to discussing poetry in a first-year university course. At the moment, manpower and other resources are limited, and this is about the only justifiable excuse for not implementing such plans in the universities of Ghana.

It has been thought important to give prominence to the place of the English language in education because, as has been made clear, the future development and role of this language in the life of Ghanaians will depend largely on how it is treated by educational policy and taught in the schools today. At the moment, for example, one of the most conspicuous trends in the cultural life of Ghana is the creative use of English. Those who are in the vanguard of this literary movement have all been educated in some of the best schools and at the universities. One manifestation of this literary awakening can be seen in the schools and training colleges themselves, where students who have the aptitude for creative writing are being encouraged by the British Council and other bodies to write imaginative prose and verse. Compared with French-using West Africa, the creative use of the second language was late in British West Africa.[3] Gerald Moore has attributed this cultural lag to a kind of philistinism (Moore, 1962) which has characterised West African countries like Nigeria, Ghana and Sierra Leone. It is likely that more careful study would reveal a different explanation: philistinism could hardly have fostered the long tradition of other non-literary art forms in these countries.

It is natural that young Ghanaian writers should be influenced by the English literary tradition and, possibly, other earlier ones which are accessible to them through English translations. The influence of the seventeenth-century metaphysical poets, of Hopkins, Eliot, Pound and Dylan Thomas is especially noticeable in the work of most of these young writers.[4] A few, like Efua Sutherland, on the other hand, exhibit the influence of the Greek dramatists. All the writers are of course influenced by their own linguistic and traditional backgrounds. The verse of George Kofi Awoonor, for example, contains not only references to traditional Ewe life and beliefs but also Ewe idioms translated into English. Perhaps the best example of this deliberate cultivation of an

'African idiom' is found in the prose work of Christiana Aidoo. It is interesting to note, however, that what might be considered the distinctively Ghanaian contribution to literary works written in English is regarded by some in Ghana as unnecessarily artificial. In his review of Abruquah's novel *The Catechist*, Joe de Graft (himself a writer) makes the point that Abruquah is refreshing to read because he does not strive to be consciously African, and he deprecates 'this almost paranoiac search for distinctively Ghanaian forms of expression'. He finds the story moving because of the following qualities of the novel:

> No pretensions to African avant-garde fiction writing; none of the rather over-played conflicts between 'traditional' and present-day Africa; not larded with folk wisdom congealed in proverbs; no attempt to show off or put over 'our beloved Africa'; no striving towards a hybrid of the English language that will pass for African – a language which, almost alas! is becoming such a tiresome feature of so much West African fiction in English.[5]

He then predicts that the novel in Ghana will follow the pattern set by Abruquah. The novel as an indigenous literary genre is practically non-existent in Ghana, and it would be too early to speculate about its probable course in future. If de Graft's prediction is a valid one, then the development of the novel in Ghana is very likely to stand in sharp contrast to trends in Nigeria.

An interesting question is whether Ghanaian creative writers can remain completely unaffected by their linguistic background in their search for a suitable medium of expression. Those who believe in the development of a distinctively African literature would say no; those who do not would ask in reply: does not the African writer need to make a conscious effort to develop an 'African' medium? There should surely be no objection to an African writer's using a distinctively African style provided he is motivated solely by a sincere urge to find a suitable medium, rather than by a desire to pander to the expectations of the foreign critic or publisher for whom African writing is worth studying or publishing because of its esotericism. One often finds that the esoteric is introduced into Ghanaian writing for reasons other than the demands made on the writer by his material. In an introduction to a recent anthology of poetry and prose by young Ghanaian writers (Sangster and Quashie, 1966) the editors urge writers to be African in their expression and go on to explain that among the criteria they used in selecting writings for inclusion in the anthology was 'whether the writing was a true expression of Ghana, rather than an attempt to use European modes of writing about topics alien to Africa'.

We still do not know how to separate Ghanaian expressions from non-Ghanaian ones, although we are able to recognise the obviously non-standard English 'mode' in a text by the fact that it deviates from the standard norms in respect of one or more linguistic rules – grammatical, collocational, etc. How far deviations of this kind should be allowed to go has not been made clear by critics who advocate cultivation of specifically Ghanaian modes. We should not forget that readers, both Ghanaian and non-Ghanaian, are entitled to apply the same set of critical criteria to Ghanaian writers as they would to any creative writer in English.

At the outset it was suggested that Ghana would continue to remain part of the international community of English users for a long time to come. This is sufficient justification for laying so much emphasis on the role of schools and educational institutions. As far as we can see the most important *practical* reason for learning English as a foreign language is to enable the learner to reach beyond his own culture. The variety of English required for this purpose cannot be region-bound, and the only places where international varieties are learned are the schools, colleges and universities. It is not suggested that other 'non-international' varieties have no place in Ghana. Their role, like the vernaculars, will be restricted to internal use. The role of the vernaculars, however, will differ from that of the 'non-international' varieties of English in that, like the internationally accepted varieties, they will be used on formal occasions and as media for creative literature.

Notes

1 Moore, 1965. Compare Quirk, 1962: 'It is unreasonable to regard any language as the property of a particular nation and with no language is it more unreasonable than with English.'
2 One gets this impression from a reading of a recent work on Jamaican Creole (Bailey, 1966).
3 See the anthologies edited by Sangster and Quashie, 1966, and Watts, 1967.
4 See the collection of poems in the journal *Okyeame*, Vol 3, 1, of 1966, and Asare Konadu's work.
5 This review is in the issue of *Okyeame* noted above. It is interesting to compare de Graft's view with that put forward by Eldred Jones in connection with Chinua Achebe's work (Jones, 1965): 'One of the most significant successes of Achebe in the novel is the sensitive use of English so that it reflects the African environment. This he achieves by drawing his images out of the environment instead of plucking them ready-made from British literary English.'

Eldred Jones

Krio : An English-based Language of Sierra Leone

Krio is an English-based lingua franca used throughout Sierra Leone as an inter-tribal language of trade and social communication. It is the mother tongue of the descendants of groups of freed men who settled in the Sierra Leone peninsula between 1787 and the early years of the nineteenth century. It is a second language for other residents in this same area whose mother tongue is one of the other Sierra Leone languages. It has also spread throughout the country principally in the more urban areas as an additional language. There are some slight phonological and structural variations in the language among these various groups of users and even among those to whom the language is a mother tongue. In some areas, for example the Fourah Bay area in Freetown where Yoruba survived for a long time, and where contact with it still continues, the incidence of Yoruba borrowings tends to be higher than in other areas. Similarly, in the speech of speakers highly educated in English there tends to be much freer borrowing from the language of their education, and hence a higher incidence of English words and structures. It is of the speech of this latter group that it can be most truly said that the whole vocabulary of English is potentially Krio.

Recent scholarship has demonstrated the relationship between Krio and the creoles and *patois* of other parts of the world. R. W. Thompson (1961) suggests a common origin of all creoles and pidgins in a fifteenth-century Portuguese pidgin of the West Coast of Africa. While this is an attractive hypothesis it still remains to be fully demonstrated. There is of course no doubt that Portuguese left its mark on indigenous languages in West Africa and large areas all over the world.[1] It is clear, at least, that the origins of Krio stretch to the other side of the Atlantic; to the United States and the West Indies where survivals seem to indicate the development of distinctive creole dialects before the return of the

Sierra Leone settlers in 1787.[2] Statements like these do not quite explain away the problem of origins. Indeed, when one compares the numbers of settlers who came back from the New World (some via England) with the much larger numbers of recaptives who landed in Sierra Leone speaking nothing but various West African languages, it seems staggering that the transatlantic influences were so virile.[3] There therefore seems to be room for something like the Thompson hypothesis referred to earlier.

The Sierra Leone settlement consisted of the following groups of people: The Black Poor, the Maroons and Nova Scotians, and the West African recaptives. The last were by far the most numerous, their arrival being spread over a number of years. The last Sierra Leone census figures give some indication as to the current numbers of Krio speakers, although since there was no direct question to elicit information about languages such numbers are the result of guesswork. The census report lists as Creoles 41,783 persons. For all of these, Krio is the mother tongue. It could be reasonably assumed that to most of the population of the Western area Krio is either the mother tongue or a very much used second language. The population of this area is given as 195,023. The language is also widely dispersed over the whole country, with a high density of speakers in the urban and semi-urban areas outside the Western area. A reasonable estimate of the number of Krio speakers in the whole country therefore would be in the region of 500,000.

See p. 14

There is evidence from various sources of a distinctive dialect or dialects of English in the peninsula area of Sierra Leone from the early part of the nineteenth century. Joaquim César de Figaniére e Marão in a letter written in Freetown in 1820 distinguishes between Settlers and Maroons, not only in their morals and customs but also in their language. Of the Settlers he writes: 'They speak English well and it is their mother tongue; . . . The Maroons . . . speak a language of their own, which is a corrupt English'. (The Maroons were the group of Settlers who had escaped from slavery in Jamaica.) According to Marão's account there were in Freetown in 1820, 691 Settlers (from Nova Scotia) and 487 Maroons, out of a total population of 4,106, or 4,736 if the 'Kroomen' are included. (These figures are for Freetown only; there were for example 1,216 persons in Regent Town, one of the several peri-urban settlements.) This account does not give details of the speech, but mentions the name of a drink 'romane' (the word now seems to be obsolete) made out of beer, rum and sugar.

I have elsewhere examined (Jones, 1962) other more detailed re-

6

ferences to the language of coastal Sierra Leone by nineteenth-century visitors, and concluded:

> All these records point to the existence in the mid-nineteenth century of two broad patterns of speech, the *talkee-talkee patois*, and the language we now call Krio, both of which seem to have flourished side by side (and still do), and which over the years may have influenced one another. Also it seems fairly clear that Krio was definitely formed in its essentials by the mid-nineteenth century. This leads one to suspect that its foundations had been laid even before the colony of Sierra Leone was founded.

Today Krio in Sierra Leone enjoys a rather ambivalent status. It is recognised as a useful language of inter-tribal communication and as such is used as a medium of news dissemination. The official news bulletin put out daily over the Sierra Leone Broadcasting Service by the Ministry of Information, as well as other important government statements, are broadcast in Krio as well as English, Mende and Temne. (The other languages of the country usually have weekly summaries broadcast in them.) Krio is also used widely in public speeches all over the country as well as at inter-tribal religious services. It is not however encouraged in the schools because of its supposedly harmful effects on the learning of English, the language of education, and is not widely used in its written form, although there have been sporadic bursts of good writing in it.[4] Its register remains largely intimate and oral. It is used as the normal means of communication in Creole homes but even among educated Creoles outside their homes it tends to be used only as a means of intimate conversation. Educated Creoles on first meeting other educated Creoles tend to use English, this being thought the more polite language. Conversation mellows into Krio as acquaintanceship grows, although it is apt to fade back into English as topics veer into the more technical fields. The appropriate occasions for Krio in Sierra Leone society can involve delicate nuances of etiquette.

Description of the language[5]

Since this contribution is appearing in a book on English in Africa, the emphasis will be on the contribution of English to Krio, and the examples will be chosen with this in mind. Krio can fairly be called an English-based creole language because English is the main source of its vocabulary although it is by no means the only source of borrowing. The language has borrowed widely from African languages, Yoruba being the main African source. No final authoritative word count can be made because of the fluid state of the lexicon arising from the continuing contact situation, but some indication of the proportion of borrowings in common speech can be given. Out of about 1,400 items listed in my manuscript Dictionary of Krio, Arnold von Bradshaw extracted some 200 of Yoruba origin (Bradshaw, 1965). (It must be explained that the Dictionary contained only Creolised English words – words which had undergone phonetic or semantic changes from English and other European languages – and words of African origin, and was still far from finished.) The contribution of all the other African languages put together would probably be less than half that of Yoruba. Words have been listed from the Sierra Leone languages as well as from several languages elsewhere on the West Coast of Africa.[6] Something like four-fifths of what may be called the kernel lexicon of Krio is derived from English.

CONSONANTS

English words generally undergo some modification when they are borrowed into Krio. The most consistent changes involving consonants will be illustrated:

English θ	> Krio t
δ	> d
three	tri
throat	$trot$
thick	tik
thief	tif
with	wit
teeth	tit
the	di
there	de
feather	$f\varepsilon da$
gather	$g\varepsilon da$
other	$\jmath da$

| English v | > Krio b |

In native Krio speech (K[1]) this change occurs in internal positions, but in the speech of some African speakers to whom Krio is a second language (K²) the change is sometimes heard initially: English 'vote' > K¹ *vot* > K² *bot*. Otherwise:

English cover	> Krio *kɔba*
over	*oba*
gravel	*grabul*
every	*ebri*
live	*lib*
devil	*dɛbul*
heavy	*ebi*
favour	*fiba*

In final positions English *v* > Krio *f*

| English leave | > Krio *lɛf* |
| move | *muf* |

English *st*	> Krio *t*
stay	*te*
stick	*tik*
straight	*tret*
strength	*trɛnk*

(The last example also illustrates the modification of the English final cluster *ŋθ*.)

English *sp*	> Krio *p*
spit	*pit*
spoon	*pun*
split	*plit*
spread	*prɛd*

English *sk*	> Krio *k*
scratch	*krach*
scrape	*krep*
scrub	*krɔb*
squeeze	*kwis*

These sound changes do not occur in all borrowings in current Krio. It may very well be that many words reverted to their English forms because of the continuing and increasing contact between the two languages, in a situation where its exclusive use in education confers a superior status on English. Possibly because of this, one or two sound changes survive in only a few words and therefore need not be elaborately commented on. For instance: English *f* > Krio *s* as in E 'shoes' > K *sus*. (But K *shem, sho, shaut*, etc, show initial *f*.) E final *d* > K *t* as in E 'hard' > K *at*. The last example also illustrates the loss of initial *h* which is ordinarily dropped from borrowings. Initial *h* is however used for emphasis on words beginning with a vowel.

The treatment of E 'oil' in Krio will illustrate how elaborate a complete statement of phonological change from English to Krio will have to be to include all the nonce examples. In K^1, English 'oil' remains *ɔil*, while in K^2 *wɛil* is sometimes heard. (The latter form is paralleled by K^1 and K^2 *bwɛl* from English 'boil'.) However when 'oil' occurs in the compounds K *pamain* and *natai* – 'palm oil' and 'nut oil' respectively – the final *l* is dropped and vowel nasalisation (rather than a consonantal *n*) is substituted in the case of 'palm oil'. It seems a reasonable assumption that *natai* at some stage showed a similar nasalisation. The form K *natai* suggests that K *pamain* too may in time lose this nasalisation.

On the whole there is not very much consonantal change in the borrowing process from English into Krio. When changes do occur they leave room for interesting speculation as to why they do. Our last illustration is: English nasal + *s* > Krio nasal + *tf* in final positions. This is now present in only a few words:

English beans	> Krio *binch*
ants	*anch*
fence	*fɛnch*
rinse	*rench*

Krio in fact has a consonant range very similar to English with the addition of a few African consonant sounds found in African borrowings, *eg: ny, gb* as in *nyanga* (Mende = style), *gbɛnɛ* (Mende = a discoloration of the slain).

VOWELS
Krio does not distinguish between long and short versions of the same

vowel sound as does English. In the process of borrowing, the English
long and short vowels are resolved into the same sound in Krio. Thus:

English hill, heel	> Krio *il* (with loss of initial *h*)
mill	*mil*
teeth	*tit*
wool	*wul*
move	*muf*
hard	*at* (with loss of initial *h*)

While there is no significant semantic distinction between long and
short vowels, vowel prolongation is often used as a device for indicating
emphasis. Thus in the word K *tif* the vowel sound could be prolonged:

I ti . . f lɛk mink. (He is as prone to stealing as a mink.)
I go . . lɛk noa dɔv. (He was away as long as Noah's dove.)

The Krio vowel system is thus more akin to that of many African languages than to English. The vowel sounds used are:

a	as in *kam*	(E come)
ɛ	as in *nɛf*	(E knife)
e	as in *eg*	(E egg)
i	as in *tif*	(E thief)
ɔ	as in *nɔf*	(E enough)
o	as in *got*	(E goat)
u	as in *muf*	(E move)

See pp. 92-93

Because the Krio vowel system is so close to those of many West African
languages, there is hardly any vowel change in African borrowings; but
the large number of English words have to be adapted to this much
more limited vowel system. A single Krio vowel sound thus has to do
duty not only for the long and short forms of its counterpart in English
but also for a number of other vowel and diphthongal sounds as well.
Again the position can only be briefly illustrated since a full statement
would require much more space than is available here.

The Krio vowel sound *a* is often substituted for the short English vowel *ʌ* with the following results in these examples.

English come	> Krio *kam*
one	*wan*
hungry	*angri*
sun	*san*
coconut	*koknat*
groundnut	*granat*
nut oil	*natai*
bumboat	*bambot*

But the same sound in Krio is also substituted for other English sounds. Thus:

English *æ*	> Krio *a*
band	*ban*
hand	*an*
man	*man*
handle	*andul*

Also:

English *ɔ*	> Krio *a*
shop	*shap*
stop	*tap*
shot	*shat*

English *a:*	> Krio *a*
sharp	*shap*
market	*makit*
bark	*bak*
lard	*lad*

The other Krio vowels similarly take the place of a number of different English vowel sounds. The Krio vowel sound *ε* not only represents the similar English sound as in E 'bend' K *bɛn*, E 'lend' K *lɛn*, E 'help' K *ɛp*, but also the diphthong *ai*.

English time	> Krio *tɛm*
lime	*lɛm*
find	*fɛn*
fight	*fɛt*
like	*lɛk*
mind (vb)	*mɛn*
knife	*nɛf*

A large number of English words with this diphthong, however, show no vowel change in Krio: *eg* E 'wine' K *wain*, E 'life' K *laif*, E 'white' K *wait* (but also *wet*, not *wɛt*), E 'pint' K *paint*, etc.

English *e, ei*	> Krio *e*
bed	*bed*
head	*ed*
bake	*bek*
pain	*pen*

English *i, i:*	> Krio *i* (illustrated earlier)

English *ʌ, au, ə:*	> Krio *ɔ*
cup	*kɔp*
some, sum	*sɔm*
mouth	*mɔt*
come out	*kɔmɔt*
(put) out	*ɔt*
shirt	*shɔt*
dirty	*dɔti*
worth	*wɔt*

English *ou, ɔ:*	> Krio *o*
goat	*got*
load	*lod*
port and report	*pot*
court	*kot*

English *u, u:*   > Krio *u*
    move   *muf*
    school   *skul*
    look   *luk*
    wood   *wud*

These illustrations give a false impression of regularity. To all these examples there are numerous exceptions. When for instance words of more than one syllable are borrowed or when compounds are made up, many nonce forms appear, *eg:*

  K *pɛtɛtɛ* for E potato
  K *mɛrɛsin* for E medicine
  K *ɛnkincha* for E handkerchief (or possibly headkerchief or a
    confusion of both).

VOCABULARY

The great majority of English borrowings, while changing their form, retain their original meanings. But there are a large number of interesting shifts of meaning, and many English words have become so incorporated in the devices of Krio word-formation that their English origin becomes very remote indeed. Sometimes it is almost impossible to trace the process by which a Krio word came to acquire its present meaning. In one or two cases a certain amount of fossilisation has taken place. Thus the Krio word *kɔmishɔn* (E commission), which means a loin-cloth in Krio, preserves a meaning which has now vanished from English. Commission was used in English to mean a piece of wearing apparel – a shirt – until the eighteenth century (*Oxford English Dictionary*, sb²). Similarly K *dɔgayɛn* (E dog + iron), which in Krio means a metal drum for carrying liquids, recalls a use of 'dog' in English to signify a metal frame for carrying water casks (*OED*, 7e). Other fossils are seen in K *bambot* (E bumboat) as in K *bambot uman* (a 'bumboat woman' meaning a loose woman). Similarly, K *kabaslɔt* (a loose gown for women) is from an obsolete English expression 'cover-slut', which designated a similar garment.

The resourcefulness of Krio for word-formation has wrought some intriguing changes to borrowed English words. These random examples are taken from my manuscript dictionary:

anko (E and co[mpany]) = bosom companion, accomplice.
big yai (E big eyes) = greed, to be greedy.

braskitul (E brass kettle) = to countenance (the process of semantic change is obscure).

brokɔngot (E broke + horn + goat) = used in simile to denote a very greedy eater.

kɛr-go-bring-kam (E carry + go + bring + come) = a tell-tale, tale telling.

kɔt-ya-put-ya (E cut + here + put + here) = double-dealing, equivalent to E running with the hare and hunting with the hounds.

gɛtnahan (E get + hand with K *na*) = over-particular

jokaki (E Joe + khaki) = an English soldier.

langa-trot (E long + throat) = to tantalise by alternately offering and withdrawing food.

ɔntoum (E Unto whom – from the verse in the 'Venite' 'Unto whom I sware in my wrath that they should not enter into my rest') = heathen, unenlightened.

tu-sai-pɛn-nɛf (E two side[d] penknife) = a person in opposite camps at the same time.

wokfɔwɔl (E work + for + world) = a person who devotes himself to other people's good while neglecting his own and that of his family.

tangens (E stand against). This was a common admonitory shout given by workmen who went to their war-time construction work in open trucks. The trucks (lorries) then came to be called K *tangens lɔri*, the men themselves *tangens man*, and the work itself *tangens*.

tik bɛlɛ (E stick (= tree) + belly) = pulpit.

The French borrowing 'beaucoup' – K *bɔku* – shows similar extensions of meaning. It is still used to mean 'plenty of' but it is applied for instance to something which in the process of being made is ruined beyond cure, particularly food. Thus *di rɛs dɔn bɔku*, 'the rice (in the process of being cooked) is ruined.' Interestingly enough, as will be seen in Bradshaw's article on Yoruba loan words cited earlier, African borrowings undergo very little shift of meaning.

Educated Creoles often amuse themselves by retranslating some of these expressions into English with results like:

You are too strong ears (K *tranga yes*) *ie* You are too stubborn.

(Harassed teachers of English against the background of Krio do not consider this a joke!) Frequently English words are compounded with words of African origin to create new words:

bresinteku (E brazen + Temne *teku* = a small, very vivacious fish) = a particularly mischievously active child.
babuoto (E baboon + Mende *woto* = ape) = a very ugly person.
mata odo (E mortar + Yoruba *odo* = mortar) = mortar.

It is probably by this method of compounding that we have the K *tɔskare* – to wander aimlessly about the world. The first part would seem to be E toss + (possibly African) *kare*.

TONALITY

Tone functions in Krio in two main ways. Words borrowed from tonal African languages usually retain their original tone pattern. But the more interesting use of tonality is to distinguish homophones derived from English borrowings. Tone is most indicative in distinguishing compounds from word sequences. The most frequent pattern is numeral + noun compound, as against numeral and noun as separate words. In such cases the numeral as the first part of the compound bears a falling tone, while when standing free it bears a rising tone,[7] *eg:*

wán pálà	one + parlour = a single parlour
wànpálà	contemptuously of a one-room apartment
wán trìt	a single street
wàntrít	contemptuous adjectival compound used for example of a small village
tú bɔ́tìn	two buttons
tùbɔ́tìn	a style (of jacket) with two buttons
wán kɔt	a single stroke of a cane, or one portion of fish
wànkɔ́t	a shift-type dress
wán sài	one side or section
wànsái	one-sided, crooked
wán pɔt	a single pot
wànpɔ́t	a dish in which all the ingredients are cooked in the same pot like a casserole
síks pèns	sixpence
sìkspéns	in my schooldays this indicated a red rubber ball sold for a sixpence

By a similar process adj + noun compounds are distinguished from their homophones:

lás bérìn	last funeral
làsbérìn	the feast which ends the observances after a death
bád yài	evil eye
bàdyái	the old-fashioned look
ɔ́p sài	top, top end, etc
ɔ̀psái	to outsmart, get the better of by trickery
bíg yài	large eye or eyes
bìgyái	greed
lángà trót	a long throat
làngàtrót	to tantalize

The role of tonality is barely illustrated here. A full investigation still needs to be undertaken. However, enough has been said to indicate how by the use of this feature the usefulness of borrowings is greatly increased.

SYNTAX

One of the notable features of Krio is its almost total lack of inflexions. Indeed, morphology of any kind is insignificant. It is interesting that Krio has even less inflexions than Jamaican Creole, which uses morphological devices, for example, in the comparison of adjectives. There is a certain amount of morphological change used jocularly to express ideas like total negation or to pour scorn on an idea. For example, to the question K *yu go gi me?* (E will you give me?) the reply might be K *a go ga yu: ga* for *gi* pours scorn on the very idea of giving. Reduplication and a certain amount of compounding would account for the other instances of morphological modification. Also, since Krio borrows concepts rather than just words from English, so that the nominal and verbal forms of the same concept are usually identical, the language relies very heavily on syntactical structure. When signals other than word order are needed to indicate function or meaning, these are usually free-standing units. These general remarks will now be illustrated.

Plurality is indicated in nouns by the use of free-standing units, the lexical item itself always remaining the same. Thus *bɔbɔ* (sing.), *dɛm bɔbɔ*, or *dɛm bɔbɔ dɛm* (plural), *viz:*

Da bɔbɔ bin kam	The boy came
Dɛm bɔbɔ bin kam ⎱	The boys came
Dɛm bɔbɔ dɛm bin kam ⎰	

Krio has borrowed from English the word 'sing'. In English this is a verb, and the particular form 'sing' is found in the infinitive and certain of the forms of the present tense. In Krio, the form *sing* occurs in every form of the verb, *eg:*

K *A de sing*   I am singing
K *A dɔn sing*   I have sung
K *A go sing*   I will sing

In addition to this verbal use, the form *sing* occurs as a nominal:

K *A lɛk dis sing*   I like this song.
K *A lɛk di sing we i de sing*   I like the song which he is singing.

Krio further extends the use of the form by using it adjectivally:

Dis sing biznes ya dɔn mɔna mi o!   I've had too much of this singing business!

Jɔn na sing man o!   John is a good singer (singing man).

(In the second example, a falling tone on *sing* indicates its adjectival function.)

This illustration shows some more of the devices by which Krio extends the range of its borrowings, making what would appear perhaps a limited lexicon go a long way. Other features which illustrate the resourceful use of borrowings will appear in the course of this article.

A full treatment of Krio syntax is not possible here. All that can be usefully done is to give a few typical structures as an indication of the nature of the language. The first example is a brief but complete general utterance:

K *Ren kam.* (E lit 'Rain came'; more idiomatically, 'It rained')

The structure is nominal + verbal. The sentence may be amplified to indicate the various functional positions in Krio:

1 *Ren kam.*   {nominal (subject) + verbal}
2 *Ren kam yɛstade.*   {n(s) + vbl + adv}
3 *Big ren kam yɛstade.*   {adj + n(s) + vbl + adv}

This example is typical of a general statement employing an intransitive verb. The negative is achieved by inserting the negative indicator immediately before the verb:

Ren nɔ kam.
Ren nɔ kam yɛstade, etc.

In the examples given, only one item, the adverb, could be put in a different position – the alternative position would be before the nominal group *ren/big ren*:

Yɛstade big ren kam.

In the negative also

Yɛstade ren nɔ kam, etc.

The next utterance involves a transitive verb:

Da pus dɔn kil da arata.   The cat has killed the rat.

This structure is made up as follows:

nominal phrase (subject) + verbal + nominal phrase (object)
da pus   *dɔn kil*   *da arata*

The sentence could be amplified further:

Da blak pus dɔn kil da ambɔgin arata.

(K *ambɔgin* = E troublesome: lit 'humbugging')

The two nominal phrases now contain an adjective each in the following pattern: article + adj + noun. This would be a typical pattern. Variations would permit the use of more than one adjective:

Da tif blak pus dɔn kil da lili ambɔgin arata.

(K *tif* = E thieving: K *lili* = E little)

Both nominal groups have the same pattern:

Article + adj[(i)] + adj[(ii)] + noun

A great number of Krio statements are introduced by the word *na* = E it is.[8] Examples of sentences introduced with *na* are:

Na God mek dis wɔl.
(E lit 'It is God made this world', or more idiomatically, 'God made this world.')

The use of *na* as an introducer where a parallel idiomatic English utterance needs none is one of the notable differences between Krio and English. Other examples and their literal renderings into English will further emphasise this difference:

na + au (K *au* = E how)
Na au dɛn luk yu na im mek dɛn aks yu.
(E lit 'It is how they look at you it is that made them ask you', or idiomatically, 'They only asked you because of their scant regard for you'.)

The Krio correlatives *na au . . . na im mek* signal a structure completely foreign to English. Compare also *na + we*:

Na we a lɛk yu mek a tɔk to yu.
(E lit 'It is because I like you made me talk to you', or more idiomatically, 'I only talked to you because I like you'.)

Krio *we* seems to be related in some of its uses to English 'what' as in *we yu se?* = what did you say? or the relative 'who'/'which'. When it is used with *na*, as in our illustration, it shows either a considerable extension of meaning or possibly that it is not in fact derived from *we* = 'what', 'which', 'who', etc. One more brief example of *na* is all our space allows:

Na wan tɛm man kin dai
(E lit 'It is one time (a) man can die', or idiomatically, 'A man can only die once'.)

This construction is one that would need to be watched in the teaching of English against a Krio background.

As far as question patterns are concerned, there are two types in Krio:

The first is introduced by an interrogative word – K *u, udat* (E who), *wetin* (E what), *usai* (E where, where from), etc.

The second is indicated by a rising tone at the end of the spoken utterance.

Examples of type 1:

Usai yu kɔmɔt?	Where have you come from?
Wetin yu de du?	What are you doing?
Udat yu de kɔl?	Who are you calling?
Au yu du am?	How did you do it?

Examples of type 2:

Yu de kɔmɔt?	Are you going out?
Yu de du sɔntin?	Are you doing something?
Yu de kɔl ɛnibɔdi?	Are you calling anyone?
Meri dɔn kam?	Has Mary come?
Jɔn bin fɔdɔm?	Did John fall?
A bin tɛl yu so?	Did I tell you so?

In neither type of question is an inversion of word order involved. Where an interrogative is used, it merely precedes a normal sentence pattern, and type 2 shows no deviation from the normal sentence pattern whatsoever: this, however, is quite common in English, where a rising intonation pattern alone can convert a statement into a question.

Most of the examples of sentences given so far have been fairly simple. By accumulation of clauses, more complicated utterances can be achieved. As has been indicated in connection with the only complex structure given, the structure of complex utterances can be very remote from English. A few further examples of more complex utterances will now be given:

Da pɔsin we tif mi fɔl, God go pe am.
(E lit 'That person who stole my fowl, God will pay him'.)

The only link between the two constituent clauses is the fact that the object *am* in the second, refers back to the subject *da pɔsin* in the first. English would require a much tighter structure. A large number of Krio sentences are constructed after this and similar patterns:

Da kau we nɔ gɛt tel, na Gɔd go drɛb in flai.
(E lit 'That cow which does not have a tail, it is God who will drive away its flies.')

In the Krio sentence, K *in* (E its), which is part of the object of the second clause, refers back to the subject of the first, *Da kau*.

Our next example involves a descriptive clause introduced by *we* (= E who, which):

Da buk we yu bin gi mi, a dɔn lɔs am.
(E lit 'The book which you gave me, I have lost it.')

We yu bin gi mi describes *buk*, and immediately follows it, intervening between the word it qualifies and the clause which completes the statement introduced by *Da buk*. Thus we have two sentences:

1 *Da buk . . . a dɔn lɔs am*
2 *we yu bin gi mi*

Da buk; a dɔn lɔs am is itself quite an acceptable Krio utterance, the semi-colon representing a pause in the vocal utterance. It is also worth noting that the whole utterance could alternatively be made with a much tighter structure. *A dɔn lɔs da buk we yu bin gi mi.* This would be very close to the English 'I have lost the book which you gave me.'

Perhaps one of the most striking illustrations of the resourcefulness of Krio and its ability to adapt its borrowings to fulfil its grammatical needs is to be found in the devices for constructing the various tenses, modes, and aspects of the verb. All the grammatical particles so used are probably from English, but most of them retain only the barest suggestions of their original meanings and functions.

Tense: Krio is equipped with a range of tense markers,[9] as may be seen from the following set, using the Krio verb *rait* (English 'write'), and given with the first person singular pronoun *a*, from English 'I':

Present	*A de rait*
Past	*A rait* (unmarked)
	A bin rait (or, for emphasis, *A did rait*)
Future	*A go rait*

Aspect: The perfective forms make use of the particle *dɔn*. Thus:

Perfect	*A dɔn rait*
Future Perfect	*A go dɔn rait*
Past Perfect	*A bin dɔn rait*

The progressive aspect marker is *de*, and can be used with all the tenses, including those which are marked for perfective aspect, *eg:*

A de rait	I am writing
A bin de rait	I was writing
A bin dɔn de rait	I had been writing
A go de rait	I will be writing
A go dɔn de rait	I will have been writing

Modals: The modals *kin* (E can), *fɔ* (possibly E for) and *mɔs* (E must)
7

may be combined with tense and aspect markers. The following are
some examples of verbal phrases involving modals:

A bin kin rait	I could write (*ie* if I wished or dared)
A bin fɔ don rait	I ought to have written, *or* I would have written (*ie* by now)
A bin fɔ mɔs dɔn rait	I would (most certainly) have written
A bin go mɔs dɔn de rait	I should (certainly) have been writing

It will be seen that modals follow the tense markers in verb phrase structure, and that the aspect markers follow these. Where the structure is
marked for both perfective and progressive aspect, the perfective marker
precedes the progressive marker.

The spirit of Krio

Comparative study of Krio and the indigenous languages of West
Africa will probably reveal syntactical affinities which will explain the
syntactical distance of Krio from English, the language which so largely
influences its vocabulary.

Krio may derive its vocabulary mainly from English but the spirit of
the language is African. A bald description of the vocabulary and syntax
of any language gives only a limited idea of that language since it describes merely the skeleton. The particular character of the language
comes out in the idioms and the images through which people express
themselves. Krio has inherited not only structures from African languages but the habit of speaking through images. It is almost paradoxical
that Krio, which is the language of the most detribalised Africans in
Africa and a language which developed in an essentially urban context,
should reflect so much of the country in its idioms. The explanation is
twofold. First, the town in Africa is never very remote from the country;
but more significantly, Krio inherited the idioms of rural Africa ready-
made. Its proverbs and wise sayings are mostly close translations of
proverbs current in the many indigenous languages of Africa. A few of
them should illustrate the point.

Yams are a kind of prestige crop and item of food in rural West
Africa. Several Krio proverbs involve yams even though Sierra Leone is
not a yam-growing country. The snub *par excellence* in Krio is:

> *Dɛn de kɔnt yams bai dɔzin, koko de rol go de.*
> While yams are being counted by the dozen mere koko yams go
> intruding their presence.

Other yam proverbs are:

If yu yams wet, kɔba am.
(lit) If your yam is white (*ie* of good quality), cover it up.
ie If you are well off, don't show off.

To a person who is pretending prudish ignorance of sex or some embarrassing facts of life, a Creole is inclined to say rhetorically:

Wetin de pan yams we nɛf nɔ no?
What is there in a yam that a knife does not know all about?

Advice to someone to carry on with the job on hand with the tools he has got (not waiting until everything is perfect) runs:

Put yams na faia, tek yai de luk fɔ nɛf.
Put your yams on the fire while you look around for a knife.

Beans, another common crop, feature in the contemptuous dismissal of a person's belated efforts to achieve success:

Wɛn binch rɔi nɔ ful blai . . . (usually left unfinished)
When the beans were fresh they did not fill the basket (now that they are dry and shrivelled up how likely is it that they will?)

Lizards, frogs and snakes also provide images for these vivid expressions:

Wɛn snek dɔn bɛt yu, yu si ɔkpɔlɔ, yu go rɔn.
Having been once bitten by a snake, you will run when you see a frog. (Rather more vivid than 'Once bitten twice shy'.)

To express the fact that external signs may not always indicate the true state of things:

Ɔl kondo le im bɛlɛ na grɔn; yu nɔ no uswan im bɛlɛ de at am.
All lizards lie with their stomachs flat on the earth, so you can never tell which one has a stomach-ache.

Frogs (K *ɔkpɔlɔ*) are usually found on the ground; so another proverb runs:

Wɛn yu si ɔkpɔlɔ klem fɛnch, yu mɔs no se grɔn wam.
ie When you see people in unwonted places the likelihood is that something out of the ordinary has happened – they are probably in bad trouble.

Other animals, wild and domestic, also feature in these proverbs. In an emergency we are likely to use whatever tools come to hand:

Wɛn man nɔ gɛt dɔg fɔ tek go ɔntin i kin tek got.
When a man fails to find a dog to take hunting, he makes do with a goat.

Several proverbs warn that he who fails to listen to verbal advice and warnings will learn a painful way. One of these uses the domestic fowl as its image:

Da fɔl we nɔ yɛri 'shi', i go yɛri ston.
The chicken which does not respond to the shout 'shi' will respond to a stone.

A person who does not behave in a way to earn the respect to which he is entitled will find himself humiliated. Again, the domestic fowl is the image used here:

Big wet fɔl we nɔ no insɛf, dɛn go dɔk am na bɔn pamain.
A big white fowl which does not behave decorously will be dipped in burning palm oil – *ie* will soon be cooked.

The colonial regime, especially the near-regal person of the governor, has left its mark on the language too. A sight of the governor becomes the symbol of achievement in one proverb. When a person with limited gifts or means aims too high – wants to have a sight of the governor – he is reminded that even those who have two eyes – greater claims – have not yet achieved this:

U gɛt tu yai nɔ si gɔvna!

The large ornate iron gates which open into the drive of Government House are humorously linked with the gaps in children's mouths when they lose their milk teeth; the gaps are called *gɔvna get*.

Other influences like Islam and Christianity have also left their mark. Creole talk is loaded with biblical expressions and bits and pieces from the Book of Common Prayer and popular hymns. The expression *ɔntoum* (unto whom) has been referred to earlier. When a man reaches the rather early retirement age in the civil service and, seeing the prospect of a long period of unemployment and obscurity ahead of him, asks for an extension of his service, his plea is usually jocularly stigmatised with a snippet of a verse from Psalm 39: 'O spare me a little . . . '; there is usually no need for the speaker to finish the quotation '. . . that I may recover my strength before I go hence and be no more seen.' Similarly, the expression 'sorrow vanquished' is usually enough to express jocularly the overcoming of one of life's hurdles. The whole line of the popular hymn is of course: 'Sorrow vanquished, labour ended, Jordan passed.' When a worthless offering is made to the church, or when a person who is quite unfit offers himself for service in it, the event is usually greeted with the expression:

Rɔtin bɔdi blant Jizɔs.
A rotten body belongs to Jesus.

Islam, with its custom of praying on mats, sometimes made of animal skins, inspires the thought that however great an Imam a rat may be, he will not pray on a mat made of cat's skin:

Arata na big Mɔriman bɔt i nɔ go pre na pus kanda.
This really means that a person always knows (or should know) how far he can dare.

These are the sort of idioms which give Krio its African quality and make it a very expressive medium of oral communication. A politician, making a speech in Freetown – most political speeches are now made in Krio – had cause to refer to an occasion when he and his colleagues had, as they thought, been induced to make concessions to a rival because they were deceived by his mild exterior into thinking that he could be easily manoeuvered. Once in power, however, the rival proved intractable. He expressed their sudden realisation of the true nature of the man by saying:

Biol na sok lɛpɛt wi bin si wi mɛmba se na pus. Wɛn san kɔmɔt i
drai ɛn shek insɛf na im wi no.
It turned out that we had mistaken a wet leopard for a cat. Only when the sun came out and he dried out and shook himself did we realise our mistake.

It is this piquancy that makes English a poor substitute for Krio in conversation among Creoles, and which keeps it alive. It is also this that keeps hope alive that one day it will come into its own as a literary medium. Already a few poets have exploited its expressiveness to great effect.

The two writers who have done most to exploit the potentialities of Krio as a literary medium have been Thomas Decker and the late Miss Gladys Hayford. Thomas Decker has been for a long time both a campaigner for the literary use of Krio and a practising writer in the language. His contributions include translations from the Bible and Shakespeare, as well as original poetry. His translation of *Julius Caesar* was performed in Freetown in 1964 to mark the third anniversary of Independence, and Shakespeare's quater-centenary, and was very enthusiastically received. Excerpts from this play have appeared in *Sierra Leone Language Review*, No. 4, 1965. Excerpts from his adaptation of *As You Like It* under the title *U Di Kiap Fit* (Whoever the Cap Fits) appear in No. 5 of the same journal.

The translation of Shakespeare's song 'O Mistress Mine' in *Twelfth Night* illustrates Decker's abilities in the sphere of translation. At his best he recreates the spirit of Shakespeare in this new medium. (In these quotations I have for convenience used the orthography preferred in this article.)

> *Us pat yu de, mi yon yon pɔsin?*
> *Tinap, opin yu yes; yu rait pɔsin*
> *De kam, we kin sing ɔl kanaba sing.*
> *Mi fain fain lɔvin, yu waka dɔn dɔn.*
> *Wɛn tu rait pɔsin mit, waka mɔs dɔn.*
> *Man we gɛt sɛns no se dat na tru tin.*
>
> *Wetin na lɔv? Lɔv nɔ to nɛks wɔl tin.*
> *Tide yon gladi gɛt tide yon laf*
> *Nɔ put at pan tin we nɔ kam yet*
> *Kam kis me ya, gud gud, ɛn plɛnti*
> *Da tin we mek yu yɔng i nɔ ba kip.*[10]

In spite of the merit of his translations, however, Decker is at his best in his own original compositions, when he is free to choose both subject and idiom. His lover's lullaby 'Slip Gud' ('Sleep Well') shows how expressive he can be:

> *Slip gud o, bebi-gial!*
> *opin yai lilibit*
> *ɛn luk mi wan minit*
> *bifo yu slip.*
>
> *A wan fɔ si da tin*
> *we kin de shain insai*
> *insai yu fain-fain yai*
> *ɛn kɔt me at.*

So! sɛt yu yai nau nɔ
a tink se a dɔn si
wetin a wan fɔ si.
Gudnait! Slip gud.[11]

Miss Gladys Hayford's poetry has never been published in full. But she too wrote a good deal in Krio; not only poetry but plays, some of them musical, for children. Her poems whether written for children or adults have an extraordinary evocativeness. Possibly her best poem in this regard is 'Courtship' which describes a brief encounter at the street corner between a girl and her admirer, at the end of which he stands watching her until she disappears in the distance. The poem illustrates Miss Hayford's sense of situation and dialogue:

I tinap misɛf tinap te a put in kalbas dɔng.
A se 'usai yu kɔmɔt bo?' 'A kɔmɔt Fula Tɔng'.
I sɛt im mɔt, mi sɛt mi mɔt; i tan lɛk spirit pas
So te a drɔ am kam klos mi fɔ kam sidɔm na di gras.
Dɛn nɔto kɔmɔn yan wi yan. If yu yɛri we a de shut,
Wails mi wan yai jɛs de spai am, frɔm in ed te rich in fut.
I luk mi, misɛf luk am. A se 'a lɛk yu bo'.
I drap in swit yai wan tɛm. I se 'misɛf lɛk yu Jo'.
I kis mi, misɛf kis am. Na so mi at de bit.
Dɛn wi tɛl gudbai. A wach am te . . . i lɔs go dɔng di trit.[12]

The next poem is equally evocative of a completely different situation – a mother giving orders, admonitions and threats to a whole lot of children as she gets dinner ready. Miss Hayford, as in the last poem, uses rhyme. But the quicker rhythm here contrasts with the last poem and is in perfect harmony with the quick movement implied in the matter.

Dinner Time
Jen go pul di fufu, Ayɔ tɔn di pɔt,
Bɔbɔ yu go was dɛn plet, mek di sup de ɔt.

Maraya nɔ kam bak yet? Lɔd da pikin slo!
A jɛs sɛn am fɔ go bai rɛs, from lɔn tɛm we i go?

Sɔni de ple bɔl na trit. I tink se in de wet
Fɔ mek a kɔl am? A nɔ ful, mi bisin if i let?

Tunu, tɛl yu sisi se if i nɔ go tap
Fɔ nak da piano bɔm, bɔm, bɔm, ɛn trai kam dɔng kam chɔp?

U ambɔg mi nɔ go gɛt wan gren drai fish sɛf.
Jen yu pas di kɔba dish we de pantap da shɛlf.

Ɔl man fɔ go was dɛn pan! ɔl man was dɛn spun
I luk lɛk una ɔl nɔ wan go skul dis aftanun.

Jen, Bɔbɔ, Tunu, Maraya, Sisi, Sɔni, Swit,
Se yu gres ɛn tek yu plet, tɛl tɛnki ɛn go it.[13]

The future of Krio

As long as English continues to hold its very powerful position in Sierra Leone (and there is no reason to suppose that it will not do so indefinitely) it will continue to influence Krio. New objects and ideas are usually introduced with their English names. Thus 'election', 'constituency', 'House of Representatives', like 'bicycle', 'flying ship' (still used side by side with 'aeroplane'), 'lipstick' are part of, and will remain part of the Krio lexicon. When a Creole gentleman is dressed for a very special occasion he will probably be wearing *trausrinɛn bɔnkash* or even *ɔgzon*. *Trausrin* is from English 'trousering' but it is now used particularly for the striped trousers worn with an ordinary black jacket (*bɔnkash*) or a morning coat (*ɔgzon* = Oxon). If however he wears what the English call a bowler, he will describe it as his *bush trɔki* (= bush tortoise). No doubt American words will also be borrowed. *Yɛnkiman* for an American is already part of Krio. It is also possible that as contacts expand, words of other languages will be borrowed. The rate of borrowing from African languages seems to be much slower than from English. But recently the labourer's handcart was introduced into Freetown with its Yoruba name – K *ɔmɔlanke*. There is no reason why more borrowings like this should not take place.

As a means of oral communication, Krio seems destined to increase its role in the country away from its home, the Freetown peninsula. As a means of written communication it seems also likely to become more widespread. On the intimate level it is used quite a good deal in letters between Sierra Leoneans when they wish to express particularly homely ideas. Most frequently this takes the form of proverbs and verbal formulas. On a more public level, newspapers sometimes employ the same technique to put over familiar ideas.

The movement for the use of Krio as a literary medium has never really got under way, although Thomas Decker's Krio poems and translations keep the medium alive. A number of translations from the Bible have been used at the services of the Sierra Leone Evangelical Group, and parts of the Liturgy have also been translated and used. It would seem therefore that Krio will come to be used increasingly at a literary level.

The question of orthography has still not been settled although several suggestions have been made. This in itself is not a great barrier to writing as the considerable body of work by Gladys Hayford and Thomas Decker shows. If the need is pressing the orthography will soon be settled.

In the following private letter a Sierra Leone Churchman decided to write to me in Krio since he was writing principally about the language. I reproduce the body of the letter as an illustration of written Krio, as well as of the interest there is in the subject of using it for more literary purposes:

Di las tɛm we wi si, a bin tɛl yu se a min fɔ rait yu, fɔ tɛl yu tɛnk fɔ di atikul we yu put na di 'Sa Lon Mɛsenja'. Wi ɔl no se di Krio tranga fɔ rait; bɔt as we wi dɔn bigin fɔ trai, wi go ebul am. Mɔs mek a no if yu min fɔ rait ɔl tɛm so a kin aks dɛm na Bunumbu Press na Bo, fɔ mek dɛm go roneo yu atikul as dɛm gɛt taipraita we go du am. A nɔ no ɔmɔs i go kɔs, bɔt a tink se dɛn go gi mi fɔ lili ɛn natin.

Yu no se a bin de trai si if a kin ɛp wit sɔm transleshɔn – lɛk di crid, di awa fada bɔt usai, – chans nɔ de! Frɔm 1938/9 na im a se mek a trai du wan pan di Gɔspɛl – a bigin wit St Mark. A du af af bɔt a nɔ ebul dɔn am. Wɛl bai we a gɛt fɔ de muf, a min wɛn a transfa, sɔm ɔf mi pepas dɛm kin lɔs. Dɛm wan we lɛf gbɔg gbɔg ɛp mi cham dɛm. Fɔ stat egen, na wok bra! So yu we de trai, yu du wɛl.

Wɛl au dɛm ɔl na os? Di wɛf wɛl ɛnti? teŋ Gɔd. A no se yu bizi, so dis du so fɔs.

Gɔd blɛs yu.

P/S Au di maskita ɔp to una na kɔlɛj? Dɛn wan we de ya dɛn so gɛt sɛns dat a de wɔnda au di wan dɛm na kɔlɛj go chupit rich.

Translation: The last time we met (lit. the last time we saw), I told you that I meant to write to you to thank you for the article which you published in the 'Sierra Leone Messenger'. We all know that Krio is difficult to write, but as we have started making attempts we will overcome the difficulties (lit. we will be a match for it, *ie* Krio). Please let me know if you mean to write frequently so that I can ask the people of the Bunumbu Press at Bo to roneo your article since they have a type-writer which will do it. I do not know how much it will cost, but I think that they will let me have it for a reasonable price, (*ie* little or nothing).

You know that I had been trying to see if I could help with some translation – like the Creed, the 'Our Father' – but could I? There was not enough time! (lit. but where? – there was no chance). It was as far back as 1938/9 that I decided that I should attempt one of the Gospels. I began with St Mark. I did bits (lit. half-half or halves) but was not able to finish it. Well, because I had to move often – I mean when I was trans-ferred – some of my papers got lost. White ants chewed up those that were left (lit. the ones that remained, the white ants helped me chew up). Starting again was too great a labour. So for attempting anything you are to be commended.

Well, how are they all at home? Your wife is well I hope: thank God. I know that you are busy, so this will do for the time being.

God bless you.

P/S How are the mosquitoes up your way at the College? The ones around here are so clever that I wonder how 'stupid' the ones in College are.

Notes

1 See, for example, Bradshaw, 1965, on the vestiges of Portuguese in the Sierra Leone languages. Further studies by the same writer are expected to include other West African languages.

2 See Turner, 1949, and Cassidy and Le Page, 1961. The latter list words which are common to the two languages. Compare also Hancock's chapter in this volume.

3 An interesting record of the broken English speech of a Bullom King in a diary entry made in 1817 makes one wonder whether an independent growth may have preceded the arrival of the settlers, since, of course, the Bulloms did not come from overseas. On the other hand there had been sufficient time between 1787 and 1817 for the speech of the settlers to have spread.

4 On the subject of literature and journalism in Krio see Jones, 1957 and 1964. Three Krio poems by Thomas Decker appeared in the *Sierra Leone Language Review*, 4, 1964.

5 *Orthographical note:* The orthography used in writing Krio words here employs the English alphabet with the addition of two symbols: ɛ to indicate the vowel sound in English 'egg' and Krio ɛbɛ; ɔ for the vowel in English 'pot' which is the same in Krio. The vowel sounds are thus:

    a approximating to vowel in English 'hat'
    ɛ as in English 'egg'
    e approximating to vowel in English 'ape'

i	approximating to vowel in English	'thief'
ɔ	as in English	'pot'
o	approximating to vowel in English	'hope'
u	approximating to vowel in English	'coop'

These are combined to form diphthongs.

Consonants: to make the orthography approximate to phonetic regularity, *q* and *x* have been dispensed with and *c* is never used to indicate the initial sound in 'cat' (this is always represented by *k*). It appears however in the combination *ch* as in English 'chop', Krio *chap*. The symbol *g* indicates the initial sound in English 'gang' and *j* the final consonant sound in English 'change'. The other consonants are used as in English.

6 For a further discussion of Krio vocabulary see Jones, 1956 and 1959, and Berry, 1959a.

7 Grave (`) and acute (´) accents are used here and elsewhere in this book to indicate low and high tone respectively.

8 It should be noted that there are two quite distinct *na* forms in Krio: the verbal here described, and the prepositional *na* (= 'in', 'on', etc.)

9 Compare Jamaican Creole, in which the tense system 'is limited to the unmarked verb for general purposes, and a particle specifying "past" ' (Bailey, 1966).

10 This poem and those of Gladys Hayford which follow later in the chapter appeared in my article, Jones, 1957.

11 Published in *Sierra Leone Language Review* 3, 1964.

Sleep well, my darling,
Open your eyes a little
And look at me for a minute
Before you sleep.

I want to see that thing
Which shines deep inside
Your so beautiful eyes
And jogs at my heart.

So! shut your eyes now
I think I have seen
What I wanted to see.
Goodnight! Sleep well.

bebi-gial < E baby + girl = K darling
nɔ: a particle used at the end of a request with the effect of 'please'.
wetin: that which, what.

12 (*I tinap*, etc)

She stopped, I stopped, then I lifted down her calabash.
I said 'Where do you come from, love?' 'I am from Fula Town.'
She shut her mouth (*ie* fell silent), I shut my mouth; it was as though a ghost had walked by,
Till I pulled her close to sit down on the grass.
Then you should have heard our love talk! you should have heard me shoot,
While my one eye kept spying her from her head down to her feet.

She gazed at me, I gazed at her. I said 'I love you dear.'
She lowered her bright eyes at that. She said 'I too love you Jo.'
She kissed me, I too kissed her. You should have heard my heart beat!
Then we said goodbye. I watched her till she disappeared down the street.

tinap < E stand + up = stand up, halt
kɔmɔt < E come + out = come from, originate from
yan   < E yarn = to engage in love talk
yeri < E hear
shut < E shoot = speak ungrammatically
13 (*Jane go pul*, etc)

Jane go serve the foofoo, Ayo stir the pot,
Bobo go and wash the plates while the soup gets hot.
Has Maria not come back yet? Lord, how slow that child is!
I only sent her to buy some rice; what a long time she's been gone!
Sonny is playing ball in the street. Does he think he is waiting
For me to call him? I'm no fool, what do I care if he is late?
Tunu, ask your sister if she will never stop
Banging that piano bom, bom, bom and bring herself down to eat?
Anyone who bothers me will not get even a shred of stockfish.
Jane you hand me the covered dish which is standing on the shelf.
Let each one go and wash his plate! each one wash his spoon.
It looks as if you all do not wish to go to school this afternoon!
Jane, Bobo, Tunu, Maria, Sisi, Sonny, Sweet,
Say your grace and take your plate, say thanks, go on and eat.

bisin < E business = be concerned with, care
ambɔg < E humbug = cause trouble, bother
gren < E grain = the smallest piece of

Bernard Mafeni

Nigerian Pidgin

It has become customary today to accept Robert A. Hall's distinction between a pidgin and a creole language (Hall, 1959 and 1966): the former being a lingua franca or trade language spoken as a second language, and the latter a first language which has developed out of an original pidgin, and, as a result of becoming the mother tongue of a community, expanded its resources and functions. While this is a useful working distinction, it does not always prove possible to make such a neat separation. This is the case with the English-based Pidgin which is spoken in Nigeria. Nigerian Pidgin is a lingua franca for many, and thus a true pidgin in Hall's sense; it is also a mother tongue for a number of families in certain areas and communities, and as such might in these cases be defined as a creole language.

Elsewhere in this volume Eldred Jones has written of Krio as an English-based lingua franca 'used throughout Sierra Leone as an inter-tribal language of trade and social communication', but also 'the mother tongue of the descendants of groups of freed men who settled in the Sierra Leone peninsula between 1787 and the early years of the nineteenth century'. Krio, though perhaps predominantly to be considered a creole, is thus also utilised as a pidgin beyond the community which maintains it as mother tongue. A somewhat similar situation exists in the western area of the Cameroon Republic, where a widespread use of Pidgin English as a lingua franca among people whose mother tongues may be any of the many African languages to be found in this area, is accompanied by its use as a mother tongue by families long settled in the urban centres of the Cameroon coast, some of them descended from nineteenth-century migrants from Sierra Leone.

If we are to postulate a West African Pidgin related to English, of which Nigerian Pidgin, Cameroon Pidgin, Sierra Leone Krio, among others, are branches, it can best be seen at the present stage of research as a dialect cluster consisting of related varieties and sub-varieties of both pidgin and creole languages in Hall's definition of these terms. Without a great deal more investigation, diachronic as well as synchronic, it is not possible to state with any certainty the nature of their relationship to one another, in terms either of their historical origins or their present similarities and differences. Since Sierra Leone Krio represents the major concentration of mother tongue speakers within this postulated dialect cluster, and is probably of primary historical and cultural significance in the extension of Pidgin in West Africa, it has merited separate treatment in this volume.

Nigerian Pidgin, then, can most conveniently be seen as part of a larger group of English-based pidgin and creole languages, or dialects, spoken mostly in coastal areas, and especially in cities and towns, but also in the hinterland, from the Gambia to Cameroon. Naturally, these dialects are to be found mainly in English-using West Africa: namely, in the Gambia, Sierra Leone, Liberia, Ghana, Nigeria and Western Cameroon (formerly the southern part of British Cameroons). But speakers of West African Pidgin are also to be found among coastal West African communities in what were formerly French – and before 1918 German – colonies, as well as in the Portuguese and Spanish West African territories. West African Pidgin thus not only covers a very large geographical area, but runs the gamut all the way from true creole – as a mother tongue and home language – to what one might call 'minimal pidgin', the exiguous jargon often used between Europeans and their domestic servants. It thus exhibits diversity in geographical terms, being a dialect cluster in the traditional sense, not all dialects perhaps being mutually intelligible.[1] It also exhibits diversity in terms of the creole-pidgin polarity referred to above. Research into West African Pidgin must thus take into account its varying social functions equally with its formal variation from area to area along the West African coast. Information of this kind must also be complemented, wherever possible, with whatever historical information may yet be found as to its rise, development and spread.

Few specimens of West African Pidgin survive in written form from the nineteenth century and earlier. One example of an English-based pidgin dating from the early years of the last century may be quoted (Dike, 1956) as an example of Nigerian Pidgin as spoken in the Niger Delta at that time:

Brudder George . . . send warship look um what water bar ab got, dat good, me let um dat. Brudder send boat chopum slave, dat good. E no send warship for cappen no peake me, no lookee face. No, no; no me tell you, No; Suppose you come all you mont full palaver, give e reason, whye do it, me tell you, you peake lie, you peake lie, you peakeed-n lie. Suppose my fader, or my fader fader come up from ground and peake me why English man do dat, I no sabby tell why.

This speech, recorded by a certain Captain Owen, is attributed by him to King Opubu. It is of course impossible to reconstruct King Opubu's actual pronunciation from this text. Indeed it is probable that it is not really a faithful reproduction, but rather an anglicised, 'edited' version of the original speech. Nevertheless, there are enough features present in the text to suggest that we are here dealing with a genuine English-based pidgin language and not with mere 'imperfect' English. It is also one of the first recorded instances of Nigerian Pidgin, though there is no reason to believe that we can therefore date its origins from about this period. It may well have a longer history; and the origins of West African Pidgin probably date from the first contacts with the English in the sixteenth century.

Nigerian Pidgin, with which we are here concerned, is itself relatively complex, and exhibits variety in form and in function from region to region and from community to community. Although the different varieties or dialects of Nigerian Pidgin are nearly all mutually intelligible, they vary in the identity of the vernacular languages which contribute, or have contributed, to their phonological, lexical and even syntactical resources. It is convenient to regard a pidgin language as consisting of a base language – in this case English – which has been, and possibly continues to be, modified by one or more other languages, which may be termed substrates (see Ross, 1964). The substrates, in the case of Nigerian Pidgin, are potentially many and varied. Thus, in Lagos the major substrate would be Yoruba, while in Port Harcourt it would be Igbo. Nevertheless, some of the variation deriving from this difference of substrate is constantly being reduced by certain standardising influences, such as the increasing mobility of peoples within the country (itself a cause of the spread of Pidgin), inter-tribal marriage, the radio, and of course the continuing influence of Sierra Leone Krio. The latter is clearly of considerable significance historically. Krio-speaking Sierra Leoneans held important positions in Nigeria in the latter half of the nineteenth century and the early part of this century, and it is very probable that Krio served at that time as a kind of model language for

Nigerian Pidgin. A good many of the older generation of Nigerian Pidgin speakers use a variety of the language very close to Krio, possibly because they came into intimate contact with Sierra Leoneans working in Nigeria.

Nigerian Pidgin is essentially a product of the process of urbanisation. While its origins lie historically in the early contacts between Europeans and Africans on the coast, its development and spread is the result of contacts between Africans. The rapidly growing towns of Nigeria have increasingly become the melting pots of the many tribes and races which constitute Nigeria, and Pidgin seems to be today a very widely spoken lingua franca, many town and city dwellers being at least bilingual, in Pidgin and an indigenous language. For the older generation, Pidgin is often the second language. In the lives of their children, however, Pidgin plays a more important role; many of the young people in the cities seem to be polyglot, using Pidgin, standard English and one or more Nigerian languages as occasion requires. In some cases it is not always easy to determine which of these is their 'first' language, either in the sense of which of them was learned first, or in relation to which is used with greatest competence. The fact that Pidgin is, for many town children, a language of primary importance is not often fully appreciated. The sociolinguistic reasons for this are perhaps worth examining.

In the first place, inter-tribal and international marriages, which used to be frowned upon by earlier generations in Nigeria, and were therefore relatively rare up to the end of the first quarter of this century, have become increasingly common in urban society. In many such cases husband and wife may not share a common indigenous language, and as a result will often use Pidgin as their chief medium of communication in the home; or, of course, Pidgin alongside standard English. Children brought up in such homes naturally speak Pidgin, sometimes alongside standard English, as their first language, although they may also speak the native language(s) of either or both parents. The children therefore learn to operate several linguistic systems, of which Pidgin is one; and in many cases it may be the primary and predominant system. However, even where both parents speak the same native language, many urban and partially detribalised children learn Pidgin very early although it is not the language of the home. Often several families live in the same compound, and if they differ in linguistic background Pidgin serves as a convenient lingua franca. The children in such compounds and neighbourhoods find Pidgin an efficient means of communication among themselves, and may also use it at home even though their parents may not approve. At school, especially among the southern communities living in towns in the North, or in towns in the South whose populations are linguistically heterogeneous, like Warri, Sapele or Benin, or large cities like Port Harcourt and Lagos, Pidgin is the commonest language used outside the classroom; while some teachers (despite the school regulations forbidding its use) may have recourse to it for explanatory purposes, especially in the early stages of primary education, where there is no other common language amongst their pupils. Pidgin is also widely spoken in the secondary schools, particularly those whose pupils are drawn from different linguistic groups, or where there is a preponderance of children of Southern Nigerian extraction, as in the missionary or voluntary agency schools which serve the immigrant elements of the *sabon-garis* (stranger-communities) in the North.

Nigerian Pidgin is thus, linguistically and sociolinguistically, a complicated phenomenon, consisting of several varieties depending upon the influence of various substrates, and also containing a variety of registers, whose formal characteristics and functional determinants cannot, without more research, be clearly distinguished. The majority of domestic servants employed by European families, for instance, almost certainly use two quite different varieties of Pidgin; one, a minimal variety, which they use to their employers – and which is the only kind of Pidgin which most Europeans come across – and a fuller variety, Pidgin proper, which they use elsewhere. Attitudes towards Pidgin are also complex, and often ambivalent. Many Nigerians, although they use Pidgin as a register in certain, especially familiar, contexts, are nevertheless ashamed to be associated with the language in public. This is probably a result of the influence of parents and school authorities, who have often discouraged its use because they consider it a debased form of English and not a language in its own right. Some amusing illustrations of the use of Pidgin by apparently sophisticated Nigerians may be found in Chinua Achebe's novel *No Longer at Ease* (1960). The Hon Samson Okoli is entertaining Obi Okonkwo, Secretary to the Scholarship Board, and Clara, a nursing sister, to drinks in his luxuriously furnished sitting-room. Obi notices Samson's 'enormous' radiogram and admires it, and the host proudly reveals that there is a tape-recorder fitted to it as well. He then plays back part of their conversation which had in fact been recorded without their knowledge:

'You will hear all our conversation, everything.' He smiled with satisfaction as he listened to his own voice, adding an occasional com-
8

mentary in pidgin. 'White man don go far. We just de shout for nothing,' he said. Then he seemed to realise his position. 'All the same they must go. This no be them country.'

In spite of traditional attitudes of disapproval towards Pidgin, however, it appears that many Nigerian novelists, playwrights, advertising agents, trade unionists and even politicians realise and have begun to exploit the great potentialities of the language as a medium of mass communication. For example, the various Broadcasting Corporations in Nigeria have in recent years done much to popularise Pidgin (however unintentionally) by allowing its use in advertisements; the NBC radio serial 'Save Journey' has been running with great success for a number of years now; Achebe has used Pidgin less apologetically and with greater success in his very entertaining and prophetic novel *A Man of the People* (1966), and Frank Aig-Imoukhuede's poem in Pidgin, 'One Wife for One Man' (Banham, 1961), is generally considered outstanding.

There are, however, two problems connected with writing in Pidgin which should be mentioned at this point: the fact that it is difficult to specify a standard form of Nigerian Pidgin; and the lack of a uniform orthography for the language. We have already noted that Nigerian Pidgin is really a dialect cluster, but there is the further complication that within a single community of Pidgin speakers, there is a wide range of pronunciation differences between the speech, say, of the younger educated people on the one hand, and that of the illiterate younger generation and the older generation on the other. On the whole, the older generation use more African loan-words; and where they have come in contact with Krio, they tend not only to use a good many Krio forms but also to imitate as closely as possible the pronunciation of conservative Krio speakers.

This pattern of usage falls in line with what Berry, in writing about Krio, calls 'hyper-creolization' (Berry, 1961a): 'the inordinate use of Africanisms and a keen awareness of the early stages of phonetic integration'. The educated younger generation on the other hand are inclined to borrow more and more vocabulary items from standard English and to anglicise their pronunciation. Thus the following Krio forms cited by Berry in his article, *bɛt* 'bite', *nɛf* 'knife', *rɛs* 'rice', *grɔn* 'ground', *klem* 'climb', would be typical of the pronunciation of the older and perhaps illiterate speakers of Nigerian Pidgin, while the younger and more educated speakers would use the more anglicised forms *bait, naif, rais, graun, klaimb*.[2]

Generally, however, there seem to be very close similarities between the varieties of Pidgin spoken by the young educated southerners born and bred in the northern states and those of educated southerners of the same generation who, although born in some part of the southern states like Enugu, Port Harcourt, Calabar, Lagos, Ibadan, Benin, Warri, Sapele, have nevertheless, at various times, lived in some of the other states of the Nigerian Federation. Pidgin speakers of the latter group are mostly children of civil servants, members of the armed forces, employees of Federal Corporations like the Railways and the Airways, who have had to be transferred periodically from one part of the country to another. Their varieties of Pidgin, like those of the young people of southern origin bred in the northern states, are, besides being anglicised, characterised by a considerable expansion of vocabulary, including words from all the main languages of Nigeria, and are easily intelligible anywhere in the country. From these varieties perhaps a convenient standard form might be selected.

Regarding the problem of orthography, I am of the opinion, from the tentative work I have done on the phonology of a few varieties of Nigerian Pidgin, that an orthography similar to that of Yoruba or Igbo would not only show clearly at least the phonetic/phonological differences between the base language and Pidgin but would emphasise the independent nature of the latter. The following passages, which are clearly Nigerian Pidgin but have been written in English orthography, illustrate this point, as well as providing some examples of Pidgin:

'Ah! I hear say 'e get one letter so from im boy dat "Kobo-Kobo" boy dem call Mr Chukwuka. Me I no know wetin 'e write for this letter. After Miss Olowu read am 'e begin do as if 'e mad. Dem don carry am go Abeokuta Mental Hospital. Some people wey know-am proper for Ilesha say na de same ting wey kill 'im papa. Dem say 'e run mad one afternoon, kill one of 'im own pikin with matchet and run inside bush . . .'

(V. C. Ike, *Toads for Supper*, London, 1965.)

'So emake two time way Mr Midman come thisi Niger Company to come and be A.G. . . . and that time I de for work, and them write come from England say Mr Midman don regin from Niger Company and then he dash government ten hundred say because he be big man and that be the time I de thatsal.'

(From a recording by Kay Williamson in Western Ijo Division in 1963. The speech is that of Chief Moke Ohihia.)

My fader before my fader get him wife borku.
E no' get equality palaver; he live well
For he be oga for im own house.
But that time done pass before white man come
Wit 'im
  One wife for one man.[3]

(F. Aig-Imoukhuede, 'One Wife for One Man'.)

A cursory glance at these three passages may give the reader the misleading idea that he is faced with some sub-standard dialect of English.
The spoken form is, however, a different matter; listening to the original
recording of Chief Ohihia's speech, for example, one cannot but regret
the false impression which the transcription has created.[4] The passage
from Ike's novel also illustrates the disadvantage of trying to write
Nigerian Pidgin according to English orthographic conventions. In the
sentence 'I no like de way you de waste your time come here', the two
words 'de' in 'de way' and in 'you de waste' are spelt alike, but they are
actually two different lexical and grammatical items with different
phonetic realisations. The first is phonetically [di] and the second is [de].
Perhaps these inconsistencies will show up more clearly when we consider the sound system of one variety of Nigerian Pidgin in the section
which follows.

A descriptive sketch of Nigerian Pidgin

It is not possible within the limited scope of this chapter to give a detailed linguistic description of Nigerian Pidgin. It would require a book
to do this. Besides, such an attempt would presuppose an exhaustive
investigation into the language, and this the present writer cannot in any
way claim at the moment; nor has anyone else so far attempted it.
Nevertheless, it may be of some interest to examine, even if in outline,
at least one variety of Nigerian Pidgin (the variety spoken by the writer
himself) against the background of one or two theories of pidginisation
which have been advanced by linguists.

We have already drawn attention to a popular theory which looks on
a pidgin language as a special kind of 'mixed' language[5] consisting of a
'base' language which supplies the bulk of the vocabulary of the 'new'
language and one or more substrates which, according to Douglas
Taylor (1956), provide 'the basic morphological and/or syntactical

pattern' of the language. Robert A. Hall (1959) holds a different view, it would seem:

> It is often assumed that a European language furnishes the pidgin vocabulary, while the 'native' language supplies the pidgin grammatical structure. Chinese Pidgin English is sometimes called 'Chinese spoken with English words'. This notion is inexact. Close examination reveals that each form of pidgin adheres to the dominant language in grammar as well as in the vocabulary. . . . However, elements of all kinds – sounds, inflections and types of word order – can and do invade pidgin from the native tongues of the subservient group.

Besides objecting to the use of the phrase 'subservient groups' in a linguistic discussion on pidgins,[6] I would claim that Nigerian Pidgin neither adheres to English (the base language) in grammar, nor is it entirely similar structurally to any of the indigenous languages which constitute its substrates. Perhaps it would be more correct to say that Nigerian Pidgin has a structure of its own with similarities at certain levels and in varying degrees to English and to the various substrates.

VOCABULARY

There can be no doubt that the bulk of the vocabulary of Nigerian Pidgin is derived from English. Indeed, every word in English is a potential loan-word in Nigerian Pidgin, but this does not mean that all Nigerian Pidgin words of English origin are easily recognisable as deriving from standard English as such.[7] There are several reasons why it is difficult to tell at a glance the English origin of a good many lexical items in Nigerian Pidgin.

In the first place, some of these words were borrowed at least three centuries ago, more often than not from various regional dialects of those days as spoken by sailors, rather than from standard English as such. A good many words which were borrowed in this way are either obsolete or archaic in English, or are confined only to vulgar speech. Thus quite perfectly acceptable, innocuous Nigerian Pidgin words like *pís* (urine or to urinate), *shít* (excrement or to defecate), *fọ́k* (to copulate) may be heard only in certain registers (usually vulgar) in English, whereas items like *bọ̀bí* (breast), *tót* (carry) and *tìtí* (girl) are more difficult to trace back to English either because they are obsolete English words or because they derive from some regional dialect.

Another reason why it is difficult to tell immediately whether certain lexical items have been adopted from English is that although these vocabulary items have some phonological resemblances to certain current English words, the Nigerian Pidgin items seem to cover completely different areas of meaning from the English. For example, it is possible for educated speakers of Nigerian Pidgin to say, *ì dè chóp fàyà wúd*, but most speakers would look at them askance if they did since for the majority of speakers *chóp* means either 'food' or 'to eat' and not 'to cut up in pieces'.

Again, there are those instances of English loan-words in Nigerian Pidgin which are capable of entering into collocations which are un-English, with resultant semantic extension or the creation of a completely new lexical item. Thus the Pidgin word *bad* in the utterance *yúù nà bád màn* ('you are a bad man') has the same meaning as the English word *bad*, but the reduplication *bad bad* as in *dì súp swít bád bàd* ('the soup is very delicious' or 'tasty') has a completely different function and certainly means the very opposite of 'not good'. Further examples of reduplication as a method of word-derivation include the following:

	English origin	Pidgin meaning
bèn-bén	bend	crooked, shady
kàtàkátá	scatter	confusion
sósó	so	always
wàkà-wáká	walk	to wander about

However, not all cases of reduplication result in as great an extension of meaning as the examples cited above. A very considerable proportion of reduplicated forms are merely intensives:

bèg-bég	beg	to ask for aid or charity indiscriminately
kòs-kós	curse	to insult thoroughly
krày-kráy	cry	to cry continuously for a long time
lùk-lúk	look	to stare at

In a few cases there does not seem to be any difference in meaning between the Nigerian Pidgin reduplicated form and the English word from which it derives. For example, *sànsán* from the English 'sand' is not an intensive, but merely an equivalent of the latter. Reduplication as a process of word-formation, it must be noted, is a phenomenon more typical of African languages than of English.

The third major reason why it may not be immediately evident that a particular lexical item in Nigerian Pidgin derives from English is that, in addition to other modifications, the loan-word may have undergone certain phonological changes as well. A good example of this is the word *kàtàkátá*, which was probably derived from the English word 'scatter'. English, then, supplies the bulk of the vocabulary of Nigerian Pidgin. A few loan-words were, however, borrowed from other European languages, notably Portuguese. It is believed that a Portuguese-based Pidgin was spoken along the West Coast of Africa as early as the fifteenth century (Christophersen, 1953), and that words like *sàbí* (know), *pìkín* (a child), *dásh* (gift, give a present), *pàlává* or *plábà* (quarrel), may have been borrowed into Nigerian Pidgin from that source. A word in common usage which is of French origin is *bòkú* (plenty, much, many), while Spanish probably supplied words like *chínch* (bed bug) and *pànyá* (a thing of inferior quality).

It would seem, however, that the African languages which constitute the substrates of Nigerian Pidgin are a far more important source of lexical borrowing than all other European languages apart from English. African loan-words in Pidgin probably account for no less than twelve per cent of the lexicon. Understandably, the relative contribution of the individual African languages varies from locality to locality. Terms for local objects, food, fauna, flora and festivals will, for example, be borrowed from the dominant Nigerian language spoken in any given area, resulting in a higher incidence of loan-words from that language in the variety of Nigerian Pidgin spoken there. In the Hausa-speaking areas of the north, for instance, the Pidgin word for 'bean-cake' is *kwósé*, whereas in the Yoruba-speaking areas and in the south generally it is *àkàrà*. In the Igbo-speaking areas the word for 'stockfish' is *ókpòrókó* but in Yoruba-speaking areas the Yoruba loan-word *kpánlá* is used.

Nevertheless, it would appear that, in general, the more widely spoken varieties have borrowed far more words from Yoruba than from any other African language. This may well be partly the result of indirect borrowing, via Krio, for the Krio lexicon contains a preponderant element of Yoruba items as compared with those derived from other African languages (Berry, 1959a). Igbo, Twi (a language of Ghana) and Hausa have to a lesser extent also contributed some widely used vocabulary items. The following is a list of a few loan-words of African origin which are common to a good many varieties of Nigerian Pidgin, irrespective of the localities where they are spoken:

wàyó (tricks) Hausa origin
yàngá or *nyàngá* (vanity) Hausa origin
ògá (master, superior) Yoruba origin

kònkòsá (gossip, hypocrisy) Twi origin
òyìbó (a white man or a light-skinned person) Yoruba origin
járá (bonus) Hausa origin
rìkíchí (trouble) Hausa origin
wàhálà (trouble) Hausa origin
kòbòkóbò (rascal) Yoruba origin
jàkí (ass, fool, slave) Hausa origin
ògìlì (a kind of soup condiment) Igbo origin
sàrá (sacrifice) Hausa origin
àjé (witch) Yoruba origin
jàgùdà (ruffian) Yoruba origin

The contribution of African languages to the lexicon of Nigerian Pidgin may, however, not be fully appreciated if we consider only direct borrowings from these languages; of far greater importance are the various processes of word-formation which it has adopted from the substrates. There are two principal ways in which Nigerian Pidgin increases its lexicon apart from the direct borrowing of lexical items. The first, which we have mentioned above, involves the phenomenon of reduplication as a method of word-derivation. In this way new words may be formed either as intensives of the words from which they have been derived, or with completely different meanings from them. The second important method of word-formation is the kind of compounding known as calquing, utilising English loan-words in combination according to the pattern of compounds to be found in Nigerian languages: *stròng-hẹ́d* or *tròng-hẹ́d* (stubborn), *bìg áy* (greedy), *lòngà-tròt* (*ie* 'long throat') and *bòtòm-bẹ̀lẹ́* (vagina), *òpùn-áy* (boldness, wisdom, or to brow-beat) are a few examples which spring readily to mind.

Briefly, therefore, although English has supplied the vast majority of the items that make up the Nigerian Pidgin lexicon, the various substrates also supply vocabulary items (however few) as well as the more important processes by which the English loan-words are made to acquire new or additional meanings.

PHONOLOGY

The following outline phonology of Nigerian Pidgin is based primarily on the speech of the present writer. The variety is that spoken in Kano *sabon-gari* and is characterised by considerable lexical borrowing from Yoruba, Igbo and Hausa while at the same time being fairly anglicised. This variety is easily intelligible anywhere in the country and differs from the very conservative type mainly in the distribution of the segmental phonemes. Although I am not here directly concerned with conservative varieties of Nigerian Pidgin, comparisons will be made wherever necessary between these and the style of speech being described.

1 *Consonant phonemes:* The consonant phonemes of Nigerian Pidgin are shown on the chart below. The symbols used have IPA values, and are in some cases different from the orthography in which forms are cited in the text. Thus, the palatal nasal /ɲ/ is represented in the text as *ny* and the palatal approximant /j/ as *y*, the palato-alveolar affricates /tʃ/ and /dʒ/ as *ch* and *j* respectively, the palatal fricatives /ʃ/ and /ʒ/ as *sh* and *ž* respectively.

	Bilabial	Labio-dental	Alveolar	Palato-alveolar	Palatal	Velar	Labio-velar	Glottal
Nasal	m		n		ɲ			
Plosive	p b		t d			k g	kp gb	
Affricate				tʃ dʒ				
Roll tap			r					
Lateral			l					
Fricative		f v	s z	ʃ ʒ				h
Approximant					j		w	

In addition to the twenty-four consonant phonemes shown on the chart above there is a syllabic nasal /N/ which is tone-bearing and is always homorganic with the succeeding consonant. In some varieties of Nigerian Pidgin /v/ does not occur as a phoneme, and thus *véks* (vex, make angry) would occur as *féks*. Also, /z/ does not occur in some, being replaced by /s/, and /ʒ/ is absent from many varieties, being replaced by /ʃ/.

2 *Vowel phonemes:* Nigerian Pidgin has seven vowel phonemes: /i, e, ɛ, a, ɔ, o, u/. Phonetic diphthongs are possible, but phonemically, these are more conveniently treated as sequences of vowel plus consonantal glide. Vowel length is not significant. The following examples illustrate the vowel system, and also the orthographic symbols, which bring it into line with Yoruba spelling:

Vowel phonemes	Phonemic	Orthographic	English equivalent
i	/bít/	bít	beat
e	/pén/	pén	pain
ɛ	/bɛ́t/	bẹ́t	bet
a	/hát/	hát	heart

Vowel phonemes	Phonemic	Orthographic	English equivalent
ɔ	/hɔt/	hɔt	hot
o	/tót/	tót	carry
u	/fút/	fút	foot

3 *Syllable structure:* The generalised formula for Nigerian Pidgin syllable structure is:

$/C_{0-2}VC_{0-2}/$ and $/N/$

where the subscript figures indicate the possibilities in terms of number of elements, for that place of syllable structure. Thus:

  V: à (I), ì (he, she, it)
  CV: gó (go), fò (for), dì (the)
  VC: ít (eat), àn (and), ég (egg)
  CVC: bít (beat), tíf (steal, thief), chóp (eat, food)
  N: ń-kǫ́ (so what? what if?)
  CCV: stǫ́ (store), pré (pray), plé (play)
  VCC: áks (ask)
  CCVCC: práwd (proud), smáyl (smile)

In addition to these structures, there is also the possibility in anglicised Pidgin of up to three consonant clusters in either syllable-initial or syllable-final positions, as in English. Conservative speakers tend to avoid clusters altogether, however, either by dropping one member of the cluster as in *pún* – one pronunciation of the word *spún* (spoon) – or by vocalic intrusion, as in the case of *sìpík* instead of the more anglicised pronunciation *spík*.

4 *Tone and stress:* Nigerian Pidgin is essentially a tone language, with two basic tones, 'high' (´), and 'low' (`). These may be correlated with two degrees of stress, high-tone syllables being normally more heavily stressed than low-tone syllables. The following minimal pairs illustrate the distinctive function of tone:

bàbá	father
bábà	barber
sìsí	sister, or a female
sísì	sixpence
fàdá	a Roman Catholic priest
fádà	father

High and low tonemes are usually realised as high-level pitches and low-level pitches respectively, but a high-tone monosyllabic word said in isolation or occurring in prepausal position in a sentence, has a 'high-falling' pitch. Thus, although *pé* (pay), for example, is a high-tone monosyllabic word, the actual phonetic realisation of the toneme depends on the context in which the word occurs. In isolation or in sentence-final position as in:

à nóbá gét má pé (I have not received my pay as yet),

it has a high-falling pitch; but in

dèm pé mí wòn shílìn (I was paid a shilling),

the tone on *pé* is high-level.

5 *Rhythm and intonation:* Nigerian Pidgin is a syllable-timed language. The syllables constituting a stretch of utterance occur isochronously and tend to be of equal duration. As far as the intonation of Nigerian Pidgin is concerned, it bears some relation to English, but may also be seen to have characteristics in common with the overall handling of tone sequences in some of the Nigerian languages. To give a detailed account of it here would be inappropriate.

In the above sketch of the phonology of Nigerian Pidgin a number of important details have been sacrificed for brevity. Nevertheless, what has been included in the phonology may be sufficient to serve as a basis for a comparison between Nigerian Pidgin phonology and those of English (the base language) and Yoruba (which seems to be the most important substrate of the variety of Nigerian Pidgin being described), as well as with other varieties of West African Pidgin.

Beginning with the vowel phoneme inventories, one notices immediately that the Nigerian Pidgin system is very much reduced in comparison with, for instance, that of English Received Pronunciation (to take an accent of standard English which has been much described). Where RP has twelve monophthongal phonemes, Nigerian Pidgin has only seven. Yoruba on the other hand has seven oral vowel phonemes, /i, e, ɛ, a, ɔ, o, u/ and four or five nasalised vowels (Ward, 1952). The Nigerian Pidgin vowels have a close qualitative correspondence with those of Yoruba, while the absence of nasalised vowels in the variety of Pidgin under investigation is probably due to the influence of standard English. It is possible that a number of nasalised vowel phonemes may be included in the vowel inventories of some of the conservative varieties of Nigerian Pidgin spoken in certain parts of the country.

With regard to consonants, one notes the occurrence of the labio-velars /kp/ and /gb/ and the nasal /ɲ/, and the non-occurrence of the English dentals /θ/ and /ð/. In these respects the Yoruba consonant system corresponds more closely to Pidgin than does the English system, although there are systemic and structural differences between Yoruba and Pidgin consonants which should not be overlooked. Angli-cised Pidgin speakers, as has been noted, have a tendency to approxi-mate their handling of consonant clusters to that of English, as compared with more conservative speakers of Pidgin, while retaining for the most part the vowel system of Pidgin unmodified.

With regard to suprasegmental features, it seems evident that both the base language and the substrate have together influenced Nigerian Pidgin quite considerably. Unlike English, Nigerian Pidgin is a tone language; but unlike any of the Nigerian languages forming its substrate, stress seems to be of some importance in Nigerian Pidgin and is closely linked with the tonal patterns. As far as rhythm is concerned, Nigerian Pidgin is like the substrates, but the former has a more elaborate in-tonation system, in some ways resembling that of English.

GRAMMAR

Even a brief grammatical sketch of Nigerian Pidgin is not possible here, and a few morphological and syntactical notes must suffice, if only to suggest that the grammatical categories of English do not necessarily fit the patterns of Pidgin. If certain types of phrase or clause structure in English are paralleled in Nigerian Pidgin, it is likely that many of these are also paralleled in one or another of the languages that con-stitute the Nigerian Pidgin substrates.

By far the greater majority of Nigerian Pidgin words are invariable in form and are usually monomorphemic – that is, not divisible into smaller meaningful units; though there are a number of compound words con-sisting of two free morphemes. English words in general are capable of inflexion, while Nigerian Pidgin words are not. Plurality, for instance, is indicated in Pidgin by the use of an independent particle. Thus, whereas in English the plural of 'driver' is formed by the addition of the plural suffix, in Pidgin this can only be done by placing the independent plural marker *dem* after *drayva*. For instance:

English	Pidgin
The drivers are coming.	dì dráyvà dèm dè kọ́m.
I did not see the teachers.	à nó sí dì tíchà dẹ̀m.

Inflexion also plays an important role in verbal construction in English, in relation to subject-verb concord and in differentiating tense and aspect. In Pidgin such inflexions of the verb radical do not occur; there is no concordial inflexion, and tense and aspect distinctions are made entirely by the use of particles (or auxiliary elements) in the verb phrase. Thus:

Run!	*rǫn!*
He runs	*ì dè rǫn.*
He ran	*ì rǫn.*
They run	*dèm dè rǫn.*

Question patterns in Nigerian Pidgin do not involve inversion of word order. Questions are distinguished either by an intonational difference from that of the corresponding statement, as is possible in English, or by the initial interrogative:

You are crying. (statement)	*yù dè kráy.*
Are you crying? (You are crying?)	*yù dè kráy?*
Why are you crying?	*wáy yù dè kráy?*

This brief descriptive sketch of Nigerian Pidgin, together with the account of its place in Nigerian life, suggests that a great deal more research is needed. Such research would have to apply itself not only to the provision of a fuller description of the language itself, in its several related varieties, but also investigate its role in the developing life of Nigeria. To do so adequately would mean accepting the premise that this is an independent language, though one which continues to draw for renewal and development both upon English, its original base, and the many Nigerian languages, its substrates, with which it remains in such intimate association in the lives of those who use it. Beyond this, comparative studies of the various English-based pidgins and creoles of West Africa might well provide, among other things, a clearer picture of the kind of contacts which, in the past, resulted in their development and diffusion.

Notes

1 During a visit to the Cameroons in 1954, I found it extremely difficult to understand Cameroon Pidgin. Again, I have not always found it easy to converse with Ghanaians who use Pidgin. I was born and brought up in Kano *sabon-gari* (the

'stranger-community' of Kano) in Northern Nigeria. My parents and I lived in the same compound as several other families from the South. Besides speaking Pidgin in the compound with Yoruba and Igbo friends, I attended missionary schools for children of Southern Nigerian families living in the North. In these schools Pidgin was the most important medium of communication amongst the pupils. I have the feeling that I speak Pidgin more fluently than any other Nigerian language which I know and use. Although my mother tongue is Isoko, Yoruba seems to be the dominant substrate in my variety of Pidgin.

2 In the pronunciation of the word 'climb' we see the influence of English spelling.

3 'borku' = bòkú, many > Fr. beaucoup; 'oga', master.

4 This transcription is by E. H. T. Gbobate, and it must be pointed out in fairness to him that when he made it he had little experience of this kind of work, and thus based it upon English orthography.

5 'The mixed nature of Creole languages is to be found in their grammatical and phonetical structures rather than in their mixed vocabulary' (Rens, 1953). This is likewise true of pidgins, of course.

6 Pidgin languages have been known to develop in circumstances where no master-servant relationship existed between the groups in contact. Pidgin Sango, spoken in the Central African Republic, is a good example.

7 It may be that the term 'loan-word' in reference to the vocabulary of a pidgin or creole language is somewhat tautological, since all words in such a language, apart from compounds, etc, constructed out of the existing vocabulary material, are borrowed from some other language, however much they may be modified semantically and phonologically after being taken over. However, it is a convenient term, and the borrowing involved in developing the word-stock of a pidgin or a creole is only different in degree as compared with that of a language with a more homogeneous lexical history. If one assumes that Nigerian Pidgin is best treated as a distinct language, or at least as a dialect of a distinctive cluster (West African Pidgin), one is justified in speaking of 'English loan-words'. Obviously, if it is merely regarded as a rather divergent dialect of English, which I should regard as misleading, then this term would not be justified.

Ian F. Hancock

West Africa and the Atlantic Creoles

A creole may be defined as a pidgin language which has become the first language, or mother tongue, of its speakers. A pidgin results from contact – especially trade contact – between speakers of two or more different languages, usually under conditions where time and circumstance do not allow for complete mastery of any particular one by either or where there is no need to learn one thoroughly in order to carry out the business of trading.

From such contacts, a vernacular may arise which is generally based on the speech of the dominant group, having a much simplified grammar and vocabulary, and which is used by both parties in their dealings with each other. Naturally pidgin languages are adequate only for the fairly limited situations out of which they develop; they are also unstable both in vocabulary and pronunciation, since their use is determined by the native languages of their speakers.

If a pidgin becomes well established – and many do not survive for long – new generations of children born in the area where it is in use may learn it in addition to, or instead of their ancestral language, from infancy. In such a case, when a pidgin supplants a 'full' language, changes must occur, since it now has to suffice as the vehicle for all human expression required by the environment. Therefore in becoming *nativised* and thereby *creolised*, it expands its vocabulary, produces more explicit grammatical constructions and becomes more fixed in pronunciation. It may do this in three ways: by drawing on the dominant (or base) language, by drawing on the indigenous languages, or by coining new words and constructions from its existing stock. In fact what happens is generally a combination of all three.

There is a good deal of disagreement as to how pidgin and creole languages ought to be classified, whether as aberrant dialect forms of the various metropolitan languages, or as new languages in their own right. Those dealt with here are called *English*-derived because it would seem that they all originate in one type of pidgin, the dominant language of which was English, and because the overwhelming majority of words in each is clearly traceable to English. It must be pointed out, however, that this is only one of several criteria; the grammatical structure of any one of these English-derived creoles is far closer to any one of the other creoles spoken in the area dealt with whose words are not English-derived – such as the French- or Portuguese-derived creoles – than it is to English. This fact serves as the basis for an alternative approach to their classification.

The accompanying word-lists (*p* 118 *ff*) compare up to 100 different items in seven different English-derived creoles, two of which are spoken in West Africa, and the remaining five in the Americas.[1] These are:

1 *Krio:* The first language of perhaps 200,000 people in Freetown and the peninsula villages in Sierra Leone, and the second language of much of the country's non-Creole population. A very similar variety is spoken by about 3,500 Creoles in Bathurst, the Gambia, in which country it also serves as a lingua franca.[2]

2 *Sranan:* Spoken by about 80,000 people in Paramaribo and along the coastal strip in Surinam, in north-eastern South America. There are several Sranan-speaking townships in Surinam in addition to the capital, Paramaribo, and like Krio the language serves as a lingua franca throughout the country.

3 *Saramaccan:* Also spoken in Surinam, by groups of so-called Bush Negroes living along the banks of two rivers in the interior of the country. This language and Sranan are mutually unintelligible but practically all Saramaccan speakers have a knowledge of the latter.

4 *Cameroon Pidgin:* Spoken by upwards of one million people in Cameroon. This is the only pidgin language discussed here, although there is evidence that this language is becoming creolised in some areas. A similar pidgin is spoken in neighbouring Nigeria.

5 *Jamaican Creole:* Spoken in one form or another by about one million Jamaicans. Jamaican speech ranges over a spectrum having a fully creolised form at one extremity and standard Jamaican English at the other, unlike the situation in other areas where the dividing line between the creole and the standard language is clearer. Many Jamaicans can understand the fully creolised speech even if they do not themselves use it.

6 *Gullah:* Gradually approximating to more standard forms of

American English, because of improved education and communication facilities, Gullah is still used by more than 125,000 American Negroes inhabiting the coastal strip and offshore Sea Islands of South Carolina and Georgia, in the United States. In earlier years Gullah was almost certainly spoken over an area far more extensive than that which it now occupies.

7 *Guyana Creole:* In use by the majority of Guyana's population of 700,000, mostly in rural areas. This creole exhibits some influences from the Sranan of neighbouring Surinam, others from Barbadian speech brought in by migrants from Barbados, and yet others from Krio or some variety of West African Pidgin, imported with the Liberated African labour force directly from Africa in the 1840s. Guyana Creole and Sierra Leone Krio share some words which do not occur anywhere else in the area.[3]

Until recently it has been taken for granted that each variety of pidgin or creole was the product of independent growth on its own soil; in a recent book dealing with the origins of Sranan, L. L. Rens (1953) remarks that '... it seems a safe assumption to state that during that period [*ie* the first fifteen years of English colonisation] the African slaves had acquired the habit of expressing themselves in English of a sort ...', and L. D. Turner (1949) writes: 'presumably the slaves coming to South Carolina and Georgia direct from Africa, unlike those who had spent some time in other parts of America and the West Indies, had, on their arrival, little or no acquaintance with the English language.'

Such ideas, even in modern works, are not uncommon. Unfortunately we lack historical records clearly indicating otherwise; since such types of language were considered 'corrupt' or 'broken' and otherwise unworthy of serious study, little mention was made of them in the diaries and ships' books which have come down to us, except an occasional sample included for interest. However, by piecing together the facts we do have, and by a careful examination of the slave trade, and by comparing features common to all these creoles, it is possible to put forward a fairly strong argument to support the hypothesis that Guyana Creole, Sranan, Jamaican Creole, Gullah, the other West Indian creoles and Saramaccan all began not in the Western Hemisphere but on the coast of West Africa; or in other words, that the initiator of all of these was being spoken by Africans, in Africa, before being taken to various parts of the New World. The same argument indicates that the origins of Sierra

9

Leone Krio go back perhaps two centuries beyond the date generally given for its origin, that is *c.* 1800.[4]

A comparison between Krio and Sranan suggests a two-way diversion from a common pidgin which history places at some time between 1651 and 1667. Not only do the two languages share words which are too similar for items which are so unlikely, such as Krio *brokobák*, Sranan *brokobáka* (vine species), Krio *wiriwíri* (pubic hair) and Sranan *wiwíri* (earlier *wiriwíri*, hair),[5] Krio and Sranan *amáka* (hammock), and the use of *na* as a copula link in both languages,[6] but they both share phonological features which occur nowhere else in the area, such as *wáka* (walk), Krio *dróŋɔ*, Sranan *drúŋu* (intoxicated), the change of vowel in items 4, 11, 12, 33, 46, 48, 85, 86, 89 and 95, and the common derivation of items from English *plural* forms, as in items 75, 82, 83, 93 and 97.

Surinam was under the English flag for 16 years (1651–1667), during which time slaves were brought to the colony from English-controlled parts of West Africa. After this time Surinam fell to the Dutch who, except for a brief period between 1799 and 1802, and again between 1804 and 1816, when it was once more under the English flag,[7] have remained there until the present day. Since, as far as is known, the Dutch did not buy slaves from the English colonies in West Africa, and since no British-owned slaves were sold in Surinam after 1667 except during the later period of control there, if Sranan was initiated in West Africa it must have been before that date. The fact that Krio contains no Dutch-derived words, but Sranan increasingly since 1667 exhibits a great number, indicates that this latter language has had no contact with Krio since their separation from each other.

Sranan has preserved many more older creole features than the other languages dealt with here since it is the only English-derived creole spoken in a country where English is not the official language. Krio, on the other hand, as with Gullah, Jamaican Creole, Guyana Creole and Cameroon Pidgin, is spoken side by side with English, which constantly exerts a 'standardising' pressure on the language, resulting in its gradual decreolisation, especially with regard to pronunciation.

Gullah demonstrates a more recent influence from West Africa; P. E. H. Hair (1965), working from material published by Turner (1949), has already pointed out that languages spoken in the Sierra Leone area account for nearly all of the African-derived Gullah ritual terms, for a quarter of all the personal names and for about one-fifth of the terms found in everyday speech in the language. Words common to both

Krio and Gullah, but not found in any other American creole, include Krio and Gullah *poŋ* (intensity of distance), Krio *bɔbɔ́*, Gullah *bábə* (little boy), Krio *tití*, Gullah *títə* (little girl), Krio *múskyat*, Gullah *máskyat* ('muskrat'), Krio and Gullah *fɛntʃ* ('fence'), Krio and Gullah *jája* (nag, quarrel) and Krio and Gullah *ɛntí* (indeed). Grammatical similarities peculiar to Krio and Gullah include the use of Krio *dɔn*, Gullah *dʌn*, placed before the verb to indicate completed action, and the use of Krio *blant* or *blan*, Gullah *blaŋ*, to indicate habitual action.

Saramaccan presents somewhat more of a problem in that it contains a much higher proportion of words derived from Portuguese than does Sranan, which is spoken in the same country; thirty per cent for Saramaccan, four per cent for Sranan. It is probable that Saramaccan was taken to Surinam as a Portuguese-derived pidgin, but in the expanding process of creolisation drew on the coexistent Sranan. Earlier samples of these languages show that they were at one time phonologically more similar; Djuka, a third English-derived creole spoken in Surinam, seems to stand between the two:

English	Sranan	Djuka	Saramaccan
believe	*bríbi*	*bilíbi*	*biíbi*
forget	*frigíti*	*figéte*	*fɛ̀ɛ̀kɛ́tɛ̀*
throw	*trowé*	*towé*	*túɛ̀*
afraid	*fréde*	*féde*	*fɛ̀ɛ́ɛ̀*
big	*gran*	*garán*	*gaán*
bread	*bréde*	*bede*	*bɛ̀ɛ́ɛ̀*
school	*skóro*	*sikólo*	*sikɔ́ɔ̀*

The process of creolising in the direction of a language other than the initiator language of the pidgin form has been rather misleadingly called *relexification*; a better term would be *supralexification*. Relexification does occur too, when for instance (in Sranan) an earlier English-derived form is supplanted by a Dutch one, *eg hánson* (< E handsome) giving way to *moy* (< Du. 'mooi'). One theory of the origin of all the European language-derived creoles maintains that they were all initiated as a Portuguese-derived pidgin, becoming relexified in the direction of the languages which they reflect today.

The study of creoles and pidgins has gained impetus only during the last fifteen years. These languages, long viewed as the product of linguistic miscegenation and therefore beneath the dignity of scholars of the more traditional schools, have for too long gone unregarded.[8] It is now known that the process of creolisation can shed light not only upon the evolution of language, but also on various historical aspects of the languages from which the creoles ultimately derive.

Much work remains to be done in creole-speaking areas from a practical point of view; ideally, workable phonemic spelling systems should be devised for public use, and the creoles taught officially in the schools. In this way the differences between the creole and the metropolitan language would be made clear, creative writers would be able to produce works in the mother tongue, and the language would gain status in the eyes of its speakers. The impetus must however come from the educationists; the linguist can only advise.

DISTRIBUTION OF THE MAIN ENGLISH-DERIVED CREOLES
A *Gullah* B *Jamaican Creole* C *Guyana Creole* D *Sranan*
E *Saramaccan* F *Krio* G *Cameroon Pidgin*

COMPARATIVE WORD-LIST[9]

A: VERBS

English	Krio	Sranan	Saramaccan	Cameroon	Jamaica	Gullah	Guyana
1 annoy	*trɔb*	*tróbi*	*toóbi*	*trɔ́bu*	*trobl*	*trʌβl*	*trɔbl*
2 ask	*aks*	*áksi*	*hákísi*	*aks*	*aaks*	*ʌks*	*aaks*
3 be	*na*	*na*	*na, da*	*na*	*a, da*	*dʌ, də*	*a*
4 bite	*bɛt*	*béti*	*kukunyán*	*nayt*	*bayt*	*bayt*	*bayt*
5 climb	*klem*	*kren*	*subí*	*klaym*	*klaym*	*klaym*	*klaym*
6 crush	*mas*	*mási*	*makisá*	*maʃ*	*maʃ*	*maʃ*	*maʃ*

English	Krio	Sranan	Saramaccan	Cameroon	Jamaica	Gullah	Guyana
7 curtsey	kɔtʃi	kósi	bukúnu	kiní	kótʃi	kʌ́ci	kɔ́rtisi
8 drive	drɛb	dríbi	diípi	draf	drayb	dray	drayb
9 eat	nyam	nyan	nyam	tʃɔp	nyam	nyam	nyam
10 fall	fɔdɔ́m	fadón	kai	fɔl	faaldɔ́ŋ	fɔldɔwn	faal-dɔwŋ
11 fight	fɛt	féti	féti	fayt	fayt	fayt	fayt
12 find	fɛn	féni	féndi	fayn	fayn	fayn	fayn
13 give	gi	gyi	dá	gif	gi	gyi	gi
14 gossip	koŋgosá	goŋgosá	goŋgosá	kuŋgusá	koŋgosé	ʃíʃi	kɔŋgəsá
15 hang	ɛŋ	áŋa	héŋi	haŋ	heŋ	haŋ	haŋ, hɛŋ
16 hear	yɛrí	yére	yéi	hía	yéri	yéri, yédi	hya
17 help	ɛp	yépi	heépi	hélɛp	hep	hɛp	hɛp
18 know	sabí	sábi	sábi, sá	sábi	núo	no	no
19 lie							
down	lidɔ́m	lidón	sáka	laydɔ́ŋ	lidóŋ	lɛdáwn	lidɔŋ
20 leave	kɔmɔ́t	k'móto	kumútu	kɔmɔ́t	komówt	gɔynáwt	go owt
21 look							
(at)	luk	lúku	lúku	luk	lúku, ku	luk	luk
22 push	ʃub, ʃɔb	ʃóbu	–	puʃ	ʃub, ʃob	ʃʌb	ʃɔb
23 remem-							
ber	mɛ́mba	mémre	mɛ́mbὲ	mímba	mémba	mɛ́mbə	mɛ́mbə
24 spill	trowé	trowé	túὲ	trowé	truwíe	tʃʌráy	trowé
25 spoil	pwɛl	póri	pói, póndi	sipɔ́l	pwayl	pʌyl	spayl
26 stab	tʃuk	júku	tuká	tʃuk	tʃuk, juk	juk	juk
27 take	kɛr	cári, ca	ca	kɛ́ri	kyay	ca	kári, ka
28 thank	téŋki	tányi	taŋgí	taŋ	táŋki	téŋki	táŋki
29 walk	wáka	wáka	wáka	wɔk	waak	wɔk	waak
30 wash	was	wási	wási	wɔʃ	waʃ	wɔʃ	waʃ

B: ADJECTIVES

English	Krio	Sranan	Saramaccan	Cameroon	Jamaica	Gullah	Guyana
31 abun-dant	nɔf	nófo	ndófu	bɔkú	nof	nʌfə	nɔf
32 afraid	frédi	fréde	fὲέὲ	fía	fríed	fed	fráykn
33 blind	blɛn	bréni	beéndi	blayn	blayn	blayn	blayn
34 bold	drayáy	dreyáy	póli	drayáy	drayáy	bol	drayáy
35 broken	brɔ́ko	bróko	boóko	brok	brokóp	brʌk	brok
36 drunk	drɔ́ŋgɔ	drúŋu	dɔɔ́ŋgɔ	drəŋ	droŋk	drʌŋk	drɔŋk
37 foolish	lawláw, tʃúpit	law	law	fúliʃ	fuúliʃ, tʃúpit	fuúliʃ	fuúliʃ
38 greedy	bigyáy	bigyáy	giíi	bigáy	bigáy	bigáy	bigyáy
39 heavy	ébi	ébi	hébi	hɛf	hébi	héβi	hébi

B : ADJECTIVES, *continued*

English	Krio	Sranan	Saramaccan	Cameroon	Jamaica	Gullah	Guyana
40 long	lánga	lána	lánga	lɔŋ	laŋ	lʌŋ	laŋ
41 only	sóso	sóso	sɔ́sɔ́	sóso	sóso	sóso	sóso
42 softly	sáful	sáfri	sáápi	sɔ́fri	saáfli	sέfli	sáfli
43 strong	tráŋga	tráŋa	taáŋga	trɔŋ	traŋ	trʌŋ	traŋ
44 ugly	wɔwɔ́, wogrí	ógri	wógi	wowó	úogli	ókli, ɔ́gli	wɔwɔ́
45 untidy	jaga-jága	yaga-yága	–	jaga-jága	yaga-yága	jug	jugajúga
46 white	wet	wéti	wéti	wayt	wayt	wayt	wet

C: ADVERBS, PREPOSITIONS, ETC.

English	Krio	Sranan	Saramaccan	Cameroon	Jamaica	Gullah	Guyana
47 and	ɛn	ɛn	ɛn	an, na	an	ɛn, na	an
48 as, like	lékɛ, léka	léki	kuma	láyka	láka	lʌ́kə, séŋkə	láykə
49 even	sɛf	sréfi	séépi	sɛf	sef	sɛf	sɛf
50 every-where	ɔ́lsay	alapé	alapέ	ɔ́lsayd	ébriwe	έβəwe	ébriwe
51 how many	ɔ́mɔs	oméni	homéni	hámə ʃ	hómotʃ	hʌ́mʌtʃ	hówmɔtʃ
52 if	ɛf, if	éfi, éfu	é	ifi	if	ɛf	ɛf
53 more than	pas	p' sa, móro	pasá, mɔ́ɔ	pas	múoran	mónə, pas	mówən
54 on top of	pantáp	tápu	tápu	ntɔp	tápsayd	pəntɔ́p	pantáp
55 only	nɔmɔ́	nomó	nɔ́ɔ	nomó	nomó	nʌ́mə	nɔmɔ́
56 outside	nadó	nadóro	–	awsáyd	adúo	awsáyd	owtsáyd
57 perhaps	sɔntέm	sontén	sɔnté	səmtáym	miebi	mébi	sɔmtáyn
58 recently	tradé	tradéy	ótodáka	no-fawé	wedíe	tʌrədé	di ɔda de
59 some-one	sɔmɔdí	súma	sɔ́mbὲ	sɔ́mbədi	smádi	sʌmbóri	sɔmbádi
60 to (pre-verbal)	fɔ	fu	fu, u	fɔ	fi	fə, fʌ	fu
61 to (lo-cating)	na	na	na, a	fɔ	a	tə, də	a
62 too much	túmɔs	túm' si	túmúsi	tumá ʃ	túmɔtʃ	tʌmʌ́tʃ	túmɔtʃ
63 until	soté, te	soté, te	téé	soté	soté	twəl	so til
64 what	wétin	osán	andí	wáti	wára, wa	wʌt	wa, wat
65 when	ústɛm	otén	té, hén	hústaym	wéntaym	wʌ́taym	wítɛm
66 where	úsay, úspat	opé, úsay	únsé, ká	húsayd	wépaat	we, wʌ́say	wisáy

English	Krio	Sranan	Saramaccan	Cameroon	Jamaica	Gullah	Guyana
67 which	we, us	di	di	we	we	we	witʃn
68 who	úda(t)	osúma	ambé	hu	hu	hudát	hudá(t)
69 why	wétin du	sáyde	andí	hu	wa mek	mɛk so	wɔ mɛk
70 with	wit	náŋa	ku	wíti	wi, wid	wid	wid
71 yet	et	éte	yéti	yɛt	yet	yɛt	yɛt
72 yonder	yánda	yána	alá, aá	yánda	yánda	yan	yánda

D: NOUNS

English	Krio	Sranan	Saramaccan	Cameroon	Jamaica	Gullah	Guyana
73 ant	antʃ	míra	ánsi	ans	hans, hantʃ	antʃ	ans
74 bee	ɔní	óni	hóni	hóni	bii	bii	bii
75 duck	dɔks	dóksi	patupátu	dɔ́kfawu	dɔk	dʌk	dɔk
76 hawk	ak	áka	gabián	hɔk	aak	hʌk	haak
77 sand-flea	jigá	síka	síka	tʃíga	jíga	jígə	jíga
78 wasp	waswás	waswási	wasiwási	manawá	waswás	wʌs	was
79 ground-nut	granát	pindá	pindá	gránɛt	pínda	pínda, gúba	gúba
80 pepper	pépɛ	pépre	pépè	pépɛ	pépa	pépə	pépə
81 thorn	tʃuk-tʃúk	máka	maká	tʃuka-tʃúka	máka	–	pímplʌ
82 yam	(n)yams	yámsi	nyámísi	nyámas	nyaamz	nyam	yam
83 ash	ásis	ásisi	sínja	áʃis	háʃiz	áʃəz	áʃiz
84 earth	dɔtí	dóti	dóti	dɔtí	dɔ́ti	dʌ́ti	dɔ́rti
85 night	nɛt	néti	ndéti	nayt	nayt	nayt	nayt
86 time	tɛm	ten	tén	taym	taym	taym	taym
87 child	pikín	picín	míʃi	pikín	píkini	cayl	píkni
88 comrade	kɔ́mpin	kómpe, máti	kómpe, máti	kɔ́mbi	kómpini	frɛn	máti
89 wife	wɛf	wéfi	muyéè	méri	wayf	wayf	wayf
90 head-scarf	ɛŋkíntʃa	ányisa	háŋísa	tayhét	bandúu	héŋkətʃə	hédtay
91 house	os	óso	wósu	haws	hows	haws	hows
92 loin-cloth	kɔmíʃɔn	kámsa	kamisa	klɔs	ráproŋ	–	–
93 shoe	sus	súsu	súsu	ʃus	ʃuuz	ʃuu(z)	ʃuuz
94 fence	fɛntʃ	périn	tʃáŋa	fɛns	fens	fɛntʃ	fɛns
95 knife	nɛf	néfi	ndéfi	nayf	nayf	nayf	nayf
96 breast	bɔbí	bóbi	bóbi	bóbi	bóbi	bʌ́bi	bʌ́bi
97 ear	yes	yési	yési	hía	íez	yíəz	ez
98 excreta	kaká	kaká	kaká	ʃit	kaká	tútu	kaká
99 lung	fukfúk	foko-fóko	fugufúgu	lɔŋ	lowŋz	fukfúk	lʌŋ
100 vulva	bombó, píma	bombó, píma	ku	mbumbú	bómbo	púsi	pus(i)

Notes

1 This chapter is a condensation of a more detailed discussion in *African Language Review*, London, 1969, in which I compare 570 items. In some instances the words taken from individual creoles (notably Guyana Creole) for the present lists represent an obsolescent pronunciation, for purposes of closer identification. Several items are non-cognate for all seven creoles.

2 Item 32 (afraid) in the lists is from Bathurst, not Freetown, Krio.

3 Examples include *tóbo* (chilblains), *ɔkú* (a Yoruba), and *wɔwɔ́* (ugly).

4 See Bradshaw, 1965, Berry, 1959a and 1959b, and Hall, 1966, for statements supporting this view.

5 This item turns up in Papiamentu, the Portuguese–Spanish Creole of Curaçao, with the meaning of 'pubic hair', and in Guyana Creole in *wíriwíri pépɔ*, a type of pepper.

6 *Na* also occurs in Saramaccan, and in the Dutch Creole formerly spoken in the Danish Antilles.

7 We know that Sranan was not introduced into Surinam during either of these later periods of English occupation thanks to fairly copious data recorded before this time, the earliest being 1718.

8 That this stigma still exists may be illustrated by quotations from Mario Pei's *The Story of the English Language* (London, 1968): 'When Pidgin English is mentioned one's thoughts run immediately to the uncouth Melanesian variety'; 'But one must not think that the natives . . . all use pidgin; some are fairly well educated'; 'It is perhaps unfair to refer to the language of Trinidad and Jamaica as pidgin.'

9 All items are marked for prominence, *ie* stress and/or high tone. The orthography employed for Saramaccan follows that outlined in Voorhoeve (1959), with the exception that his *è, ĕ, ò* and *ŏ* are here written *è, é, ɔ* and *ɔ́*. For the Jamaican Creole entries *o* has the value [ə].

Anthony Kirk-Greene

The Influence of West African Languages on English

The study of the influence of West African languages on English may be undertaken at two levels, one minor and one major. The minor one is concerned with the trends and shifts in the English of native English speakers resident in West Africa. Such a study – suggestive, if the lack of literature on the subject is a valid guide, of an untapped area of socio-linguistic research – may not at first sight seem very germane to a consideration of the modifying forces on English in its West African context. But when we recall the powerful Anglo-Indian precedent, with its marked influence on both the enrichment of the vocabulary of the English in India and the way in which some of it was subsequently exported and eventually incorporated into standard English, such a linguistic phenomenon begins to merit more than a cursory reference. This aspect of Englishmen's English as influenced by West African languages could be examined on two planes: the language of the English resident in Africa, and the language of the colonial after his return to England. Since, however, these two fields are related, and because this is not the major area of our study, I propose to take them here as a single element in the influence of West African languages on English.

The incidence of West Africanisms adopted into standard English is, for reasons discussed below, not very high, and is probably even smaller than that from East or South Africa – where, in the event, the vocabulary that has established itself is more Boer than Bantu: *stoep, sjambok, kloof, kopje, kraal, hartebeest*; the Zulu wars brought *impi* and *indaba*, but their *assegai* is properly of Arabic extraction. Such a situation induces us to raise the question why the period of British contact with West Africa – indeed, with Africa as a whole – has brought no influence in any way comparable with that of the Indian impact on the vocabulary of English where, as Rao (1954) and *Hobson-Jobson* (Yule and Burnell, 1886) show, many hundreds of additions to the

English language have been made. A number of postulates may be put forward.

First, the arithmetical fact of a shorter time-period of sustained contact, barely a century in most of Africa as opposed to three times as long in India. Secondly, the sheer size and age and unity of Indian culture, with scholarly works dating back two millennia, and languages like Sanskrit and Tamil known to the rest of the world of learning and capable of standing as cultural media beside Latin and Greek and Chinese. If, Arab genius apart, parallel scholarship in the sciences and humanities existed in Africa proper, it has yet to come to light and has so far not been reflected in the mainstream of international learning. Thirdly, India had, for all its diversity of tongues, the advantage of one or two languages spoken by scores of millions of people, whereas Africa has, even today, no indigenous language spoken as a mother tongue by more than, at the most generous estimate, fifteen to twenty million people.

Fourthly, West Africa has had few planters, no retired British officials, no family tradition of generation after generation born and brought up and destined to serve on the Coast: nothing, in short, comparable to the Indian experience of the British, whose continuing identification with the country has been so well symbolised by the Savage family of John Masters' novels. For it was these *dramatis personae* of the imperial linguistic scene who were the principal culture-carriers, both while resident abroad and even more so when returning to the United Kingdom. Especially is this true of the transference of lexical items. Familiarity breeds more than contempt; in language, it gives rise to adoption. To find a second-generation man working in West Africa, that is, one whose father also served there, has been the exception; in India, it was a commonplace. Consider, then, the linguistic carry-over that such vast numbers of expatriates diffuse into their own language.[1]

The English vocabulary is the poorer for the fact that West Africa never left its mark on the English language in the way that India did. Some parallel to the Anglo-Indian situation can, however, be found, linguistically, in the *petit-blanc* circles of ex-French West Africa and in the *colon* society of the French settlers of Algeria, who have been responsible for the introduction into standard French of a number of African and Arabic words (*eg*, see the excellent glossary of Mauny, 1952); whereas the only comparable settler community of anglophone Africa, Kenya, has contributed relatively little to the English vocabulary apart from *safari* and its constituent fauna like *zebra*. Nor, by and large, have representative English novelists of West Africa (Joyce Cary), East Africa (Elspeth Huxley) and South Africa (*eg* Alan Paton) succeeded, if they ever seriously sought to do so, in inseminating into the English language the local vocabulary in the same way as writers like Rudyard Kipling and E. M. Forster did for India. What African novelists (Achebe, Ngugi, Ekwensi) writing in English themselves achieve in this direction remains to be seen.

As another strand of this African-Indian dichotomy in linguistic influence on English, and a source which has not yet had the recognition that I believe it deserves, account must be taken of the profound difference in the far-reaching social role of the army personnel in the two countries. As compulsory military service showed in England, and as national service has long proved in France (witness the introduction into standard French of such African words as *toubib, gris-gris, broussard, blédard, couscous, kif-kif, spahi*), the army is a very potent force for spreading slang and neologisms far beyond its ranks in its home-country. One differential was the contrast between the career-structure of the British officers in the West African Frontier Force and the Indian Army. The officer in West Africa was only seconded to a Nigeria or Gold Coast battalion; he rarely felt this was his regiment or his career, and in most cases he reverted to his parent British regiment after a couple of tours. Hence he seldom became steeped in the country and it was the exception to acquire fluency in the language. Few commanding officers ever made their way up from subaltern in a WAFF battalion. In India, on the other hand, the British officer was commissioned into an Indian regiment, and there he expected to spend the rest of his career. Nor was this linguistic opportunity confined to the officer class. From 1857 British battalions were stationed in India for years at a time, whereas this chance was never given to British troops in West Africa till, briefly, the 1939–45 war. Thus hundreds of thousands of British Tommies learned in India, in Kipling's phrase, to '*bolo* the *bat*' ('talk the lingo'). Here indeed was a language transmitter of very wide influence, so that scores of words like *Blighty, cha* and *dekko* found their way back to 'civvy street' and have remained in the army, today firmly anglicised with a fine disregard for provenance or pronunciation.[2]

The result of this totality of circumstances has been the marked lack in England of any West African equivalent to match the Cheltenham or Tunbridge Wells colonies of *jodhpur*-wearing *pukka sahibs* or *jangli-wallahs* taking their *chota peg* or *gin-pani* before a *tiffin* of *pilau* at the *gymkhana*, nostalgically – and vainly – crying *koi hai*. True, in Africa itself instances exist of such execrable *patois* as Kitchen Swahili, 'Ki-Settler', Silunguboi and Fanagalo (Cole, 1953) in the East and South, or in the West semi-pidgin, with plenty of reduplicated intensifiers of the 'now-now' variety: fractured vernacular conversations consisting of a string of commands plus the minimum of syntax spread over a few hideously concatenated lexical items. This recalls E. M. Forster in *A Passage to India* describing the Collector's wife meeting with Indians: 'She shook hands with the group and said a few words of welcome in Urdu. She had learnt the lingo, but only to speak to her servants, so she knew none of the politer forms and of the verbs only the imperative mood.'

But whereas the Indian parallels have established themselves in English (*bungalow, verandah, pukka*, etc), very few of the Africanisms have survived the chill climate of England. It is indeed difficult to think of many West African words that have been accepted into standard English, and those that do exist are often either specialised (*gorilla, plantain, harmattan, chimpanzee, iroko*) or have derived from a corruption of another European language in use on the Coast (*palaver, juju, savvy, yam*). In this, the standard dictionaries, not excluding the Skeat and Onions repositories of etymological history, abet the situation; for while the source of Oriental words is carefully noted as Hindustani, Bengali, Malay, Chinese, etc, the few African entries are seldom more specific than 'African'.

So much for the secondary consideration of the influence of West African languages on standard English, in the context of English speakers themselves. The major area of analysis, and the focus of the remainder of this chapter, is the influence of West African languages on the English of those who are native speakers not of English but of one of the West African languages, to whom English is a second or even a third language.

Contemporary scholars have had little hesitation in agreeing that a legitimate area of linguistic study is 'the emergence of varieties of English that are identified with and specific to particular countries from among the former British colonies' (Halliday, McIntosh and Strevens, 1964). It has been claimed that 'nowadays more sophistication is creeping in', with educated West African varieties of English being deliberately adopted as models for particular teaching circumstances in Ghana and Nigeria, 'on grounds of public interest' (Strevens, 1965). On the other hand, a Ghanaian scholar has defended the teaching of British Received Pronunciation in Ghana in order to 'increase the chances of mutual comprehension' (Amonoo, 1963). Organic growth, and debates about norms, are inevitably true to the nature of language and the concerns of the users. Historically, standard English developed out of a number of competing dialects. The English of Bernard Shaw is not that of Shakespeare. There is no reason why the English of twentieth-century Lagos or Lucknow, especially in its colloquial ranges and in its pronunciation, should be identical with that of London or Los Angeles, though it is to be hoped that all users of English everywhere will remain mutually intelligible.

What follows is an attempt to investigate some of the features which characterise the use of English by Nigerians, with particular reference to the influence of the vernacular languages upon such usage. The material presented may suggest in which directions some kind of colloquial Nigerian norm – or norms – in spoken and written English may develop. I do not doubt that, *mutatis mutandis*, similar phenomena characterising the outlines of what may become Ghanaian or Sierra Leonean English could also be identified. A leading Nigerian literary figure has suggested that all developing regional varieties of English 'add life and vigour to the language, while reflecting their own respective cultures. Why shouldn't there be a Nigerian or West African English which we can use to express our own ideas, thinking and philosophy in our own way?' (Okara, 1963.)[3] Our duty as linguists is to take up John Spencer's call, made at Ibadan in 1961, for research into how English and French are reacting to their new and constantly changing environment in Africa (Spencer, 1963); not seeking to condemn, or artificially to control, change and development in the English of West Africa – to do so would be Canutian folly – but, in accepting its legitimacy, to examine its particularities and the causes which lie behind them. The discussion and exemplification which follow represent an attempt to do so within a limited compass: the investigation is limited to Nigeria, and a good deal, though by no means all, of the emphasis is upon the usage of English by Northern Nigerians, in the context of the Hausa–English contact situation.

*   *   *   *   *   *

An awareness both of the formal characteristics of African languages as well as of the sociolinguistic role of English is of major importance to our assessment of the relative influence of West African languages on English. Non-professional observers and visitors have not failed to notice the difference in the spoken English of the Hausa student and that of the Yoruba, for example. If, as such observers suggest, and years of experience on the part of the present writer confirm, there are fewer vernacular 'overtones' in the English of the former, there are a number of reasons why this should be so, in part linguistic and in part social, historical and educational.

In the first place, the role of tone and stress in the Kwa group of languages, of which Yoruba is one, is of such a nature that it seems bound to interfere with the learning of stress and intonation in English more than the similar features in Hausa. Secondly, in the classical emirates of Northern Nigeria, the strong preference for the use of Hausa as the language of wider communication outside school has relegated English to the status of a classroom language. By comparison, in the southern areas of Nigeria, where the Kwa languages are dominant, the lack of an alternative lingua franca means that English is very much the daily language of schoolchildren both outside and inside school. So dominant is the use of English by students at secondary school and university further south that I have been assured by many that after a year away at one of these institutions – many of them being boarding establishments – they may experience initial difficulties in maintaining normal home conversation in their mother tongue with their parents, relatives and friends. This does not seem to be the case with Hausa speakers in the North, and two cultured Hausa men who know English are more likely to converse in Hausa than are two educated Igbos in Igbo.[4]

A third reason is that a connection can be traced between the cultivation of Hausa and the educational policy inherent in a planned furtherance of 'indirect rule'.[5] This policy was, to quote Westermann's summary, based on the assumption that 'native political institutions contain values which are capable of development and whose loss would be detrimental to the people. Its object, therefore, is to preserve these values and enlist them in the service of the new administration' (Westermann, 1949). Among these values were the vernacular languages, as assiduously nurtured in parts of British Africa as they were ignored by the French colonial administration. But Southern Nigeria never experienced the vernacular cultivation that the North knew. Hausa newspapers, Hausa novels, a Hausa translation bureau, official Government documents and legislative instruments in Hausa, all became features of the indirect rule scene in the emirates from the mid-1930s, in a way that Yoruba and Igbo never became. Fourthly, it must be noted that, for political reasons that do not concern us here, expatriate English teachers continued to dominate Northern Nigerian schools longer than they did

in the South, carrying on the remarkable language teaching traditions of
the old Katsina College which produced Nigeria's 'Golden Voice', the
late Sir Abubakar Tafawa Balewa, and many other speakers of impeccable English. The position is, and was, very different in the South
where, without insinuating any value judgment, much English has for a
long time been taught by Nigerians who were themselves taught English
by Nigerians. This may accelerate nationalistic reactions to standard
English. It may be noted that, after some traditionalist sentiments were
expressed, a credit in the English language is now no longer insisted
upon by the West African Examinations Council as an indispensable
condition of the award of the School Certificate.

One subsidiary linguistic problem emerges from this last point. There
is already, I feel, scope for research into how enduring is the effect of the
regional accent of the English teacher on the West African student. Can
the trained listener perceive traces of the long line of German and Swiss
teachers of English in Ghana and Nigeria? For how long will so many of
the Northern Nigerian secretarial grade speak with a Glaswegian intonation acquired from their sole instructor for eleven years? Now comes a
new influence. This is the steady inflow of American Peace Corps teachers
to West African schools, over a thousand in the past few years. I suspect
that they may, willy-nilly, bring yet another dimension into the study of
English in West Africa. Already some students write *labor/honor/
neighbor*, and answer, 'sure'; one Hausa grammar renders *sannu* by
'hi!'; and 'fine!' for *lafiya* has become a commonplace at several
Northern Nigerian colleges. The influence of American English in West
Africa and its changing status may soon become a field of profitable
research.

Given these arguments, I consider that in the context of English in
West Africa sociolinguistic considerations must be given high priority in
examining the direction and causes of change and development. Only by
understanding both the structure of the first language and the method by
which English is acquired as well as the purposes for which it is used can
we account for the deviant forms in bilingual usage, for these are often
conditioned by non-linguistic factors. I am proposing that the principal
disseminative factors in developing a Nigerian variety of English, as
revealed in what for the sake of argument may be generalised as student
speech, are: conversations with others in English where this is a second
language for all participants; news broadcasts from the various Nigerian
radio corporations; public advertisements, including those on the radio
(*eg* 'go gay', 'life more abundant', 'top people'); newspapers, though

the general standard of English in the press is high; and the hundreds of cheap booklets published in Onitsha, Aba, Ibadan, Port Harcourt, Lagos, etc (some of which have sold 50,000 copies), here referred to as 'Onitsha novelettes', and including political pamphlets.[6]

To these leading carriers of 'Nigerian English' listed above must be added such 'factories', often specialising in transforming the raw materials imported from these sources, as educational institutions, with their truly remarkable richness in slang (Kirk-Greene, 1966); and the whole of the junior civil service and commercial cadres – what I find it helpful to label the 'GCE élite'. These together manufacture, retail and distribute substantial supplies of English of a particularly West African flavour. Civil service jargon tends to establish itself in West Africa largely through this source, so that even students will talk of 'leave' instead of holidays, 'quarters' instead of house, 'station' instead of town, and a graduate 'Onitsha' novelist writes of how 'they look out for flimsy excuse to issue you queries'. In Hausaland, too, the higher public service have made a linguistic contribution by their unconscious adoption of *malamanci*, the nonchalant switching from Hausa to English and back to Hausa which produces such sentences as 'Definitely, *babban* ultimate aim *namu* economic independence *ke nan*', and even such hybrids as 'good morning-*ku*' (Kirk-Greene, 1963).

There are available to me ten principal collections of source material for examining English in its Nigerian setting: (i) personal letters; (ii) taped public addresses and impromptu conversations; (iii) essays submitted in tutorials; (iv) scripts of the English Language paper in the GCE examinations; (v) recordings of the new oral English test devised for the West African Examinations Council; (vi) school slang; (vii) the Onitsha novelettes; (viii) news and talks on the radio; (ix) newspaper reports and editorials; (x) 'letters to the editor' column. These all represent the age and education groups falling more or less within the high school range, whom I consider to be the most active distributors and exponents of special Nigerian variants of English; for, like E. M. Forster in his *A Passage to India*, I too have been 'struck with the liveliness with which the younger generation handled a foreign tongue – they altered the idioms but they could say whatever they wanted to say quickly'. Of these sources, I have elsewhere dealt at length with (vi) (Kirk-Greene, 1966), and would consider using (iii), (iv) and (v) a breach of professional etiquette unless an official research project was approved, though I am confident they would unambiguously substantiate my findings from other sources.

In what follows, therefore, I have used as my corpus personal letters, supported by confirmatory data from taped public speeches and impromptu conversations, as well as the Onitsha novelettes. The multiple origins of the data have the advantage that while the first source, personal letters, is largely from a Hausa-speaking group, the other sources derive from those for whom Igbo and Yoruba, and possibly other Southern Nigerian languages, are the mother tongue. Readers with more knowledge of Yoruba and Igbo than I possess will readily be able to discern vernacular influences in the instances cited which have, to me, been merely hunches. Such influences have been confirmed by Yoruba and Igbo informants who, on scanning the relevant texts, had little difficulty in identifying linguistic and conceptual patterns deriving from their languages. I would also submit that a number of instances of the vernacular influence that I have demonstrated to be of Hausa origin could be shown to reappear as Yoruba and Igbo influences as well.

As far as I am aware, sources such as these have not previously been used in published work by those concerned to investigate West African usage in English.[7] In regard to the spoken material, I have chosen not to explore the phonological aspects (*cf* Nuttall 1969, Dunstan 1966 and 1969) because not only would it involve technical statements of some complexity, but it would only doubtfully admit of generalisation. I have thus preferred to examine some of the lexical, idiomatic and grammatical features of the data, and to present specimens of these, believing them to be susceptible of checking by others (which phonological statements would not be) and also to have wider appeal and interest. Especially is this so to those many West Africans who, while not professionally engaged in language study or language teaching (Hofstad 1969), are earnestly interested in their own languages and their own use of English.

*   *   *   *   *   *

GRAMMAR

The generative mechanics of English in West Africa would often seem to be that when on to the kernel forms of the standard English sentence already adequately learnt are built additional, novel elements transferred, in the instant-translation situation, from the vernacular, there may result an English surface structure with a vernacular deep structure. The same thing occurs, of course, in a European's instant-translations into, say, Hausa or Yoruba, where the result may be a modified syntac-

10

tic structure or a hybrid lexical formation, intelligible but deviating from the norm.

On occasions, the vernacular embedding would appear to be too deep for communication without a closer knowledge of the first language. For example, it is not easy to explain fully sentences like the following examples taken from Onitsha novelettes: 'The effect of this attitude was compensating'; 'I can wipe off any uncalled for time of assumptions in any person's mind'; 'Majority of boys everywhere have been shooting inside the ocean'; 'Today will be marked at the boards of your hearts.' It is possible in extreme cases for the vernacular deep structure so to obliterate the English surface structure that, although the cumulative effect may be meaningful in general terms, a closer examination of certain sentences and their referential meaning may defy explanation; the reader may not see the sentential woods for the lexical trees. In case it be thought that the citations above have been distorted by being out of context, here is an example taken from a published item of continuous prose:

> It is now known to my poorself the hows and whys of politics. As from now I shall call group of politicians – Peoples of varied wishes that assume one name. Politics is forced out tears by intense anger. One can not remember any time both in dream and normal life that poorself stood among honourable ones, expressing in opposition terms against a number more than one, of course, except in concerts. That eyes, so unforeseeing have forced the youths to talk with anger, what they have tried with all politeness. . .. It is therefore the idea to exchange ideas. The exchange of ideas in plays and conversation about down fall or up lift of any part of earth. This will result to total wipe off of ignorance and plant eternal freedom of thought with unlimited progress and wide knowledge.

Nevertheless, that this subconscious building of English sentences out of favoured vernacular (here Igbo) sentence models is not more apparent is worthy of note. It is, for instance, rare to find a Hausa interposing a personal pronoun between subject noun and verb in English ('the chief *he* came'), although such an obligatory construction (*sarki ya zo*) is basic to Hausa syntax.[8] Again, the influence of the Hausa dual gender system on the ascription of gender to English nominals does not seem to be nearly so pronounced as it does in the proverbial Frenchman's 'the water, she is hot, no?'. Nor does the passive transform, wanting in Hausa, where it is replaced by the impersonal subject pronoun *a/an* +

V^{tr}, carry over strongly enough for a Hausa speaker's English to be peppered with clumsy 'one has . . .' sentences. It is perhaps a truism to suggest that if a person knows, say, Yoruba, he will understand more of the syntax – and hence perhaps more of the meaning – of a mediocre Yoruba candidate's English essay than if he does not. Likewise, I suspect that a West African linguist might be able to deduce a good deal about the structure of, say, Kikuyu or Swahili by reading the English essays of such students. The sub-stratum syntax is there, and now and again it comes to the surface.[9]

Specific vernacular influences (mainly in relation to Hausa) on English calling for separate comment are as follows:

1 A marked case of local transference occurs in the non-use of the article, mostly the definite but on occasions the indefinite too. Examples from letters include 'full to brim', 'let strong football team be organised', 'he won by overwhelming majority'. It would be easy to cite examples from the novelettes, along the lines of 'he gave me tough time'. Here is a clear and common instance of the vernacular carrying over its influence into English, for, in round terms, it may be stated that Hausa, Yoruba and Igbo have no separate word for what in English is recognised as the definite article. Thus in Hausa, *sarki* may be rendered as 'chief' or 'the chief', subject to contextual inference. True, where referential emphasis is required, the diectic suffix can be added to the nominal: *ta kawo abinci, abincin ba kyau* 'she brought food, [the] food was not good'. But to the fact that no separate morpheme exists for 'the' in many West African languages can certainly be ascribed this common feature of English in West Africa. Sometimes, of course, the opposite phenomenon occurs, and a redundant article appears. Thus in 'before I say a cheerio', we have a case of nominalisation of what in standard English still retains undertones of direct speech. We find also 'we are not free to discuss matters in the public' and 'a food for thought'.

2.The Hausa words *wani* and *wane* are influential. For instance, the sentence *wani sarki ya zo* is often rendered as 'another chief came' instead of 'a chief came'. This can be traced to the multiple meanings of *wani/wata*, including 'another' and 'a certain' as well as the indefinite article. Related is the nominalisation of *wane*, giving sentences like 'you are a big somebody'. This derives from the standard Hausa construction *X malami ne wane*, 'X is a distinguished scholar'. It may also be connected (and, *mutatis mutandis*, in Yoruba and Igbo as well) with the personalisation of *wane* as 'so-and-so', hence 'you are a very social somebody'.[10]

3 The redundant pluralisation of English uncountable nouns is a not uncommon example of a transferred morphological construction in primary sentence building. The tendency to pluralise mass nouns as if they were countable nouns has its counterpart in the habit by indifferent speakers of Hausa as a second language of using the singular, since pluralisation patterns are so varied, *eg: mutum [mutane] nawa ne?* 'how many people are there?' Favourite examples include 'I lost all my furnitures and many valuable properties'. 'Accommodations' antedates the advent of American usage, where it is standard. The novelettes provide 'this season is full of foul plays . . . so full of movements', 'there were thunderous noises of laughter and chats', 'pay in his own coins', 'they appeared in white apparels', 'she walked in such paces that combined her college learnings of how to behave', 'the capital of all these advices'. Examples from letters include 'have you found any new slangs recently?' (letter from a Hausa), and 'thank you for the three quids' (letter from a Yoruba). One of the Departments of the University of Ibadan uses a rubber stamp 'Printed Matters'. The plural greeting of 'good-morning, sirs' is often met in colloquial usage, being the only way of indicating that the salutation is to all present. Sometimes the reverse holds good: *eg* 'I have not written because of lack of fund to buy stamp'. This is also found with numerals, as in: 'please send me ten shilling', reflecting the Hausa rule that a singular noun is sufficient with numerals unless there is an intention of emphasising the individual items: *sarki* (sing) *goma*, 'ten chiefs', but *yana da motoci* (pl) *uku,* 'he has three cars'. Dunstan (1966) quotes sentences like 'three man came', but I believe this to occur only at a very elementary level, whereas all the examples in this chapter are characteristic of users of English with a fairly extensive educational experience of English.

4 Negative questions are another area where the influence of Hausa on English is readily identifiable. In Hausa, the answer to a negative question is the opposite to what it is in standard English:

Q. *bai zo ba?*   'hasn't he come?'
A1. *i*   'yes' (*ie* 'yes, what you have said is right: he has *not* come').

A2. *a'a*   'no' (*ie* 'no, what you have said is wrong:
                   he *has* come').

English would expect 'no' in A1 and 'yes' in A2. Hausa acts here
on faultless logic. The same kind of influence can be discerned in
the handling of the negative element embedded in the 'hope' type
of sentence. For example, whereas in standard English one would
reply 'I hope not' to the comment of 'I hope you won't have any
difficulty with your fees next term', I have recorded many instances of 'I hope so'; *ie* 'I hope that what you have said will
indeed be the case'. Similarly standard English 'I hope not' is
often rendered as 'I don't hope so', being a direct translation of
the Hausa construction *ba na fata haka*.

5 The comparative sentence tends to carry across its vernacular deep
structure. Thus, in a novelette, 'they like the streets than their
homes'; and, in a letter from a Yoruba, 'people overseas know
much news about the coup than we do here on the radio'. The
origin of 'I am happy at school than at home' in a letter from a
Hausa is related to the Hausa construction *ya fi ni dadi*, 'he
exceeds me happiness' where the comparative adjective as such is
wanting.

6 The form 'I could remember' (for 'I can remember') reveals a
strong carry-over from the vernacular. In Hausa, where aspect
rather than tense dominates the verbal system, *na iya* can be used
for 'I can' or 'I could'. Is it perhaps a conscious effort to show
awareness of the English tense system rather than aspect that leads
to a confused conjugation of the modal? Similar difficulty may be
encountered with other verbs which in Hausa rely on an adverb of
time to indicate 'tense': *na sani* 'I know/knew', *na ji* 'I hear/
heard', *na gani* 'I see/saw', *na tuna* 'I remember/remembered'. A
sample check on speech by even the best English speakers among
the Katsina College graduates revealed that here too, over the
course of time, local usage had eroded careful instruction. In
Nigeria, 'I could remember' today ranks as a major trait of
English usage.

7 Since in Hausa the infinitive form of the verb is 'deficient', certain
characteristics of Hausa speakers' English may have their origin
in this. The omission of 'to' is therefore not surprising and is
quite usual with the verb 'to wish': 'I wish I know her soon'
translates *ina so in san ta* 'I wish (that) I know her'. Similarly, one

of the novelettes has 'I wish you talk endlessly', 'I wish you take part', 'I wish I attend'. Conversely, sentences of the pattern 'he made me to sit down' are common, especially in translating Hausa causative verbs.

8 In Hausa, the possessive follows the noun, while the demonstrative adjective precedes it: *wannan littafi naka*, literally 'that book yours'. But since a Hausa student has been taught that English requires the possessive pronoun to precede the noun it modifies, his English often demonstrates the construction 'that your brother, will he come?' Again, a novelette has 'saying Amen to those his prayers'. A related instance of vernacular-induced confusion in word order obtains with 'both': 'Placing his both hands on the table . . .' (from a novelette), 'Your both friends greet you' (letter from a Yoruba).

9 The influence of the Hausa word for 'each other', *juna*, interferes with the standard usage of the reflexive pronoun. Thus we find 'we like ourselves too much', from the Hausa *muna son juna* [*mmu*] *kwarai*. Similarly, a novelette has 'we must know ourselves before we exchange gifts' and 'such friends that within a second . . . they kissed themselves'. 'They shook themselves' is also met with for 'they shook hands'.

10 The persistence of the construction aux. + ever + p.pt is another direct vernacular influence. English allows 'I have never been to Kano', in Hausa *ban taba zuwa Kano ba*; but whereas in Hausa the affirmative is simply a denegatived version of the same sentence, *na taba zuwa Kano*, the same process produces the common 'I have ever been to Kano'.

11 Since the particle *sai* in Hausa numbers among its many nuances both 'unless' and 'except', the English of Hausas often adopts the vernacular-influenced 'I cannot succeed except you help me'.

12 The common Hausa tag-word *kuwa*, like its Kwa counterparts, causes some vernacular interference. It is, at times, rightly rendered by 'again', but it is often better left untranslated. Hence 'have you eaten again?', *ka ci kuwa?*, does not refer to a rapid second helping, but is a simple question. *Cf* 'I was very busy at that time again' (letter from a Yoruba), where 'again' is semantically superfluous.

13 Hausa dialectics enjoys the legitimate balance of *ko da shi ke . . .*, *amma . . .*, 'although . . . , but . . .'. English, however, considers the 'but' redundant. Hausa users of English often follow the vernacular: 'although you are away, but you do not forget . . .'

14 The Hausa negative of quantity is effected by simply negativing the verb: *Kana da kudi? Ba ni da kudi.* A similar transformation in English, however, breaks down: 'Have you any money? I have no any money'. 'No any' often does service for 'no/not any'.

15 The Hausa *duk abin da* sometimes transfers as 'all what' instead of 'all that': 'The contents have been carefully gone through and I have understood all what you say'. *Cf* 'let all what may be our conclusion be exactly carried out', from a novelette.

16 A Hausa says *ni kadai ne a dunya, ba ni da uwaye,* 'I am alone in the world, I have no parents'. This may appear in the English of a Hausa speaker as 'I am lonely in the world', possibly through the force of the analogy of 'only', which also translates *kadai*.

17 The use of 'too' for 'very' is common in the English spoken by West Africans. This may derive from Pidgin, but is supported by vernacular influences of a more direct nature. Thus 'I am too happy' (letter from a Hausa), 'I like French too much' (letter from a Yoruba), and 'our politicians are too fond of zigzag' (from a novelette), the latter being perhaps ambiguous.

18 Another syntactic influence is revealed in the habit of not repeating the nominal in sentences where there is an opposition of qualifiers: 'girls never love an indigent man but a rich' (from a novelette).

LEXICON

This is the area where, to the sociolinguist, the pace of growth is at once marked and at its most exciting. For here English in West Africa, especially in its imaginative creation of new verbals, is dynamic. In the realm of vocabulary, the observer soon learns to expect that he will come across a lexical gem at any moment; seldom is he disappointed. These lexical items consist of creation in two ways: deliberate coining and misascription. For the former, the creation may be either the extension or the reshaping of established words, modelled in the final analysis on either a vernacular or a standard English analogy. For the latter, the new dimension in the semantic field may derive from a mishearing, a miscomprehension, or a misprint. Typical examples of the extension of accepted meanings and collocations are: 'every now and then' to mean 'continuously', *ie* 'every now and every then'; 'wonderful' as a cry of amazement at a surprising event, *eg* 'He died yesterday morning' – 'Wonderful!'; 'good talk' for the parliamentary 'hear, hear'; 'tight friend' for 'close friend'. The phrase 'to try all my possible best', and the constant use of 'stranger' for 'guest' (the Hausa *bako* can translate both words) are standard instances of a lexical item owing its readjust-ment to a direct vernacular influence. Examples of the adaptation of words include the verbs 'to be chanced' for 'to have the opportunity' and 'to impregnate' for 'to make a girl pregnant'; and the adjectives 'bluffy' for 'fresh-complexioned' and 'trickish' for 'full of guile'. Accidental creations include 'to cope up with my work', 'by hooks or crooks', and 'next to your door' for 'next door'.

For the newcomer to West Africa, so exuberant has been the growth of fresh ideas and expressions deriving from the wildfire spread of English by the mass media as well as by far-reaching educational pro-grammes that he is likely to be confused when first meeting terms that are simply taken for granted by West African speakers of English. This is no less true of East and Central Africa. Richardson has noted how 'the most striking feature of Northern Rhodesian English is the eccentric use of many expressions which are not so misused as to result in incom-prehension but which are sufficiently strange to cause the uninitiated from the United Kingdom to hesitate in their acceptance of the utter-ance' (Richardson, 1964). There can exist a local vocabulary and idiom in the understanding of which a knowledge of standard English may be of no help, and yet which is locally commonplace. I am thinking less of the classical Pidgin words like *dash*, *chop*, *palaver*, *juju*, than of integrated neologisms drawn from the vernacular. Examples from my corpus in-clude 'loo', 'bone-to-flesh dance', 'beware of wayo people', 'long legs', 'senior service', 'been-to', 'me-and-my-darling', 'he allowed part of our land for erecting storeys', all taken from novelettes.[11]

In considering these dynamic extensions to and enrichment of the English vocabulary in West Africa, it is important to bear in mind the circumstances of their origin. Some may be by sympathetic analogy; some may be by direct translation; some may be semantic shift rather than lexical rebirth; others may be by mistake (*cf* the etymology o English 'adder'). In brief, all or any of the vernacular influences of blend, contamination, miscegenation, analogy or plain error in the acquisition and use of a second language may be at work. In such a luxuriant growth atmosphere as that of English in West Africa today, it does not take long for the seeds of neologisms to take root and flower to maturity.

Most of the lexical items to which I wish to draw attention fit con-veniently under the rubrics of nominals, verbals and modifiers. Im-mediately noticeable is the incidence of new nominals engagingly derived from adjectives and fresh verbal forms constructed from standard English nominals. But there is one area, a purely conversational one, which is best discussed separately. That is the influence that greetings, important to the point of ritual in most West African languages, have on English usage in West Africa. British English, by comparison, seems barren of such niceties. What African visitor to Britain has not been embarrassed by the stony contempt, tinged with actual resentment, which meets his courteous 'good morning' as he enters a crowded commuter compartment and then sits in silence for the rest of the journey, unhappily recalling the gregarious atmosphere of a similar transportation situation back home? The range of salutations in English is impoverished. Thus the Hausa, faced with 'good-bye' to express the varying intervals of separation inherent in *sai gobe, sai an jima, sai ka zo*, finds himself saying 'until tomorrow!', 'till later!', 'until you come!' So too, may his native English friend, at least until those on the High Street stand and stare at his farewells and wonder how long it will take him to relearn his own language now he is no longer speaking 'African'!

Some of the following examples require no commentary. A gloss has been given only when I have felt additional information would be helpful. Many of the most striking are drawn from the novelettes.

Nominals

'Both U. and E. had pre-knowledge of one another's *wheretos* of going and whereabouts.' (analogy)

'There's no *rigging* it, I've got to learn French.' (Derived from electoral behaviour in Western Nigeria, 1965.)

'*Poor-self* has merely stood here.'

'They have great *likeness* for you.'

'The girls are facing a lot of *hardcap*.' (portmanteau: hardship/handicap)

'The ladies of the town conferred them [titles] on me after a very ripe *deservation*.'

'His wife to whom he has given nothing *coinable*.' ('coins' = money, hence 'no money')

'Their invectives and *sardonics* are terrible.'

'Let's look at a well-to-do man among many financial *mediocres*.'

'Be you assured that members are *impossibles*, *impregnables* of the country.'

'It is inevitable we must die. The *fun* is that many people seem to forget this.' (*fun* = 'a funny thing')

'Greet all *known faces*.' (Hausa, *idon sani*, lit 'eye (face) of knowing' = acquaintance)

Verbals
'Some primary schools *converted* colleges.' (converted into)
'He *posed* forward.' (*ie* his pose was one of leaning forward)
'Your head is *crazied*.'
'*Cyclotyped* copies of records.' (Portmanteau: cyclostyled/typed.)
'U. with his dazzling red eyes . . . *shadowed* R. much.' (to shadow = to follow)
'Each and every one was well informed to *cope up* with any eventuality.' (*Cf* 'I must *pen up*' for bringing a letter to a close. One letter, influenced by the military take-over news, has 'to coup up with my studies'! The verbal 'to manage' has also established itself in this context; *eg* the answer to 'how are things?' can be 'I am managing' or even 'we thank the Manager (= God)', *mun gode Allah*.
'My gentleman *naked* himself.'
'I *complained* him.' (*Cf* 'Government replies editor'. The standard English use of prepositions is a notorious obstacle.)
'I was *coupled* at the dance.' ('couple' = find a dancing partner)
'That photograph you *took us*.' (Hausa *wanda ka dauke mu*, governing two direct objects)
'Will he come and *carry* students to USA again this year?' (Hausa *dauka* = take, pick up, carry)
'Are you *nauseating* for Nigeria yet?' (analogy from nausea > sickness > homesickness)
'Hardly did U. finish his sentence when some girls rushed.' (*ie* rushed in)
'They *drove* six boys from the university for lack of fees.' (Hausa *kora* = drive away)
'He is *scandalized*, he is slandered.' (analogy)
'Any persons who were interested in any of the social clubs he had mentioned or *unmentioned*.'
'The marathon speech of the gallant young man *conjured* everybody throughout his speech.' (conjure > cast a spell, mesmerise)
'I opened the door and *visualised* a very familiar face.'
'All contributed to *flower up* the occasion.' (flowers > beautiful > beautify + up)
'How long will they *backbite* him in his absence?'
'Sorry not to have been *chanced* to write before.'

Adjectives and adverbs
'Friends and comrades who rendered a most *gristable* aid.' (? from 'grist to the mill')
'A *flabbergasting* tidings . . . disclosed the death of my father.'
'A *full-dressed* lecture.'
'*Goldly* written in the book of history.'
'That *plumpy*, *bluffy* and happy man.'
'(His address) was so *bewitchery* that his audience forgot their *ached* backs.'
'*Vitaminous* foods and drinks'.
'*Confessionally*, I have misused my life.'
'U. can talk *labourately*.' (Portmanteau: labour/elaborately)

Phrases
'Your house is a stone thrown from mine.'
'At all.' (frequently used as an emphatic negative for 'not at all': (*cf* Hausa *ko kadan* = '(not) at all')
'Sorry.' (widely said even when the speaker is not, as in the standard English context, at fault; *eg* chorused by a class as the lecturer stumbles on entering the room. In Hausa, a sympathetic *sannu* would be very much *de rigueur* here.)
'Isn't it?' (a tag phrase to express the Hausa *ko ba haka ba*, is sometimes as obstinate as the Indians traditionally find it and defies metamorphosis into 'aren't you?', 'weren't they?' etc.)

*   *   *   *   *   *

What synopsis can be offered from these sample data? We have noted the flourishing existence of a developing variant of English which may in due course take its rightful place alongside such other variants as, perhaps, Indian English or even West Indian English. The English used in West Africa reveals in varying degrees vernacular influences at the morphological, syntactic and semantic levels; as well, of course, as at the phonological level in spoken English. In examining the sample drawn from the corpus and presented above, I have paid particular attention to the extent to which characteristic deviations from standard English usage may be ascribed to the influence exercised by a dominant West African language, Hausa, with an occasional suggestion in relation to similar influences from Yoruba and Igbo. From this examination, which has related only to the Nigerian context, it is surely clear that further and more extensive investigations need to be made of developments in usage in other English-using societies in West Africa. By so doing, some clearer notion of the drift and deviation, the normalising tendencies and the instabilities, of English as used in West Africa generally may be gained.

The linguistic chapter of the history of post-colonial developments in Africa has yet hardly begun to be written. There remains abundant opportunity for experiment, adjustment, and realignment in language use. In the context of this chapter of the present book, the indications seem to be that once English in West Africa settles down, after distilling and levelling off the diverse experience of its vernacular influences, a respectable and workable *koine* may emerge, possibly with regional variants. If enough people use English in West Africa, the obvious influence of the vernaculars, prominent (as we have seen here) at the outset of educational expansion, is likely to grow less obvious with time, as communal needs for a shared norm become more insistent. Practitioners of neologisms, loan-words and slang have short memories, and in due course assimilation often covers up its tracks. It is to be regretted that in the past expatriate teachers have for the most part been too keen to regard African anglicisms as an amusing collection of 'howlers', without always having the initiative, or the competence, to look for the source of such dialectal variations from standard English usage in the influence of the student's own vernacular. Today's short-term contracts for expatriate teachers are likely to reduce still further the chance that many of them will ever acquire an adequate grasp of an African language.

The study of the emergence of West African regional variants of English should provide a meeting-place for teachers of English and West African linguists, a focus of research where inter-disciplinary collaboration and very practical linguistics have a central place. It is my belief that the study of problems raised by languages in contact – for which the African continent provides the field situation *par excellence* – yields the highest rewards to those committed to a warm-hearted sociolinguistic approach rather than to an aloof and formal 'laboratory' analysis.

Notes

1 My grandparents, and even my mother who left India when she was seven, would thirty years after their retirement recite the roll-call of a typical Anglo-Indian household, with its *khansama, khitmatgar, dhobi, ayah, syce, chaprassi, chowkidar, mali, darzi,* etc, against which I from West Africa could match but the

generic 'boy', occasionally modified by house/small/horse. Francophone Africa, with Gallic gallantry, has added *la boyesse*! It is these items inseparable from daily life that persist in linguistic exile, encouraged, of course, by the writers of empire.

2 The army was no less an instrument of linguistic conversion among the local inhabitants. In India, Urdu, 'the language of the camp', became the lingua franca of the many regiments recruited from the northern plains, that storehouse of superb soldiery. In Nigeria, Hausa to a lesser extent played the same unificatory role until its use was forbidden by the General Officer Commanding during the 1939–45 war and English became the army's language of communication.

3 See also Achebe (1965b). Many issues of *Transition* and *Ibadan* carry valuable contributions on the role of English in Africa, of linguistic as well as literary relevance. So, too, do several of the inaugural lectures by Professors of English at African Universities, such as Christophersen (1948).

4 Even at the university, the preferred linguistic lowest common denominator of students speaking among themselves and to domestic servants is Pidgin, English being reserved for more formal contacts or for talking to staff. This at least was so up to 1966, when the chapter was written and I was head of the Department of Languages at Ahmadu Bello University in Zaria, Nigeria. Thus it is that, from the point of view of raw research, two West African students on an American or British campus may make a better field for the study of English as used by educated West Africans than they would on a Nigerian campus, since abroad they often prefer to talk in English (or their own language) rather than be overheard comfortably conversing in Pidgin.

5 See my introduction to Sonia Graham's study of Sir Hanns Vischer's contribution to educational policy in Northern Nigeria (Graham, 1966).

6 This genre of publication has been well reviewed by Ulli Beier (1964), Donatus Nwoga (1965) and, since this chapter was written in 1966, in continuing articles by Bernth Lindfors. Nwoga shrewdly sums up their significance thus: 'We have a new life and a new language. In the unassuming simplicity and directness of Onitsha Market literature we find authentic evidence of what these new elements mean to the common man and what are his reactions to them.' I have deliberately excluded from the factors influencing West African use of English the writings of distinguished novelists like Achebe and Ekwensi. Despite Alexandre's fear that 'I often have the impression that the typical Englishman instinctively mistrusts any foreigner who handles the English language too well' (quoted in French in Spencer, 1963), the writings of these authors have received a warm welcome, portraying standard English at its best, save where, as in *No Longer at Ease* or *Jagua Nana*, they wish to inspire their prose with the breathtaking tempo of contemporary Lagos or when, as in *A Man of the People*, Pidgin is deliberately selected as a mode of speech presentation. Unlike most of today's Indian novelists, the top Nigerian authors write for a public anxious and able to read in English rather than in the vernacular – a point that has given rise to frequent literary controversy. Tutuola's English is, of course, *sui generis*, 'the sort of English which is non-Ibadan and non-Makerere', I once heard the Nigerian writer Obiajunwa Wali say of him at Northwestern University, and it raises quite separate linguistic problems from any we are discussing here.

7 Since writing this chapter, however, the relevant work of Hofstad (1969) and Dunstan (1969) has appeared, and B. Tiffen is completing his research based on recordings of English spoken by West African students.

8 Curiously, I have found a tendency for Hausa students to revert to this construction when learning French; although it is in French, of course, an optional construction available for emphatic use, *eg* 'le roi, il est venu'.

9 Similarly, Parsons has noted how, while the direct influence of English grammar on Hausa is slight, the prevalence of certain types of relatival construction in Hausa newspapers suggests an immediate imitation of English. He goes on to cite the influence of parallel copy where the original was in standard English, giving rise to such journalistic phrases ('of doubtful normality in Hausa') as *gwamnati a shirye ta ke* for 'the government is prepared to . . .' (Parsons, 1964). I have elsewhere commented on the same phenomenon in the Hausa version of White Papers and official press releases, etc, presented as bilingual texts (Kirk-Greene and Aliyu, 1966). On the whole, those linguistic watchdogs like the Hausa Language Board and the East Africa Swahili Committee have been more occupied with the formation of loan-words than with the threatened distortion of syntax.

10 In the student world, to be 'a social somebody' is a high compliment to one's friendly accessibility, indicative of 'moving with' all and sundry, without airs: *cf* 'I like people who are sociable and plain in their ways', where 'plain' or 'simple' indicates the virtue of not putting on airs.

11 Today 'loo' is a widespread term for money, and is a modified form of 'loot', an earlier slang term in Nigeria and elsewhere, including England of course, where it is still current. In its standard English meaning, 'loot' is a loan-word from India. 'Bone-to-flesh' denotes a man dancing with a girl, in contrast to the 'bone-to-bone' style sometimes necessitated by the shortage of girls. 'Wayo', of Hausa origin, is now widely used to imply cunning or guile. 'Long legs' is a commonplace for using influence in high places to secure a service. 'Senior service', a civil service grading for the higher cadres, is used to suggest 'upper class' in economic terms. 'Been-to' is one who has been [to] overseas. 'Me-and-my-darling' describes a small sofa. 'Storeys' are houses higher than the usual bungalow style.

Gilbert Ansre

The Influence of English on West African Languages

The following sentences are genuine utterances by speakers of three West African languages; the first is from an Ewe speaker, the second from a Twi speaker and the third from a speaker of Yoruba.

Mele very sorry, *gake mena* every conceivable opportunity-*i hafi wò* let-*m* down.

Se wɔbɛ-report *wo ma me bio a mebe*-dismiss *wo* without further warning.

E arrange *re* for my convenience.

As is clearly noticeable, parts of each utterance are English. In the Ewe example we have 'very sorry', 'every conceivable opportunity' and 'let-down'. The Twi example has '-report', '-dismiss' and 'without further warning', and the Yoruba one has 'arrange' and 'for my convenience'. The translations of each of these sentences into English are as follows:

1 'I am very sorry, but I gave him every conceivable opportunity and yet he let me down.'

2 'If you are reported to me again I shall dismiss you without further warning.'

3 'Arrange it for my convenience.'

These are examples in which the Ewe, Twi and Yoruba languages may be said to be influenced by English. In these particular cases, if the speaker of each of these languages did not want to have the English items in these utterances he could have said it all in the West African language in question. For example, 1 and 2 could quite easily have been said thus:

1 *evem ŋutɔ, gake mena mɔnukpɔkpɔ ɖesiaɖee hafi wò do ŋukpem.*

2 *sɛ wɔbɛtoa wo ma me bio a meyi wo adi ntɛm pa ara.*

As will be seen later, there are other cases in which only an English item can be used, because it is the only one available.

Strictly speaking, it is not quite correct to say one language has influenced another. It is necessary to refer to the speaker or speakers of the languages concerned. Language itself is an abstraction from human social behaviour and one language cannot influence another except through the mediation of a user or users of these two languages. The only connection between two different languages is the speaker. Thus what we really mean when we say that language x influences language y is that the speakers of y incorporate items of x into their own rendering of y. A discussion on the subject of the influence of English on West African languages cannot therefore be complete if it does not take some account of the human factors that precipitate this influence. In a brief treatment of this kind, these social factors can be given only summary reference and discussion. Moreover, much detailed investigation in this area is required before we can describe them adequately.

Another important fact to bear in mind is that it is not always necessary for current native speakers of the 'influenced' language to be speakers of the 'influencing' language. In fact, in many cases they are not even aware that particular items they have in their speech have their origin in another language. Several actual instances come readily to mind, but a striking one occurs in the Peki dialect of Ewe which is spoken in south-eastern Ghana. The name of a cluster of several oranges on one stock is called *mprabεɖi*. Many speakers of this dialect are unaware that this comes from the Twi *mpra bedi* – 'the lover will eat it'. The meaning implies that such beautifully clustered oranges are best presented to a lover. They use the term solely for oranges bunched together and for nothing else, not even for lemons or other similar fruit, and they need not know any Twi to use this Twi term in their Ewe. Even more significant is the fact that current Twi does not have the word *mprabedi* for 'a bunch of oranges' at all. There are many of us who use what are popularly called loan-words, but are quite oblivious of the fact that they are 'loans' and totally incapable of telling their origin.

Nevertheless, for every instance of a language influencing another we have to postulate prior or contemporary intercommunication between speakers of these languages. This intercommunication may be due to large sections of speakers of both languages living side by side, or a relatively small number of speakers of one of the languages residing among large groups of speakers of the other and a consequent development of bilingualism, as has been the case with English and the various

West African languages. Nor must we rule out the possibility of further speakers of one language acquiring items from another language by means of yet a third language.

It seems quite certain that in the earliest instances of English language influence on the West African languages, speakers of the indigenous languages acquired some English items – how many is immaterial – from native English speakers, and found it convenient to use them in their own languages. These were accepted by the speech community and the items became incorporated into the indigenous language. The kinds of item readily acquired and the factors that influence their acceptance will be discussed later.

Another way in which English has been observed to influence the West African languages is the way speakers who are bilingual in English and a West African language insert varying 'chunks' of English into their performance of the West African language. The examples quoted at the beginning of the chapter show this kind of influence. The size of the pieces of English found in this type of utterance varies from a single morpheme to whole sentences, and it is often not immediately clear whether the speaker is speaking English or the West African language. Essentially, however, in cases of both monolinguals and bilinguals incorporating loans, the results seem similar.

The casual observer often assumes that the kind of English loan items incorporated by a monolingual West African into his indigenous language are much the same as those which a bilingual person who knows both English and the indigenous language incorporates into his speech. This in fact is frequently not the case. The examples cited at the beginning of the chapter can be obviously traced to speakers of Ewe, Twi and Yoruba who also speak English. Another example of this kind of bilingual's performance is that in which a linguist friend said in a discussion

Megye di se ade no nyinaa ye a cline in which you cannot distinguish the one from the other.

in which the first section, which is Twi, translates: 'I believe that the whole thing is . . .'.

On the other hand, one normally hears monolingual West Africans say such things as:

Car *no kɔ* fast *dodo*. (Twi)
The car goes too fast.

11

Me pass ball *la nyuie o.* (Ewe)
He didn't pass the ball well.

The differences in the kinds of English elements incorporated will be discussed later but there are borderline cases in which it is hard to decide. A medicine man with hardly any formal education was once heard to say about a patient:

Efe condition *mele* well *o.* (Ewe)
His condition is not good.

Reaction to the use of English items, and for that matter, all foreign items in West African languages, differs tremendously with different individuals and societies. Some people take strong exception to what they term the 'adulteration' of their language. They are at pains to preserve what they consider the 'purity' of the language. Often most of these people are quite oblivious of foreign elements that succeeded in getting into the language in earlier times. Those who are aware of them draw a line between loans which have already been incorporated into the 'system and feeling' of the language, and new ones, which in their opinion are being forced into the language. The former may be acceptable; in any case they cannot be helped. But the latter must be opposed and the tendency to encourage them eradicated. This is the purist point of view. The purist view may be held by a single individual or by many members of a given society. If a sizeable group of the language community is purist and influential enough, it can succeed in minimising the influence of other languages on their native language. Such a language could then be said to be a *resistant* language. However, in actual fact it is not the language itself that is resistant but rather the attitude of its speakers.

Others take the opposite viewpoint. They are anxious to introduce loans from other languages into their own. Various factors, social, psychological and others determine their attitude. This is often the case, for example, when the foreign language is such that its use, either as a completely separate language or as part of the native language, gives prestige to the speaker. Here, the more versatile the user of the language, the higher his social standing. People who readily accept foreign elements into their language may be said to be *accommodating*; and the language which they speak, and which contains (as a result of this attitude) a lot of foreign elements, may, for our purposes, be referred to as an *accommodating* language.

Between these two extreme positions is a whole cline of attitudes to innovations from foreign languages. In West Africa today, the majority of speakers of the indigenous languages seem to have a moderate and tolerant attitude to English items (and French, for that matter, in francophone areas) occurring in their speech. The extent of this toleration, as well as other facets of language attitudes, are yet to be investigated and offer great opportunities for socio- and psycho-linguistic research on a large scale. It is however true to say that unlike the Asian countries, the rise of nationalism has not created much conflict in the minds of West Africans in the area of language. The languages of the former colonial masters continue to play important roles, not only as independent languages but in the way in which elements from them continue to find their way into the indigenous languages; and there is no reason to believe that this process will terminate in the near future.

The process of influence from English should be distinguished from the process of pidginisation and creolisation. Whereas the process termed here *accommodation* is that in which a speaker allows foreign items into his native language while still speaking this native language, pidginisation or creolisation is the process whereby the native speaker of one language attempts, not fully successfully, to speak another language but retains marked traits of his mother tongue in his rendering of the foreign language. It may be said that accommodation is mother tongue oriented in aim and foreign element incorporation in result; and that creolisation, on the other hand, is foreign language oriented in aim and mother tongue element incorporation in result. The question whether it is possible to have, as a result of both processes, the same kind of language phenomenon – that is, a pidgin or creole language – is a moot point. An answer to it might be verifiable in West Africa some decades from now. For the moment, what the linguist can do is to examine the influence of the English language upon the indigenous languages of West Africa, and vice versa.

In the rest of this chapter, an attempt will be made to outline the main areas in which English may be said to influence West African languages, and to examine the linguistic characteristics of these 'loans'. Geographical and demographic data on the indigenous languages will be kept to a minimum. Some remarks will be made on the sociocultural situations in which these influences are known to be prominent. Most of the illustrations used will be from languages spoken in Southern Ghana and Togo because this happens to be the area with which the author is most acquainted. But preliminary investigations and consultations indicate that generalisations from this area are valid for most of English-using (anglophone) West Africa.

Countries and circumstances of influence

In West Africa, it is only natural to expect that those countries which have had English-speaking colonial rulers and associates would have languages that exhibit English influence.[1] These countries are the Gambia, Sierra Leone, Liberia, Ghana, Nigeria and the western section of present-day Cameroon. Each of these countries has had close associations with either Great Britain or (in the case of Liberia) the USA. In addition, these West African countries have had more to do with each other than with other West African countries. Throughout this association, English has been the language of communication. It has been taken for granted that English is and must continue to be their common language. Hardly any specific policies were ever formulated, either by the English-speaking colonial authorities or by West Africans, regarding the use of an indigenous language (perhaps with the exception of Hausa in Northern Nigeria) as a medium of inter-communication.

The result of this intensive exposure to English has been twofold. First, many Africans speak English to some extent, and many more understand it. The degree of proficiency varies a great deal from one person to another and from one place to another. But compared with an area such as East Africa, where Swahili has often been the main medium of communication between English speakers and the indigenous peoples, the number of English-speaking West Africans is very considerable. The second result is that a great many items from the English language have found their way into the indigenous languages, mainly through the medium of bilingual West Africans. These people, in their use of their native language, incorporate English items of various kinds.

Generally speaking, the amount of influence that English has on a West African language depends on two factors: the length of time the two languages have been in contact, and the intensity of the contact. The longer English and a West African language have been in contact the more items from English are likely to have been introduced into the latter. In Ghana, for example, an examination of Fanti and Chokosi will illustrate the point. Fanti is a dialect of the Akan language and is spoken on the coast. It has had the longest period of contact with English of all the Ghanaian languages. This contact dates from 1631 when the first British settlement in the then Gold Coast was founded. Chokosi is a language genetically related to Akan. It is spoken in the north-eastern corner of Ghana. We find that the proportion of English borrowings in Fanti is very considerable. English loans in Chokosi are almost non-existent. This difference is seen even in the two closely related dialects of the Akan language, Fanti and Asante. Because English has been in contact with Fanti over a longer period of time, and because this contact has been greater with Fanti than with either Chokosi or Asante, more items from English have found their way into Fanti than into the other languages and dialects.

Secondly, it is generally assumed as a matter of course that the more areas of life a second language covers the more will the native language be influenced by the second language. Thus, a speech community which only hears English when the European administrator speaks, will have fewer English elements in its language than that which hears English at work, in the shops and on the radio.

Social and technological factors

The mere coexistence within a society of two languages over a long period of time does result in the interchange of items between them. The direction of the flow of these items, however, is determined by factors that are other than just their coexistence and the linguistic characteristics of these two languages. It is determined by sociocultural factors. Given such coexistence, and also a situation in which the culture of the speakers of one language is regarded as socially and technologically dominant, the major flow of linguistic items will be primarily from the direction of the language of the dominant cultural group to that of the dominated speech community.

Throughout anglophone West Africa the cultural situation has been one in which the speakers of English with whom West Africans have been in contact have been socially and technologically dominant. Western culture as manifested by the British and Americans has not only proved to be an effective colonising tool; it has been generally welcomed by the vast majority of West Africans. This is especially so in the field of technology and social institutions. Tools and artefacts by the thousand have been introduced from Europe and America into these countries and have, in many cases, proved to be more useful and satisfactory than their indigenous predecessors. In other cases, there was nothing that the newly introduced commodity replaced. Together with the objects, the names by which they were called, as well as words connected with their specialised uses, have been adopted from English.

Examples of names of objects and terms associated with their use may be found in the following illustrations. The language in which these occur is given in brackets at the end of each example:

Medi be ma reverse car *la gake* gear *la menyo o.* (Ewe)
I wanted to reverse the car but the gear was out of order.

Start-*i* fan *no ma me.* (Twi)
Start the fan for me.

Hall-*ɛ mli* fuse *fɛ* e-blow. (Ga)
All the fuses in the hall have blown.

Ne me wind *nye* watch *la vɔ ko ma blɛ.* (Ewe)
When I finish winding my watch I shall wear it.

Me focus *me* camera *nɔ* lens *yiye enti na* pictures *no yɛ* sharp *sa.* (Twi)
I focus the lens of my camera well (and) that is why my pictures are so sharp.

Meɖee' ku type letter *ya kimɛ to mize* post. (Avatime)
Please type this letter for me for posting.

In the field of social institutions introduced into West Africa, education and government are among the most far-reaching in their effect on the languages. Obviously there were systems of education and government long before the arrival of the white man. But the traditional concepts and systems of education and government were quite different from what we have today. The way they were organised and the media of communication were unlike what exists at the present time. New organisations and ways of dealing with situations have been introduced for which the indigenous languages had not been equipped to cater. It is only natural therefore that new terminology has found its way into the indigenous languages from the language of those who brought in these sociocultural institutions.

Examples of loans which are related to the modern patterns of education in anglophone West Africa are *school, syllabus, examinations, pass* and *fail*. The indigenous system of education was not organised along the lines of a full-time institution like a present-day *school*, which follows a systematically worked out *syllabus* and *passes* or *fails students* in their *examinations* for the purpose of *promotion*. So contemporary West African languages have had to incorporate these terms for daily use. Thus:

> *Kofi* pass *efe* final exam *eyata wo* promote-*i*. (Ewe)
> Kofi passed his final exam and therefore was promoted.
> Syllabus *yi ye ma sa sukuu yi*. (Twi: note that *sukuu* represents the naturalised form of the English loan 'school')
> This syllabus is good for this particular school.

In the same way, new concepts, methods and procedures which were introduced into the forms of government have resulted in the incorporation of a large stock of terminology into the West African languages. For example, new political units have emerged which are different from the mainly linguistic and tribal groupings called *ɔman* in Twi. The *ɔman* has its subdivisions of potential fighting sub-units such as *nifa* 'right wing', *benkum* 'left wing', and others. Now the *country* has become the largest unit, with such subdivisions as *regions*, *districts* and *constituencies*, and these terms have also been taken into the languages of the people. It is true that by means of what is called local authority government in some countries, an amount of the old system of government has been preserved. But such institutions as *parliamentary democracy* (an often-used borrowing) has brought in terms like *parliament, election, vote, veto, opposition* and others into virtually all West African languages. Also, new terms used for enforcing law and protecting the individual and society have brought into the indigenous languages such terms as *police, bail, detention, prison* and *protective custody*. In the very recent past the frequency of occurrence of the loan *coup* has increased beyond all expectations, for obvious reasons.

It must be mentioned that the alternative to borrowing terminology from the language of the contributing culture is the coining, sometimes by means of calques, of new terms in the language of the receiving culture. This phenomenon occurs in the West African languages, but does not come within the scope of the present discussion. Often, though, a lot of the coined alternatives that purists suggest and which are sometimes tried out on the radio and in other mass media are not accepted. They then become topics for joking and ridicule by the 'accommodating' members of the society.

Another area of the life of West Africans in which we observe a highly marked influence of English on the languages is that of games and entertainments. The following are but a sample of English loans in practically all the languages in anglophone countries:

football, penalty, corner, half-time, referee, goal, goal-keeper
wicket, cricket, out, innings, l.b.w., bat
serve, love-all, deuce, stroke, net
100 yds, mile, relay, high jump, putting the weight
cinema, dance, waltz, etc.

From the foregoing discussion, it is obvious that the influence of English on West African languages is most marked in those areas of the life of speakers in which European culture has made the deepest inroads – those of technology, artefacts, education, government and entertainment. It remains to be said that in some other areas of West African life the traditional culture has not been deeply influenced. We notice, therefore, very little influence of English in concepts and terminologies in these fields.

One such is agriculture. Although cash-crop farming has become a major aspect of the life of West Africans, the agricultural methods employed have not been much affected by European ways. Mechanised farming is still at the experimental stage. The tools used have hardly changed at all and the traditional methods of shifting cultivation are still practised. Little surprise, therefore, that the terms used for what is called a farm (which is quite different from a European or American farm) still remain indigenous ones. Words and items connected with preparing and tilling the land, tending and harvesting the crop, are not influenced by the English language. Nor do the terms used in the native languages coincide with English equivalents. They are also highly specialised, as such terms are in their usage, and often cannot be used outside of agriculture. A few are given here from Ewe as illustrations:

flu	'piece of land cultivated in previous season(s), which may or may not have crops on it.'
kplɔ ho	'to clear area that has been burned and rid it of tree trunks and branches before crops are planted.'
fo dru	'to make special kind of mounds for planting yams.'
bu koko[2]	'to ferment cocoa in banana leaves before drying.'

But a recent innovation is:

spray koko	'to spray cocoa trees with insecticide.'

Another area which has not been invaded by English loans is that of the rites of passage: birth, puberty, marriage and death. In many West African countries, although there has been a revolution in the thinking of people, the fundamental world view of many has only been slightly altered by European concepts. With others, there has been a change in cosmology and general world view but hardly any in rituals and observances. The result is that many rites are still performed during the critical periods of birth, puberty and death, and the terms used in association with them in the indigenous languages still remain. Thus, for instance:

wɔ ŋkeke enyi	'to perform the necessary rites on the eighth day of childbirth' (Ewe)
ɖe ɖe xexe	'to go outdoors in connection with birth, chieftaincy, etc' (Ewe)
gbeleɛ	'a young woman undergoing puberty rites' (Ewe)
no aha ɖe nyɔnu ta	'to perform the necessary social duties, including giving gifts of drink to relatives of a fiancé, thus committing them as approving witnesses of the marriage' (Ewe)
tiri nsa	'one of the stipulated drinks required before marriage' (Twi)
ayefade	'debt paid to a husband by male offender who is found guilty of adultery with his wife' (Twi)
dzogbe-ku	'death due to socially specified and sudden accidents which renders the corpse taboo and therefore unacceptable in the township and the public burial ground' (Ewe)

The lengthy glosses necessary to translate these items, which are 'simple and commonly used' as far as the native speaker is concerned, indicate how inappropriate the English language is in some areas of West African life, and why it is not used in discussing matters relating to rituals. Both that aspect of life and the terminology used to discuss it remain hardly affected by the English language.

Two further commonplace but necessary observations may be made on how English is used in the indigenous languages of West Africa; first, by the formally educated bilingual as against the monolingual, and second, by people who do not speak other West African languages well, but can speak English. The non-English-speaking West African uses English loans which consist only of well-established items in his native language, or another West African language which he knows how to speak. He himself cannot increase the number of these loans from English into his own language. The English-speaking West African, on the other hand, is often found using a great deal of English in his native language, or in those other West African languages which he speaks; and much of it does not consist of established loans. The English-speaking bilingual is thus the spear-head of the influence of English on West African languages.

This innovation by the bilingual is intensified when two or more of them discuss technical subjects, in academic study, for example. It is not unusual for the discussion to contain so much English that an English-speaking monolingual may be able to follow it within reasonable limits. The following is typical of academic conversations and discussions in West Africa:

> Geiger counter *no a*-locate radio-active matter *no* (Twi)
> The geiger counter has located the radio-active matter.
> *Mepε* George Orwell satire *wɔ* Animal Farm *mo sen* Nineteen Eighty
> Four *mo de no.* (Twi)
> I prefer George Orwell's satire in *Animal Farm* to that in *Nineteen Eighty Four.*
> *Ne* phoneme *nye* minimal phonological unit *eye* morpheme *nye* minimal grammatical unit *la, ekema* lexeme *anye* minimal lexical unit. (Ewe)
> If the phoneme is the minimal phonological unit and the morpheme is the minimal grammatical unit, then lexeme will be the minimal lexical unit.

The other observation is that when two West Africans who speak English try to communicate in the native language of one of them, and in which the other is not quite fluent, the one who does not speak the language fluently uses a lot of English items as an aid to fill in the gaps that exist in his language competence. This often increases to almost unacceptable limits the number of English items above what might normally be used by the native speaker. For example, the non-native speaker of the Ga language may say:

> *Kɛ mi*-finish homework *lɛ maya fia.*

Whereas the native speaker would prefer

> *Kɛ migbe* homework *lɛ na lɛ maya fia;*

both meaning 'When I complete the homework I shall go home.' But the non-native speaker, not being quite conversant with the complicated use of *gbe . . . na* 'to complete', might use 'finish' – a frequent West Africanism – instead.

Structural characteristics

So far, we have been discussing the historical, cultural and social factors involved in the influence of English on speakers of West African languages and consequently on the languages themselves. We must now apply ourselves to structural questions. Some of the questions that may be asked are: What are the structural characteristics of the items that are accepted into the various West African languages? Can these be said to be linguistically patterned in any way, and if so do these enhance their ready acceptance? What happens to the structure of the mother tongue when these new items are introduced? Do they maintain their structures and systems? What classificatory rules do the new items obey? Are there any linguistic generalisations and predictions we can make about this process of accommodation?

In answering these questions we should avoid over-generalisation. This is especially important in a treatment like this which attempts to deal with many languages at once. It is common practice to assume that close structural affinities exist between the various languages of West Africa. This seems more obvious to the non-West African than to the West African, but to some extent it is true. For example, most of the languages of the region use pitch in their phonological patterning in a way which has earned them the term 'tone languages'. It is also true that many of them exhibit similarities in their grammatical patterning, such as the occurrence of a sequence of verbal forms within the same sentence which has come to be known as 'serial verbal construction'.[3] But a close examination of both these features, tone and seriality, shows that there are many differences in detail from language to language. In the use of tones, we have the distinction in West Africa between 'terrace level' tone languages and 'discrete level' tone languages (Stewart, Schachter and Welmers, 1964). Another distinction is also between those languages in which main tonal differences are determined by other phonological features, such as the consonants, and those in which they are determined by grammatical features. Also, tone is used in some languages predominantly to make lexical distinctions, and in others to make grammatical distinctions. In the case of the serial verbal constructions, some languages such as Twi require agreement in given cases between the constituent verbal elements of the series, others do not.

There is, for instance, a difference in negative formation within serial constructions between Twi and Ewe.

With such diversity in detail, therefore, we cannot readily lump West African languages together in contradistinction to English when discussing the influence the latter has on the former. Despite interesting similarities (and near-identity in a few cases), a serious treatment of their structural characteristics must make clearer distinctions. Moreover, the common characteristics we find among a number of languages are often quite absent from others. Therefore generalisations for all languages are bound to be too sweeping or contradictory.

Ideally what is needed is a number of careful contrastive studies, (i) of pairs or selected groups of West African languages with each other, and (ii) of individual languages with English. These studies would include an examination of the influences that these languages have had on each other. But this cannot be attempted here. All we can do is to use certain specific languages to answer some of the questions on structural features posed above. These discussions will cover aspects of phonology, grammar and lexis.

PHONOLOGY

Very little has been accepted phonologically from English in the several West African languages examined. Of these, [l] in Twi and Ewe, and [p] and [r] in Yoruba are good examples. In Twi [l] was not a phoneme until quite recently, when words like lɔ́yà 'lawyer', lɔ́rì 'lorry', pláǹ 'plan' and fiìl 'feel' were borrowed into the language. Two ways of handling this innovation in the phonology of Twi have been observed. On the one hand, those who are bilingual in English and Twi and use English frequently make a special effort to imitate the English sound in pronouncing these words. On the other hand, non-English-speaking Twis and those who do not use the English language frequently tend to make this new sound conform to the phonological pattern of Twi. The words listed above are therefore pronounced approximately thus: nɔ́yà or dɔ́yà, rɔ́rì or nɔ́rì, pìráǹ and fiìdì. The speakers in this case seek the nearest approximations to the newly introduced sound from their indigenous phonological repertoire.

In Ewe, [l] and [r] are allophones of the same phoneme. Their distribution is best described in terms of two dimensions: (i) initial and non-initial position in the syllable and (ii) articulatorily central and peripheral. In other words, [l] traditionally occurred in initial syllabic position and [r] did not. Secondly, in consonant clusters [r] occurred only with what may be termed centrally articulated consonants (dental, alveolar and palatal) and [*l*] occurred with peripherally articulated ones (bilabials, labio-dental, velar and glottal). Thus we have *ló* 'to gather up', *lé* 'to catch', *kpàlà* 'to rinse' and *bàlà* 'ringworm', but not *[rV] nor *[CvrV] canonical forms; and also *dró* 'to lower load from head', *trú* 'to vomit', *yrá* 'to bless' on the one hand, and *bla* 'to tie up', *flù* 'to confuse', *kló* 'to wash' and *ylá* 'to conceal'.

One would therefore have expected that words like *rénkòt* 'rain coat', *rídà* 'reader' and *grìñì* 'green' would be pronounced thus: *lenkot*, *lida* and *glìñì* respectively. But somehow, the former is the generally accepted pronunciation of these loan-words in Ewe. The allophonic constraints imposed by the language do not seem to apply in these cases. Perhaps this is due to the fact that these items were brought in fairly recently, and by bilingual speakers of English and Ewe who have learnt to maintain the distinction between the English phonemes /l/ and /r/. This explanation needs further investigation and substantiation, however.

Incidental to this discussion of the loan item, but of interest, is the habit of non-English users of the loan-words of inserting vowels between members of such consonant clusters as do not occur in the phonological structures of their languages, as well as, in many cases, after final English consonants. Thus

piran	for 'plan'	(Twi)
bòlù	for 'ball'	(Ewe)
paipu	for '(water) pipe'	(Yoruba)

This phenomenon, however, belongs to the topic of the influence of the indigenous language on English as spoken by West Africans and is not within our immediate area of concern in this chapter.

The way in which English loan-words which have the English phoneme /p/ are rendered in Yoruba is further illustration of a variation in usage by speakers, from those who make the distinction in most words to those who do not. It also illustrates the point made above that earlier borrowings were subject to fuller phonological integration than more recent ones. Yoruba does not have a phonemic /p/. Thus when *halfpenny* was borrowed it was rendered *hékpénì* (ie [kp] instead of [p]). This form is used today, even by very highly sophisticated English-speaking Yorubas when they speak their mother tongue. The monolingual Yoruba also uses the same form. On the other hand, the English *pin* may be rendered by the monolingual as *kpini* but by the bilingual as *pini.* Another predictable but interesting fact is that unlike the adaptations that the Yoruba-English bilingual would make in the case of /p/, he is often heard using /l/ for the English /r/, especially in initial position: *eg: lesɔlt* 'result', *lekaunt* 'recount'. Some phonological loans are more easily integrated than others.

GRAMMAR AND LEXIS

A casual look at any given piece of a West African language that has been influenced by English leaves one with the impression that it contains many English lexical items but hardly any influences relatable to the grammatical categories of structure, system or class. Closer examination however shows that the grammar is also more deeply affected than is realised. We shall consider the lexical features first and then the grammatical ones.

In the vast majority of cases the presence of an English lexical item is the predominant marker of influence. Virtually all the examples cited earlier are of this kind, and to most people it is these that strike them. However, there are a limited number of instances in which there is no overt lexical borrowing. This type of influence is very difficult to identify. It has been observed, for example, that the Twi sentence:

Ne bo kɔ soro
Its price has gone up

seems to be a recent innovation in the language, as a result of the English equivalent, and that the indigenous rendering is:

Ne bo ayɛ den
lit 'Its price has become hard'.[4]

If this is so, this is one instance in which grammatical, lexical and even semantic innovation has taken place in the Twi language without the introduction of any loan-word. Careful investigation is bound to unearth a number of similar interesting examples of this kind of influence.

The lexical items that are borrowed from English are related to the grammar of English and of the adopting languages in varying ways. Some of them are monomorphemic in both languages; *eg: ball, gallon, pin.* Many are co-terminous with the grammatical word unit in both languages. But some are not. The use of the two items *disappoint* and *let . . . down* in Ewe illustrate the point:

E disappoint m.
He disappointed me.

E let *m* down.

He let me down.

In both sentences the use of the loan in Ewe coincides with its use in English. Noticeable is the occurrence of the object after *disappoint*, and between *let* and *down*, as is the case in English. Both *disappoint* and *let . . . down* may be said to form a single lexical item, but the former is one grammatical word while the latter is two, and the discontinuity possible in English structures with *let . . . down* is maintained in Ewe.

On the other hand, one can find cases in which unusual things get done to a loan. In one instance a lady who hardly knew any English was heard to use the verb *close* (which she pronounced as *klósù*) in Ewe thus:

Yekayi wo klo-na su ya?

When do they close?

It is obvious that to her *klo-* was the verb-stem to which the habitual post-stem particle *-na* could be suffixed, and that *su* (which is actually the final 's' of the English word, to which she had added the final vowel *u* to indigenise it) had become a noun operating as object in the clause. *Close* had become two grammatical words to her (*klo* and *su*).

Moving into the area of strictly grammatical categories, we find that loan items found in West African languages are predominantly in grammatical classes whose membership consists of open sets. Classes that are closed systems, and whose members can be exhaustively enumerated, tend not to be easily violated. Thus, loan items are more frequently found in word classes like nouns, verbs, adjectives and adverbs, or their approximate equivalents in the various languages, than in classes like articles, specifiers, pronouns and postpositions. Statistical counts are not yet available, but it is clear that by far the most commonly borrowed items are incorporated into the noun word class. This is natural, since the greatest influence, as has been noted, is in the area of artefacts and sociocultural institutions. Items from the verb class are not as readily borrowed as those from the noun class. Conjunctions are sometimes borrowed, especially by those who have had more formal education in English. Any serious study of the innovations in the West African languages from English should examine all the grammatical units of that language: sentence, clause, group and word structure. Here we can only illustrate such aspects of this influence as have been observed in the structure of the nominal group and the unit word in Ewe and Twi.

In both languages the places in structure of the uninfluenced simple nominal group may be represented thus:

h(adj qnt sp pl int)

where h is expounded by an obligatory head, the brackets ( ) are to be read as 'optional', *adj*, *qnt*, *sp*, *pl* and *int* are expounded by items from the word classes: adjective, quantifier, specifier, pluraliser and intensifier respectively and represents recursion of the element above which it occurs.

Thus we have the following examples of the simple nominal group in both languages:

Nnaka kɛse anan yi (nom) nyinaa (Twi)
Aɖaka gã ene sia wo katã (Ewe)
All these four big boxes.

When, however, various kinds of English loans are introduced into this linear ordering, changes take place. In this sub-class of nominal group, the word classes which usually lend themselves to influence are the noun, adjective and quantifier. The specifier and intensifier resist loans. The pluraliser reacts differently in different cases.

When only the noun head is from English the normal rendering is maintained:

Box(es) *kɛse anan yi (nom) nyinaa* (Twi)

When the adjective is from English, the noun head is usually also expected to be in English and the adjective precedes the noun head thus:

Big boxes *anan yi (nom) nyinaa*.

One does not usually hear

*Nnaka big anan yi nom nyinaa.

nor

*Big nnaka anan yi nom nyinaa.

When the quantifier is also from English it is normal to have the English items in the way they are ordered in English and the others in the way they are ordered in the indigenous language:

Four big boxes *yi (nom) nyinaa.* (Twi)
Four big box *sia wo katã.* (Ewe)

One occasionally hears:

Nnaka kɛse four *yi (nom) nyinaa.*

Words borrowed from English into indigenous languages are given different morphological 'treatments' depending mainly on the word structure patterns that exist in the receiving language. In Ewe, for example, pluralisation is by means of the pluraliser *wo* in the nominal group. So *wo* is added to loan-words to form the plural:

Trik-wo le esi fũu.
He has many tricks.

In Twi, however, where pluralisation is achieved either by various plural prefixes or the use of the pluraliser *nom*, 'tricks' has been known to have the forms *triks* or *n-trikis*, the latter being the more indigenised form with the *n-* plural prefix and also *-is*, the phonologically indigenised form of the English plural. The general tendency in word structure seems to have been in the direction of indigenisation, but more knowledge of English and sophistication in its use seems to be reversing things. Often one finds a 'literate' and an 'illiterate' version of the same item.

The above discussion shows that the influence of English pervades all linguistic levels of the West African languages. It is not limited just to the lexical items, which are those that are more readily noticeable. Rather, we find its effect in the phonology, grammar, lexis and semantics of the indigenous languages.

Conclusion

Finally, we may ask whether one can hazard a prediction about the long-term results of this influence of English on West African languages. Such a venture, admittedly, is not strictly speaking the business of a descriptive linguist; but an outline of the kind given here points in certain directions which the linguist is perhaps best equipped to indicate.

If there is a continuation of the social, technological, educational and political influences which, as outlined earlier, anglophone West Africans have received from the English-speaking world, more and more linguistic items associated with these influences will continue to be incorporated into the local languages. It is true that purists will make

12

attempts either to stop or lessen the flow. They may succeed in a very limited number of cases, especially if they use persuasive methods rather than force and legislation. But what they prevent from entering the languages will be insignificant compared with what will enter them. Also, as more people who do not speak the same West African languages come together, and for example, intermarry, they will be more likely to use English as a common language. In such cases, they may tend gradually to lose the ability to speak their mother tongue fluently; and, as for their children, the prospects of their ever knowing a West African language well would be very slight. Nor must we forget some members of the upper middle-class 'élite' in West Africa who, for various reasons of their own, teach their children to speak English instead of their mother tongue. It seems most unlikely, though, that the West African languages will disappear in the foreseeable future. The strong sense of pride in their use that is noticeable in most places, the feeling for indigenous identity and the special efforts on behalf of these languages being made in educational institutions, especially in the universities and in government departments, are all positive factors which will contribute to the preservation of the indigenous West African tongues. The trend is in the direction of multilingualism rather than the loss of the local languages. However, perhaps some day many of the West African languages will be similar in composition to present-day English, which is basically a Germanic language, but has a lot of loan items from Romance languages, especially French, and is also heavily indebted to Latin and Greek. In other words, our indigenous languages would continue to exist, but would contain a great many foreign elements, especially from English.

Notes

1 It would likewise be expected that countries with French connections would exhibit French influence. Earlier pre-colonial contacts in West Africa, with the Portuguese, Dutch and Germans, are not discussed here.
2 *Koko* is of course itself a loan, originally deriving from Mexico, and entering Ewe either from English via Spanish, or from Portuguese via Spanish.
3 In connection with the brief discussion of structural features in the West African languages cited, the following works were particularly used: Christaller, 1881; Westermann, 1930; Ward, 1952; Stewart, 1963; Ansre, 1961 and 1966; Williamson, 1965; Boadi, 1966; Bamgboṣe, 1966.
4 This example was pointed out to me by my colleague I. K. Chinebuah.

Peter Young

The Language of West African Literature in English

The emergence of West African writing in English is by no means as sudden as is generally supposed. As early as 1789, Equiano published his autobiography, *The Interesting Narrative of the Life of Olaudah Equiano or Gustavus Vassa the African.* In the nineteenth century, A. B. C. Sibthorpe in Sierra Leone wrote his *History* (1868), and C. C. Reindorf published his *History of the Gold Coast and the Asante Peoples* (1895). Earlier in the present century East translated Akiga's *Story* (1939), Adelaide Casely-Hayford was writing in Freetown, as she continued to write almost until her death in 1959, and her daughter Gladys is remembered for her Krio poetry. Akiga did not write in English, it is true, but much is owed him and his translator for awakening interest in the possibilities of an autonomous West African literature in English. More recently, Paul Edwards, with his anthologies of African prose (Edwards, 1966a and 1966b) and his abridged edition of Equiano's *Interesting Narrative* (Edwards, 1967), has done much to stimulate interest in African writing as a distinct branch of English literature of long standing. Importantly, he has attempted to do so where it must ultimately count, in the schools, and in a direct appeal to a general readership. More recently, others have followed his example.

The most notable feature of any list of the earlier writers in English is that they were seldom writers of fiction. It is difficult to suggest why this should have been the case, unless it was that such writers were essentially outward-looking. They were displaced from, or, in the case of the Freetown settlers, replaced in, an African environment. Their education was modelled on an educational system evolved to cater for the needs of a monied English middle class. The whole effect was to distract their attention from themselves, to deny them awareness of West Africa's potential as a source of artists, unique experience and a literary expression enriched by traditional oral literature. Naturally enough, the language they used was similarly drawn from an external environment and it was to be a considerable time before increased literacy and national awareness lifted the inhibitions and the barriers to a uniquely African expression.

The suddenly accelerated growth of a literature in English in West Africa can be said to be concurrent with the growth of a more widespread nationalism. Nationalism brought with it self-awareness, and its early success, confidence. It directed inwards the thoughts of the educated and stimulated an awareness of the past, the present and possible future of West African countries. It demanded to be heard. For the purposes of the present discussion, the most significant result of this awareness was the recognition of oral literary traditions of unparalleled richness and diversity. A literature did not simply arise from a British literary tradition. West African literature in English should not be seen as lacking a history but as the natural result of a rich native inheritance in conjunction with an imported literary tradition.

Ulli Beier, writing some years ago on West African poetry, pointed out the paradox of the West African writer's situation (Beier, 1957):

> The West African poet writing in a European language finds himself in a difficult position. He is almost bound to be a nationalist and more often than not he is actively engaged in the fight for self-government. His poetry is naturally concerned partly with a criticism and rejection of European values – and yet he has to use a European language to express the same rejection.

This was, perhaps, always more valid for French-speaking West Africa than for the English-speaking regions where the writer has been less concerned with the rejection of European values for its own sake; and the fight for self-government is now over for English-speaking West Africa. But the paradox remains in that the most important figures in the struggle for the recognition of a truly West African literature in English are, as Beier points out, probably the most westernised.

The West African writer's choice of a language was very largely decided for him, for a world ear demanded a world language, and the diversity of languages within the new nations required a common language for national literatures; though there has long been a tradition of writing in indigenous languages (cf Ramsaran, 1965). In some countries the most obvious choice combining these possibilities was English, in others French. This has been the situation until now, but with the political establishment of national identities and the eventually lessening need for a world audience, the possibilities of literatures in indigenous languages can be explored. It is unlikely that a literature in English will cease to exist in West Africa, but the emphasis could well shift.

The most likely result is that English will continue to be the main vehicle of expression, but that it will be considerably modified to meet the needs of a West African literature instantly recognisable and distinct from all other branches of English literature. Chinua Achebe, writing in 1965, did not see the continued use of the English language as the road to sterility or a lack of adventurousness, but as 'a new voice coming out of Africa, speaking of African experience in a world language' (Achebe, 1965b). Hand in hand with the realisation that a tried and tested language such as English is of immense value as a vehicle for the new literature has gone a consciousness of the problems likely to arise in its new role. Achebe in the same article expressed this consciousness when he wrote:

> . . . I feel that the English language will be able to carry the weight of my African experience. But it will have to be a new English, still in full communion with its ancestral home but altered to suit its new African surroundings.

The Indian novelist R. K. Narayan, speaking on English in India at the Leeds conference in 1964 (Narayan, 1965), had this to say of English as a literary language in a new environment, which is here taken in expansion of Achebe's view:

> English has proved that if a language has flexibility any experience can be communicated through it, even if it has to be paraphrased sometimes rather than conveyed, and even if the factual detail . . . is partially understood. In order not to lose the excellence of this medium a few writers in India took to writing in English, and produced a literature that was perhaps not first-class; often the writing seemed imitative, halting, inapt, or an awkward translation of a vernacular rhetoric, mode or idiom; but occasionally it was brilliant. We are still experimentalists. I may straightaway explain what we do not attempt to do. We are not attempting to write Anglo-Saxon English.

Alan Warner and others (*eg* Warner, 1963, Mphahlele, 1964) have spoken of the possibility of a new English in Africa. Warner saw three types of English in Nigeria; the 'westernised', the 'folklore type' of Tutuola and others, and the 'new mad type' of the Onitsha pamphlet writers. The final result will not be any one of these. The increase in education will tend to eliminate many of the more obvious differences in the last type and the increase in experimentation is likely to adapt the first. Usage generally current among the educated sections of society will almost certainly limit divergence from forms of standard English. In all probability the language of West African literature in English will lie eventually somewhere between the westernised and the folklore types – and closer to the westernised. In short, it is most likely that a distinct West African variety of standard English, which will be as immediately recognisable as any other, will arise.

This is, of course, only speculation on a possible form of written English. It seems unlikely that there will be a single distinct variety of spoken English in West Africa, and this must effect some differences, mainly lexical, in the written language from each area. The growth of modern transport and communications is likely to ensure mutual intelligibility, and the more universally agreed forms of the written mode are bound to have a further stabilising effect; but the distances involved, for instance between Sierra Leone and Nigeria, will necessarily result in the development of regional varieties within West Africa. Most important, the influences of indigenous languages and differences in the oral traditions from country to country will probably have significantly different effects on the kind of English that is written in them. Jack Berry (1961b) has pointed out the wide similarities in the oral literatures of all parts of West Africa, but there are differences. Proverbs differ from place to place, so does traditional imagery, and as writers draw more and more deeply upon the richness of the oral traditions, regional variations must arise in the written literature.

Almost as important is the history of education in the different countries. The school system founded in Freetown by the missionaries disseminated a form of English somewhat different from that to be found in schools such as Bo School in Sierra Leone and the schools of Northern Nigeria, which were loosely based on the English Public School system. It is interesting to note, for instance, the biblical flavour of the English used by those educated within a missionary-based system, and the echo of the quadrangle in the speech of many from schools with less unworldly initiatives. This, however, is becoming less the case as state education systems supplant the older opportunities for a European style of education.

The influences upon experimentation with literary English in the Creole environment of Freetown, up-country Sierra Leone, in Ghana or the separate regions of Nigeria will be different, especially where such experimentation involves attempts to apply features of syntax in indigenous languages to English, as well as literal translation and the borrowing of vocabulary, all of which have been suggested or attempted already. The extent of such differences will naturally depend on how widely the transfer of the lexis and syntax of indigenous languages is accepted as a literary technique. The situation is thus extremely complex. As Achebe has said in a wider context:

> You cannot cram African literature into a small, neat definition. I do not see African literature as one unit but as a group of associated units – in fact the sum total of all the *national* and *ethnic* features of Africa.

He might well have added 'linguistic features'.

An awareness of the need for language experimentation on the part of writers is essential; but it is only half of the battle. A factor often overlooked is that very important one, the audience. How much experiment is it prepared to accept? This in itself is a further possible stabilising factor. At present the subject of a distinct variety of English in West Africa is often an extremely delicate one among educated users. Difference is all too often taken to imply inferiority. Recognition, and even prestige, is accorded the other world varieties of English, whether American, Indian, West Indian, Australian or British; while the suggestion of a distinct West African form is treated with scepticism and, at times, indignation. The attitudes Cassidy met with when he published his study of Jamaican English (Cassidy, 1961) were sadly not exceptional, for he was attacked for studying corrupt and broken English.

Artistic experiment will not be inhibited for this reason, but it remains to be seen whether it will become so much a matter of national pride as to overcome this conservatism. Amos Tutuola, to his distress, has been constantly attacked for his 'corrupt' English, mainly by his countrymen; and the potentially rich literary source he has revealed in the Yoruba oral tradition has been obscured by adverse criticism of what to him is a serious means of expression. Tutuola is not typical, he is probably not even indicative of the future as far as his use of English is concerned, but he is part of the history of a future West African literature in English.

Comment on a distinct form of West African English is again not as new as more recent interest would suggest, though it has been less specialised. Hannah Kilham, for some years a missionary in Sierra Leone, observed in 1837:

> From observing how generally a few words are adopted by the tribes here, as 'done' and 'for', and used on so many occasions to express what others would express in a great variety of ways, I am ready to conclude that the time may arrive in which a kind of general vocabulary may be formed on a limited scale, whether in English or in a mixture of languages, and be adopted, not to supersede any more complete or extensive vocabulary, but as a common medium for communication when people of some education meet from different quarters of the globe, to facilitate their intercourse with each other. 'Done' is used for the past tense of any verb in the liberated African English, and even among Maroons, and 'for', for any purpose in view, or object to be attained. 'Done go' – I have been. 'I done full 'em' – I have filled them. 'I done tell him' – I have told him. 'I want thread for sew' – I want thread to sew with, etc.

A Residence at Sierra Leone, by 'A Lady', published in 1849 (Norton, 1849), included an appendix of letters in a highly distinctive form of English still in use almost unchanged in similar circumstances today. What is now needed is an examination of West African varieties of English in the light of modern linguistic perspectives. It seems that the early observers had the perspicacity but not the means, and the present age, having the means, has given rather less attention to the area than it warrants. Amusing and endearing as some may find such passages as those quoted, there is no longer a place for the kind of curiosity that prods Mother Nature with walking-sticks in English country lanes, no matter how valuable it has occasionally proved in the past. Whether one agrees with Hannah Kilham's views on the limitations of the kind of English she noted or not, or whether one approves of Mrs Melville's collection of linguistic curios, these two works indicate that the emergence of distinct forms of usage in West Africa has been going on for a considerable time and that some of them are firmly established as features particular to a 'West African English'.

The view that African writers mainly have a European and American audience in mind is often exaggerated. Most African writers would, while welcoming a wider audience, acknowledge a primary duty to an African readership. This is, of course, fundamental to any decision on the choice of a language for a literature. If English is chosen, those literate only in an indigenous language are excluded from the readership; though the spread of a European type of education and the political advantages of retaining a non-indigenous, and therefore neutral, official language for the new nations, will considerably lessen the number of readers in this category.

West African oral tradition has always possessed a verse and prose closely bound up with the dramatic element, though the formal conventions within which the modern African writer attempts to contain them in English are largely imported. The language of West African poetry in English, by its very nature as poetry, demands a highly specialised and separate study. It is perhaps more the concern of the literary critic than of the person interested in attempting observations on the use of language more general than the poet's natural individualism would allow. As Ian Watt (1963) puts it:

> It would appear . . . that the function of language is much more largely referential in the novel than in other literary forms; the genre itself works by exhaustive presentation rather than by elegant concentration.

The formal conventions of poetry require special linguistic consideration. This is especially the case where, as with West African poetry in English, the process involves attempts at a union of alien formal traditions.

Before going on to fuller discussion of some of the characteristics of the English language in West African literature, it is necessary to make the nature of our interest clear. It is important not to overlook the fact that the African writer has his place in a modern society; he is not a resurrection of the dim past, a colourful, conjured ghost to be smiled on by the connoisseurs of the quaint. First of all he is Africa's 'new voice'; but, in quite another way, he is also the voice of a language in the process of adaptation and change. It is this latter which is of particular interest to the student of language.

There can be no room for the kind of considerations that prompted the attacks on Cassidy's *Jamaica Talk*. For our present purposes there can be no corruption, only change. Language carries with it nothing but what it gains from a particular situation at a particular time. As this study is an attempt to draw general conclusions about the use of language in West African literature in English, it has been necessary to restrict it, with one outstanding exception, to a certain established level of literacy. As a rough guide only, this has been set here at the level one might normally expect to be the attainment of candidates for the Advanced level examination of the West African Examinations Council.

Chinua Achebe suggested (Achebe, 1965b) that 'African writing in English or French should attempt to secure verisimilitude by rendering African speech literally into the metropolitan language'. In varying degrees, consciously or unconsciously, the indigenous languages have influenced the imported languages. This belief in the need for writers to use English in an unusual way to reflect unique material depends for its realisation on how the process is seen by the writer. It must be decided whether experiment is a search for an adequate medium of expression for particular purposes, or an attempt at establishing a highly individual form of English for its own sake, or as a means of national identification. For most West African writers the question is literary first and, as their writing is the expression of the African situation, national or regional only second.

Alongside experiment runs writing drawing upon the indigenous languages unconsciously because of the amount of European education the writer happened to receive. Amos Tutuola is the best known representative of this group. In a recent conversation, Tutuola had much of interest to say which would perhaps shed light on the complexity of the influence of indigenous languages, in this case Yoruba, on the language of writing in English. He writes first in his own language and himself then translates it into English. This naturally has its effect on the language of his works. He also expresses a preference for indirect speech in his writing as more fitting the role of a storyteller, and this necessarily dictates significant features of his style. Indeed, such features are likely to be, in part, the product of the changing role of the literary artist in West Africa, as was suggested by Michael Crowder (Crowder, 1966): the traditional relationship was the direct one of artist to audience, speaker to hearer, whereas the modern relationship involves the indirect relation necessitated by a written literature. This shift from the spoken to the written mode must affect the artist's style.

Tutuola is, also, consciously attempting to disseminate his knowledge of Yoruba folklore, and he shares this informational approach with not a few of his more orthodox countrymen. Moral didacticism, as Achebe points out (Achebe, 1965a), is expected of the West African writer by a considerable portion of his West African readership. It is hardly surprising, therefore, that he should be conscious of this and that it should affect his use of language. It surely lies at the root of what Ronald Dathorne has called the 'flat informed account', the selection of an inappropriate register, the use of a form of the language in a social role with which it is not customarily associated.

So far we have been concerned with both deliberate and non-deliberate deviation. For the purposes of further discussion I shall refer to deliberate deviation as 'experiment' and reserve 'deviation' for such distinctive characteristics as may have arisen from social or historical causes. It is true, of course, that all creative writing entails deliberate deviation by virtue of the fact that the writer sets out with the intention of creating a literary work. There is, however, a distinct division between the selection of a suitable existing register and the attempt to create a new one. A novel, then, can be seen as an amalgam of registers within a wider register of literary endeavour. This duality in the nature of literary language demands that all valid comparisons (and all linguistic study of literary language must be comparative) must be, in a case such as the examination of the language of West African writing in English, a comparison with the language of a more established regional literature in English. As it is the most important influence and source of models, genres and styles, British literature in English is the obvious choice for such a comparison; though comparison with other regional literatures might offer other insights, especially a comparative view of the processes of imitation, adaptation, break-away, and the struggle for literary autonomy.

The following passage from Onuora Nzekwu's *Wand of Noble Wood*, typical of this novel as a whole, illustrates a tendency to select an inappropriate register which is apparent in much West African writing in English:

> Among us the *ozo* title was the equivalent of the sacrament of Holy Orders. It was the only passport to officiating at offerings to ancestral spirits. *Ozo* was also a form of insurance policy which was neither transferable (except by the Obi) nor inherited. It guaranteed for the initiate a share of the fees paid by anyone who was initiated into the society after him. It was an expensive title which cost well over seven hundred pounds.

The information continues to roll over the reader for another few pages. The reasons for this formal, informative language are several. First of all, there is the conscious didacticism stemming from the traditional function of the storyteller in the oral tradition. It is likely that this influence is more considerable than is generally supposed, since the effects of tradition are as much unconsciously absorbed as consciously learned.

When combined with the obvious need to inform an extensive reader-ship, this tendency towards the informational adds greatly to the formal tone of much West African writing in English.

A further important reason for this formality of tone is undoubtedly the spread of a formal system of education on the European model, depending as it does on a series of examinations in a second language. Attention to the special problems of the second-language learner are sadly recent; it is only in the last few years that material specially intended for West African learners of English at any level has been available, and techniques are still far from perfect. The pressures upon a student in West Africa to succeed are enormous and more re-sponsibility falls upon him than is generally felt by his European counterpart. Consequently, he spends a great deal of time on books required for examinations. He is bound by highly formal requirements and reading for pleasure is for most a luxury. His linguistic limitations bind him to an environment of textbook language, and it is hardly surprising that for him this is often the most normal type of English. It is this that gives rise to a kind of English deriving from the didactic impulse; perhaps, indeed, both influences are in force here. The follow-ing passage, taken from N. U. Akpan's *The Wooden Gong*, reflects once again a highly informational type of language:

> A girl's fattening involved spending at least three months – in some areas it could involve as many and more years – in a secluded place, under heavy, and regular enforced feeding. During this period she would do nothing whatever but eat, wash and sleep. Any type of food she wanted would be provided, and the more she ate the more she would please her parents and her prospective husband. To avoid her doing any form of work, many maidservants were placed at her service. As an additional means of achieving as much weight as possible, a lady specialising in the trade of fattening girls would be hired for the task of regularly massaging the girl, who would lie flat with belly on the floor . . . The amount of weight put on at the end of the period would indicate the wealth of the girl's parents, and the efficiency of her fattening woman and of her maidservants.

The writer continues in the same fashion for some time. There is no need to quote further, for the passage illustrates, in its detailed, prosaic de-scription, what has become known as the 'anthropological' West African novel. There is no reason why 'anthropological' content should preclude the possibility of a good novel. It depends on the emphasis it receives, the way in which it is woven into the whole, and upon the language used. Achebe's *Arrow of God*, which he sees as a mirror of his 'ancestor worship', is 'anthropological', but it is also a better novel. The fact remains that the informational style has the advantage of familiarity for varying reasons. It is possible for the writer to ignore it, but as it is the most normal English to him, the motive is absent.

It is unlikely that the situation will change suddenly in this respect, if at all, but the reasons for the confusion of usual distinctions of register are more complex than has been suggested so far. To return to a suggestion made earlier, the reasons are both social and historical. In the first place, apart from the missionaries, English was imported by administrators and those engaged in business in West Africa during the colonial period. Consequently, their dealings with the local people were mainly either commercial or administrative. This had its effect on the form of English used from the earliest days, and there emerged as a result a type of English, simplified for its mainly utilitarian roles, and drawn from a severely restricted number of situations, which were for the most part formal. It is often boasted that, unlike the French, the British were always willing to recognise the indigenous languages. It would be fairer, perhaps, to suggest that they were not much worried as long as the people with whom they were dealing had sufficient English to make their jobs possible. Again, the education of Africans for posts in the civil service brought them into contact with a highly formal language environment.

It is also possible that historical reasons can be found to account for the highly declamatory style also favoured by West African writers. This derives, in all probability, from missionary influence. The main aim of the missionaries in teaching English was to make the Bible and the hymnal available to their new congregations. These missionaries were not always themselves native speakers of English, but often German, Danish or Dutch. This also had its influence on the kind of English taught, as did the fact that the English the newly literate then went on to read was usually the English of the King James version of the Bible. The language of the King James Bible is magnificent, but hardly appropriate to the demands of modern everyday language situations away from the church pew. However, the biblical flavour so often commented upon in much West African writing seems to have deeper roots even than that. While the missionary influence is without doubt important, there may also here be a link with notions of linguistic skill within the indigenous cultures.

Traditional notions of linguistic skill, and hence prestige, in many West African cultures related to a person's knowledge of traditional literature. This *ipso facto* involved a mastery of a declamatory style of speech. The Bible too, of course, has similar origins. The readiness to use a declamatory style, then, may derive as much from indigenous cultures as from the comparatively short-lived, if powerful missionary influence. The following passage is from a chapter of a novel by D. O. Fagunwa (Beier, 1963), and it seems to represent the common declamatory factor:

> Then I called him a third time and said: 'Akara-Ogun'. Then he burst out laughing and slapped his hand on his chest and raised up his body, he said: 'Akara-Ogun' is my name, yes I bear a very mighty name, I bear the praise names that befit me, I have been wandering through the world according to my nature, I am your friend of old time and indeed my power has not diminished; there are still bones in the body of the man . . .

> . . . When he said this, my soul was sweet, like the soul of a man in danger of prison who has been freed by the judge, because I had found what I had been seeking, and I had come across the thing I liked, and God had buttered my bread. And I dipped my hand into my pocket and I found writing materials indeed, and I sat down on the rock and I began the work of my hand. And Akara-Ogun sat down on the rock beside me and began to talk as fast as a parrot.

What is interesting here is that this is a translation from the original in Fagunwa's native language, Yoruba. It is striking how greatly the written mode in the original shows traces, even in translation, of its close relationship with a spoken mode. As Beier points out in his introduction to the translation, Fagunwa 'created his own stories but used the style and bizarre humour of traditional storytelling'. This seems to be the point: the language of the Bible was in accord with certain features of a traditional oral literature; it did not of itself bring about a declamatory style in West African writing. What is taken to be the use of a declamatory, or a 'biblical' register, sometimes inappropriately according to current European or American standards of usage, could, in many cases, be more fittingly described as a stylistic echo of tradition.

An entirely separate biblical influence, however, is the direct borrowing of language from the Bible. Such borrowing is mainly lexical, the lifting of lexical items and collocations from the Bible for use in registers very different, and can give rise to language such as the following from a letter to an employer:

> In this period of my perils brought upon me by no fault of mine, I am pleading to enjoy your understanding heart and I know the Architect Divine will show you how to continue to govern Israel.

There is, of course, no reason why such language, especially in literature, cannot be perfectly appropriate. Ezuelu, in *Arrow of God*, often uses a highly declamatory kind of language, but it is matched to the situation.

> If my enemy speaks the truth I will not say that because it is spoken by my enemy I will not listen. What Nwaka said was the truth. He said: 'Go and talk to the white man because he knows you'. Was that not the truth? Who else among us could have gone out and wrestled with him as you have done? Once again, *Nno*. If you do not like what I have said you may send a message not to come to your house again. I am going.

This is indeed a mixture of informal and declamatory registers, but no less successful for that. Success is, though, in this respect delicately balanced, and the following passage from Nzekwu's *Blade Among the Boys* is an example of what is far more typically the result of the handling of register. In the case just quoted we have the use of a register appropriate to the situation; in the following we have the use of a register divorced from its typical situation:

> 'As punishment for not having prepared my lesson he slapped my face and asked me to fill a thirty-page copybook with the Pater Noster. This I did. Unfortunately, I wrote it in English instead of in Latin. When he saw what I had done he became furious with me, called me a liar when I told him I didn't realize I had to write in Latin, promised this would be the last time I would ever lie to him and swung a blow at me. I ducked just in time and there was a muffled exclamation from the class. In his anger he chased me around the class and finally asked me to report myself to you.'

The language here is more that of the written report than of a pupil explaining himself nervously, or even indignantly, to his headmaster. 'There was a muffled exclamation from the class' and 'swung a blow at me', as well as the punctuation, are journalistic devices to give immediacy to the account, and 'didn't' comes as the only concession to the spoken mode.

Such confusion, as opposed to deliberate and appropriate juxta-position of registers, seems to be the direct consequence of a largely bilingual language environment. Whether the vernacular is an indigenous language or, like Pidgin or Krio, based on imported as well as indigenous languages, complete bilingualism is almost impossible. The languages will have specialised purposes in the life of the user. The first language takes first place in everyday living and in his affections, while English is for him the language of formality, the language of the school and the struggle for social advancement. It is rarely the language of relaxation. The natural result of this is that, at a level below only the most proficient users of British or American English, there is in general no occasion for informal registers in the English the West African uses, for their place is taken by the vernacular.

A tacit admission of this can be seen in the work of West African writers using Pidgin in an attempt to gain verisimilitude. This is particularly the case with those writers who use Pidgin in conjunction with English, as in Wole Soyinka's play *The Trials of Brother Jero*, in place of informal registers of English. In the following extract, the proportion of Pidgin to English can be seen to increase naturally with the change in the degree of formality, as the speaker waxes enthusiastic:

CHUME: Father forgive her.
CONGREGATION: Amen.
CHUME: Father forgive 'am.
CONGREGATION: Amen.
CHUME: (*Warming up to the task*) Make you forgive 'am Father.
CONGREGATION: Amen.
They rapidly gain pace, Chume getting quite carried away.
CHUME: I say make you forgive 'am.
CONGREGATION: Amen.
CHUME: Forgive 'am one time.
CONGREGATION: Amen.
CHUME: Forgive 'am quick, quick.
CONGREGATION: Amen.
CHUME: Forgive 'am Father.
CONGREGATION: Amen.
CHUME: Forgive us all.
CONGREGATION: Amen.
CHUME: Forgive us all.
And then punctuated regularly with Amens . . .

Yes Father, make you forgive us all. Make you save us from palaver.
Save us from trouble at home. Tell our wives not to give us trouble . . .
The penitent has become placid. She is stretched out flat on the ground.
. . . Tell our wives not to give us trouble. And give us money to have a
happy home. Give us money to satisfy our daily necessities. Make you
forget those of us who dey struggle daily. Those who be clerk today,
make them Chief Clerk tomorrow. Those who are Messenger today,
make them Senior Service tomorrow.

Indeed this seems a wholly reasonable way out of the difficulty, though
more than usual skill is required to develop its possibilities into a successful technique. It results from the recognition of the possibility that
English, because of its high degree of specialised usage in West Africa,
has become restricted in use to a limited range of registers for clearly defined formal situations. It is not a palatable possibility to many, perhaps, but English may no longer be relevant in every situation the West
African writer has to face. Unless English becomes the language for
every situation, and emotionally and politically this is unlikely, even
undesirable, in the near future, the handling of register will hardly be
seen in the same terms by a West African writer as it is by his counterpart in Britain or America, for whom English is a whole language in the
sense that it is applicable to all situations. In this respect, English in
West Africa is a divided language, and adaptation or experiment in
literature must be concerned to some extent with establishing its autonomy and developing its resources as a distinct West African variety.

There are, however, factors now operating which may contribute to a
widening of the range of English used by West Africans, and this may
in the long run affect the opportunities open to the writer. In the first
place, there is an increasing number of West Africans who have spent
considerable time, often with their families, in Britain or America, either
as students or skilled workers. In so far as their children may attend
school in English-speaking countries, even for a short time, their
familiarity with a wider range of informal linguistic usage in English is
bound to be extended. A further factor of importance in this connection
is the increase in the amount of light popular reading among certain
sections of the community. Few students are unfamiliar with Cheyney,
Charteris or Ian Fleming. The effect of casual reading of this kind on the
English they use can only be a matter of conjecture. It is not good
literature, perhaps, but its language draws directly upon fairly informal
first-language register ranges. It is an influence to balance the language of

13

the textbook, of formal language in general, and its effect may be far-reaching.

Nevertheless, it is possible that English will continue to be restricted largely to use in formal situations, and as a result a rigid literary language may evolve, producing stagnation or extreme esotericism. It is also possible that such factors as those mentioned above will accelerate a swing towards norms of British usage without halting the development of a distinct regional variety of English for West Africa.

Most noticeable in the area of literary experiment is that involving adaptation of normal English syntax. Once again both experiment and non-deliberate deviation are involved. The area of non-deliberate change, that is change due to the influence of the indigenous language on the imported one, offers one of the richest areas for linguistic research in the immediate future. Like the enlightened examination of indigenous languages, this type of investigation requires trained first-language speakers. Here our concern is mainly with deliberate deviation in syntax, as illustrated in a work by the Nigerian poet and novelist, Gabriel Okara. His novel *The Voice* exhibits a highly idiosyncratic syntax obtained, according to Okara, by a direct substitution of the syntax of his native Ijaw for normal English syntax. How direct this substitution is requires a knowledge of Ijaw, but there is little doubt that there is a deliberate attempt to evolve a new style of writing in English.

I have killed many moons, many years in that hut thinking of the happening things in this town. My feet know not the door of a school but Woyengi who all things created gave each of us human beings an inside and a head to think. So the many years I have killed in the hut have put many thoughts into my inside which have made me see differently. To speak the straight thing, I was beginning to see things as if through a harmattan fog when they called me a witch and I was put out of the way by the Elders like a tree that has fallen across a path. I put a strong fear into their insides because they thought I was going to turn the insides of the people against them.

Achebe's contention already referred to above that African writing in English or French should attempt to secure verisimilitude by rendering African speech literally into the metropolitan language, could, then, have far-reaching consequences, though it is to be supposed that such an attempt would have to be judiciously handled. The aim of a distinct West African form of the English language for literary purposes is only useful and admirable in so far as its individuality goes hand in hand with a new awareness. The 'new voice', at least a valuable and instantly communicable 'new voice', cannot be found in extreme esotericism. This would establish individuality, but far from releasing the expression of African experience from bondage, it would restrict it within a new one. However, the call for experiment has been made, which is the important thing for the student of the English language; value judgments must be the concern of the literary critic. Such successes or failures as there may be in new forms of the English language in literature will be purely individual; and individual experiment does not presuppose a universally accepted new form – languages are not radically changed for the general user by single efforts, no matter how successful they may be as literary works. Once again there is the division between experiment and non-deliberate deviation. It seems likely that ultimate success will go to the writer able to choose wisely among the already developing forms in more general use. Ideally, of course, the language he uses in a particular work will be judged on its artistic success, though its relevance to the development of a distinct form of literary English will depend on the general acceptability of his choices.

A further area of change, and perhaps the most obvious to the casual observer, is that of vocabulary. It would seem that this process of change involves three distinct types. The first is quite simply that of extensive borrowing from the indigenous languages. This can be seen in the work of nearly every novelist, in particular those from Nigeria, and has at times reached proportions exceeding those demanded by the immediate literary need. Chukwuemeka Ike, for example, in his novel *Toads for Supper*, has felt it necessary to attach a considerable glossary of words from Igbo and Yoruba. This is perhaps the natural result of an informational approach and the search for a world audience, and goes hand in hand with the anthropological element in so many West African novels.

> Their instruments were few and simple – a pot with a long neck and a circular hole in one side, called the *udu* and used to provide the beat, a *shekere* made out of a calabash with a network of dark seeds on the outside, and small drums which the women beat with little art.

This type of borrowing is quite different from borrowing for an artistic purpose, or when a word in the mouth of a character in a novel has to be drawn from an indigenous language because no other will do. It will often be necessary, as Achebe has said, for the West African writer in

English to use language in an unusual way to express his unique environment. The English language is having to operate more and more in situations which it has never previously encountered; and survival, for a language, lies in adaptability to new situations.

A form of borrowing closely akin to this is the use of literally translated proverbs, though the literary result is perhaps even more pronounced than that produced by lexical borrowing. It is really the job of the literary critic to discuss the effectiveness or otherwise of proverbs in translation. The fact that they are literally translated is what may interest the student of the English language most, though this would require specialist study on its own. There is little doubt, however, that English can be enriched in this way now that our own proverbs, with long use, invite scorn as cliché.

Cyprian Ekwensi suggested (1956), in discussing the African writer and his traditions, that

> He may choose to set down the oral literature of his people. Oral literature opens up a wide field of fantasy, of the irrational and the incredible. But its values lie in fostering an awareness of national identity which can only come through a sound knowledge of folklore, proverbs, art and music.

This is certainly a valid point of view. Though I would tend to agree with Wole Soyinka that the African Renaissance is not an easy refuge for literary nationalism, that this is self-indulgence and no substitute for art, and that Tutuola's wildly spontaneous English hit the European critics at their weakest point – boredom with their own language and the usual quest for titillations. The 'usual quest for titillations' is no more invalid, perhaps, than deliberate deviation in West African literature in English. The possibility remains that it is from Africa and its more recent users of English in literature that the language will be enriched with the new and the 'wildly spontaneous'.

Adaptation of English by analogy is to be found in certain writers, whereby such nominals as *the deads* and *the dumbs* are derived from adjectives or from the corresponding uncountable noun (*the dead, the dumb*). Similar analogical adaptations noted are *havocs*, *refuses* (n pl from *refuse* – 'rubbish'), and *the pesters* (ie 'those who pester'). Another class of analogical extensions is the attachment of the adverbial suffix -*ly* to adverbs which do not possess it: *He grasped her waist hardly*, *talking fastly*, etc. It is not easy to determine whether these are unintentional deviations, and if so whether they reflect widespread usage in

West Africa. It is of course difficult as yet to predict how far and in what directions deviation and experiment will go. Possible lines of influence, on the English language in West Africa generally, and, more particularly, on the language of West African literature in English, may be represented diagrammatically as follows:

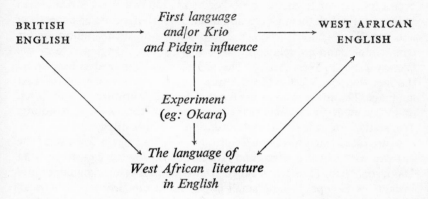

Here it can be seen that the development of the language of West African literature in English and the possibility of a West African English are seen as two separate processes. A significant feature is the cross-fertilisation, represented by the double arrow, between the two. The English used in West Africa in everyday life will, to some extent, restrict literary deviation; just as it is itself partly restricted by the need for communication beyond the immediate speech community. The result could be a standard form of West African English. A great deal of speculation is naturally involved here, but at this stage little else is possible.

There is, at present, much evidence of a considerable increase in written literature in the indigenous languages and the effect of this upon West African literature in English, as Banham and Ramsaran (1962) have pointed out, will ensure the uniqueness of African literature. Indeed, the problem of the choice of a language mentioned by Ekwensi is to be seen in the work of Tutuola. The dramatised version of *The Palm Wine Drinkard* was published in English originally, but performed as a play-opera in Yoruba at Ibadan. Tutuola was so deeply impressed by the fact that the Yoruba version was more exactly what he was trying to convey that, when the present writer suggested that it might be performed elsewhere in English, he expressed doubts that it would be at all successful. For him, at least in some aspects of life, English must be an inadequate vehicle of expression. In view of what the Sierra Leonean writer and scholar Davidson Nicol (1964) has called Tutuola's 'vivid and attractive African para-literate' use of English and the striking possibilities it has revealed, in spite of its failure at some points, there is even more reason to encourage experimentation in a West African form of literary English through a union of an imported means of expression and a rich indigenous heritage. The problems of such a union are far from simple, and are related in some ways to the changing role of the literary artist in West Africa. The situation is complicated further by the fact that the West African reader rarely has English as his first language. The adaptation of the fruits of an oral literature into a written literature in a foreign language requires sensitive, skilled handling. Translation, or at least literal translation, is not enough.

More established forms of English have much to gain from what the African writer has to offer, and Africa has no less to gain from what Davidson Nicol (1961) has called 'the tried and tested languages and insight' of Europe. It is no small hope that in this process the African writer may be able to forgive 'the agony' that their acquisition entailed.

References

The list of works which follows is not a bibliography of the English Language in West Africa, but a consolidated list of references from the chapters of this work.

ACHEBE, CHINUA 1960 *No Longer at Ease*, London
1963 *Arrow of God*, London
1965a 'The Novelist as Teacher', in Press, J., 1965
1965b 'English and the African Writer', *Transition*, 18
1966 *A Man of the People*, London
AJAYI, J.F.A. 1965 *Christian Missions in Nigeria, 1841–1891*, London
AKIGA, BENJAMIN 1939 *Akiga's Story: the Tiv Tribe as seen by one of its Members* (trans R. M. East), London
AKPAN, N. U. 1965 *The Wooden Gong*, London
ALEXANDRE, PIERRE 1961 'Problèmes linguistiques des états négro-africains à l'heure de l'indépendence', *Cahiers d'Etudes Africains*, 2
AMONOO, R.F. 1963 'Problems of Ghanaian *Lingue Franche*', in Spencer, 1963
ANSRE, G. 1961 *The Tonal Structure of Ewe*, Hartford
1966 *The Grammatical Units of Ewe*, London (PH D thesis)
ASAMOA, E. A. 1955 'The Problem of Language in Education in the Gold Coast', *Africa*, 25, 1
BAILEY, B.L. 1966 *Jamaican Creole Syntax*, Cambridge
BAMGBOṢE, AYỌ 1966 *A Grammar of Yoruba*, Cambridge
BANHAM, M. (ed) 1961 *Nigerian Student Verse*, Ibadan
BANHAM, M. and RAMSARAN, J.A. 1962 'West African Writing', *Books Abroad*, 36, London
BEIER, ULLI 1957 'The Conflict of Culture in West African Poetry', *Black Orpheus*
1963 (ed) *Black Orpheus: An Anthology of African and Afro-American Prose*, London
1964 'Public Opinion on Lovers: popular Nigerian Fiction sold in Onitsha Market', *Black Orpheus*

BERRY, JACK 1959a 'The Origins of Krio Vocabulary', *Sierra Leone Studies*, 12
1959b 'Creole as a Language', *West Africa*, 19 September
1961a 'English Loanwords and their Adaptation in Sierra Leone Krio', in Le Page, 1961
1961b *Spoken Art in West Africa*, London

BOADI, L. 1966 *The Syntax of the Twi Verb*, London (PH D thesis)

BOWEN, T. J. 1857 *Adventures and Missionary Labors in Several Countries in the Interior of Africa from 1849 to 1856*, London

BRADSHAW, A. T. VON S. 1965 'Vestiges of Portuguese in the Languages of Sierra Leone', *Sierra Leone Language Review*, 4

BROSNAHAN, L. F. 1958 'English in Southern Nigeria', *English Studies*, 39
1963a 'Some Aspects of the Linguistic Situation in Tropical Africa', *Lingua*, 12
1963b 'Some Historical Cases of Language Imposition', in Spencer, 1963

CASSIDY, F. G. 1961 *Jamaica Talk*, London

CASSIDY, F. G. and LE PAGE, R. B. 1961 'Lexicographical Problems of the *Dictionary of Jamaican English*', in Le Page, 1961

C.C.T.A. 1964 *Symposium on Multilingualism*, London

CHRISTALLER, J. G. 1881 *A Grammar of the Asante and Fanti Language called Twi*, Basel (reprinted London, 1964)

CHRISTOPHERSEN, P. 1948 *Bilingualism* (inaugural lecture), Ibadan
1953 'Some Special West African English Words', *English Studies*, 34

CLARK, JOHN PEPPER 1968 'The Legacy of Caliban: an introduction to the language spoken by Africans and other 'Natives' in English Literature from Shakespeare to Achebe', *Black Orpheus*, 2, 1

CLARKE, ROBERT, MRCS 1843 *Sierra Leone*, London

COLE, D. T. 1953 'Fanagalo and the Bantu Languages in South Africa', *African Studies*, 12

CROWDER, MICHAEL 1966 'Tradition and Change in Nigerian Literature', in *Three Essays on African Art and Literature*, Chicago

CUST, ROBERT NEEDHAM 1895 *Linguistic and Oriental Essays, Fourth Series*, London

DEUTSCH, KARL W. 1953 *Nationalism and Social Communication*, New York

DIKE, K. O. 1956 *Trade and Politics in the Niger Delta, 1830–1885*, London

DUNSTAN, ELIZABETH 1966 *The Sound Systems of the Main Nigerian Languages and English*, Ibadan
1969 *Twelve Nigerian Languages*, London

EDWARDS, PAUL (ed) 1966a *Modern African Narrative*, London
1966b *Through African Eyes*, 2 vols, Cambridge
1967 *Equiano's Travels*, London

EKWENSI, CYPRIAN 1956 'The Dilemma of the African Writer', *West African Review*, 27
1960 *Jagua Nana*, London

FERGUSON, CHARLES A. 1959 'Diglossia', *Word*, 15

FORDE, DARYLL (ed) 1956 *Efik Traders of Old Calabar*, London

FULLER, HELEN 1966 *Handbook on Nigerian Education*, British Council, Nigeria (mimeographed)

GRAHAM, SONIA F. 1966 *Government and Mission Education in Northern Nigeria, 1900–1919, with special reference to the work of Hanns Vischer*, Ibadan

GRIEVE, D. W. 1964 *English Language Examining*, Lagos

GROVES, C. P. 1948 *The Planting of Christianity in Africa*, London

HAIR, P. E. H. 1965 'Sierra Leone Items in the Gullah Dialect of American English', *Sierra Leone Language Review*, 4

HAKLUYT, RICHARD 1598–1600 *The Principal Navigations, Voyages, Traffiques and Discoveries of the English Nation*, London

HALL, ROBERT A., JR 1959 'Pidgin Languages', *Scientific American*, 200 (2)
1966 *Pidgin and Creole Languages*, Ithaca

HALLETT, ROBIN (ed) 1964 *Records of the African Association, 1788–1831*, London

HALLIDAY, M. A. K., MCINTOSH, A. and STREVENS, P. 1964 *The Linguistic Sciences and Language Teaching*, London

HARRISON, T. W. and SIMMONDS, JAMES 1966 *Aikin Mata: The Lysistrata of Aristophanes*, Ibadan

HMSO 1927 *The Place of the Vernacular in Education*, Colonial Office, London

HOFSTAD, DAVID H. 1969 *English Drills for Hausa Speakers*, Zaria

HYMES, DELL (ed) 1964 *Language in Culture and Society*, New York

IKE, CHUKWUEMEKA 1965 *Toads for Supper*, London

JOHNSON, SAMUEL 1759 Introduction to *The World Displayed*, London

JONES, ELDRED 1956 'Some Aspects of the Sierra Leone Patois or Krio', *Sierra Leone Studies*, 8
1957 'The Potentialities of Krio as a Literary Language', *Sierra Leone Studies*, 9
1959 'Some English Fossils in Krio', *Sierra Leone Studies*, 12
1962 'Mid-nineteenth Century Evidences of a Sierra Leone Patois', *Sierra Leone Language Review*, 1
1964 'Krio in Sierra Leone Journalism', *Sierra Leone Language Review*, 3
1965 'Academic Problems and Critical Techniques', in Moore 1965

KIRK-GREENE, A. H. M. 1963 'Neologisms in Hausa: a sociological approach', *Africa*, 33, 1
1966 'The Vocabulary and Determinants of Schoolboy Slang in Northern Nigeria', *Journal of African Languages*, 5, 1
KIRK-GREENE, A. H. M. and ALIYU, Y. 1966 *A Modern Hausa Reader*, London
KNAPPERT, J. 1965 'Language Problems of the New Nations of Africa', *Africa Quarterly*, 5, 2
KOELLE, S. W. 1854 *Polyglotta Africana*, London
KUP, A. P. 1961 *A History of Sierra Leone, 1400–1787*, Cambridge
LADEFOGED, PETER 1968 *A Phonetic Study of West African Languages*, rev ed, Cambridge
LE PAGE, R. B. (ed) 1961 *Creole Language Studies* II, London
MBASSI-MANGA, FRANCIS 1968 *The English of the Students at The Federal University of Cameroon: A Study in Error Analysis*, Leeds (M PHIL thesis)
MAUNY, R. 1952 *Glossaire des expressions et termes locaux employés dans L'Ouest Africain*, Dakar
MOORE, GERALD 1962 *Seven African Writers*, London
1965 (ed) *African Literature and the Universities*, Ibadan
MPHAHLELE, E. (ed) 1964 *Modern African Stories*, London
NARAYAN, R. K. 1965 'English in India', in Press, J., 1965
NICOL, DAVIDSON 1961 'West African Poetry', *Africa South*
1964 *Africa: a Subjective View*, London
NORTON, THE HON MRS (ed) 1849 *A Residence at Sierre Leone, by 'A Lady'*, London
NUTTALL, CHRISTINE 1966 'Interference Phenomena of Hausa on English', *Ahmadu Bello University Department of Languages, Occasional Paper 5*, Zaria
NWOGA, DONATUS 1965 'Onitsha Market Literature', *Transition*, 19
NWOSU, C. G. (no date) *Miss Cordelia in the Romance of Destiny*, Onitsha
NZEKWU, ONUORA 1961 *Wand of Noble Wood*, London
1962 *Blade Among the Boys*, London
OKARA, GABRIEL 1963 'African Speech . . . English Words', *Transition*, 10, 3
1964 *The Voice*, London
PARSONS, F. W. 1964 'Some Observations on the contact between Hausa and English', in C.C.T.A., 1964
PRATOR, CLIFFORD H. 1968 'The British Heresy in T.E.S.L.', in Fishman, J. A., Ferguson, C. A. and Das Gupta, J. (edd) *Language Problems of Developing Nations*, New York
PRESS, JOHN (ed) 1965 *Commonwealth Literature*, London
PURCHAS, SAMUEL 1619 *Hakluytus Posthumus, or Purchas His Pilgrimes, Contayning a History of the World in Sea Voyages and Lande Travells by Englishmen and Others*, London

QUIRK, RANDOLPH 1962 *The Use of English*, London

RAMSARAN, J. A. 1965 *New Approaches to African Literature*, Ibadan

RANKIN, F. HARRISON 1836 *The White Man's Grave: A Visit to Sierra Leone in 1834*, 2 vols, London

RAO, G. SUBHA 1954 *Indian Loanwords in English: a study in Indo-British cultural and linguistic relations*, Oxford

REINDORF, C. C. 1895 *History of the Gold Coast and the Asante Peoples*, Basel

RENS, L. L. 1953 *The Historical and Social Background of Surinam Negro English*, Amsterdam

RICHARDSON, I. 1964 'Linguistic Change in Africa', in C.C.T.A., 1964

ROSS, A. S. C. 1964 'On the Historical Study of Pidgins', in C.C.T.A., 1964

ROWLANDS, E. C. 1963 'Yoruba and English: a problem of co-existence', *African Language Studies*, 4, London

SANGSTER, E. G. and QUASHIE, C. K. A. (edd) 1966 *Talent for Tomorrow*, Accra

SIBTHORPE, A. B. C. 1868 *A History of Sierra Leone*, Freetown

SOYINKA, WOLE 1963 'The Trials of Brother Jero', in Soyinka *Three Plays*, Ibadan

SPENCER, JOHN (ed) 1963 *Language in Africa*, Cambridge
1970 'Language Policies of the Colonial Powers and their Legacies', in Berry, J. and Greenberg, Joseph H. (edd) *Current Trends in Linguistics* VII: *Linguistics in Sub-Saharan Africa*, s'Gravenhage

STEWART, J. 1963 'Some Restrictions on Objects in Twi', *Journal of African Languages*, 2, 2

STEWART, J., SCHACHTER, P. and WELMERS, W. 1964 *The Typology of the Twi Tone System*, Legon

STREVENS, P. D. 1965 *Papers in Language and Language Teaching*, London

TAYLOR, DOUGLAS 1956 'Language Contacts in the West Indies', *Word*, 12

THOMPSON, R. W. 1961 'A Note on some possible affinities between Creole dialects of the Old World and those of the New', in Le Page, 1961

TIFFEN, B. W. 1968 'Language and Education in Commonwealth Africa', in J. Dakin (ed) *Language in Education: the Problem in Commonwealth Africa and the Indo-Pakistan Sub-continent*, London

TURNER, LORENZO 1949 *Africanisms in the Gullah Dialect*, Chicago

TUTUOLA, AMOS 1952 *The Palm Wine Drinkard*, London

VOORHOEVE, J. 1959 'An Orthography for Saramaccan', *Word*, 15

WARD, IDA 1952 *An Introduction to the Yoruba Language*, Cambridge

WARNER, ALAN 1963 'A New English in Africa', *Review of English Literature*, 5, 2

WATT, IAN 1963 *The Rise of the Novel*, London

WATTS, M. E. (ed) 1967 *The New Generation*, Accra

WESTERMANN, D. 1930 *A Study of the Ewe Language*, Oxford
1949 *The African Today and Tomorrow*, London
WILLIAMSON, KAY 1965 *A Grammar of the Kolokuma Dialect of Ijo*, Cambridge
YULE, H. and BURNELL, A. C. 1886 *Hobson-Jobson: a glossary of colloquial Anglo-Indian words and phrases, and of kindred terms, etymological, historical, geographical and discursive*, London (reprinted 1966)